JACOB'S WELL

Joseph A. Amato

Jacob's Well

A Case for Rethinking Family History

Minnesota Historical Society Press

www.mhspress.org

Book design: Wesley B. Tanner/Passim Editions

The Minnesota Historical Society Press is a member of the Association of
American University Presses.

Printed in Canada

10   9   8   7   6   5   4   3   2   1

♾ The paper used in this publication meets the minimum requirements of
the American National Standard for Information Sciences—Permanence for
Printed Library Materials, ANSI Z39.48–1984.

International Standard Book Number

ISBN 13: 978-0-87351-613-6 (cloth)

ISBN 10: 0-87351-613-3 (cloth)

Several passages in this book that discuss the author's immediate family first
appeared, in altered form, in *Bypass: A Memoir*, by Joseph A. Amato, © 2000
Purdue University Press. Reprinted with permission. Unauthorized duplication not permitted.

Library of Congress Cataloging-in-Publication Data

Amato, Joseph Anthony.

Jacob's well : a case for rethinking family history / Joseph A. Amato.

    p. cm.

Includes bibliographical references and index.

ISBN-13: 978-0-87351-613-6 (cloth : alk. paper)

ISBN-10: 0-87351-613-3 (cloth : alk. paper)

1. Amato family. 2. Genealogy—Authorship. I. Title.

CS71.A4816 2008

929.1—dc22

2007046458

Frontispiece: The author and his parents, Joseph and Ethel Amato, about 1950.

To my parents and grandparents,
and their parents and grandparents

Immigrants and migrants all

Contents

Preface: Family History, a Way to Know Our Selves and Our Times   ix

Introduction: Putting on the Coat of the Past   3

1   Rosalia, a Misery as Ancient as Sicily   15

2   "Forty Acres, and All Mine"   43

3   Banished from Acadia, Exiled in Plymouth Colony   63

4   Up and Down the Hills of Maine, and Off to Wisconsin   87

5   Migrants West   105

6   A Memorable Death, a Common Lot   126

7   Jacob, the Rise and Fall of a Plebian Patriarch   147

8   Cousins of the Tongue   176

9   Workers to the Bone, East Siders to the End   200

Conclusion: The Reason For, and The Matter Of, Family History   241

Appendix: Amato, Linsdeau, and Associated Families   247

Source Notes   251

Family History,
A Way to Know Our Selves and Our Times

Family is the well of self. It makes childhoods, imprints memories, and offers models for a lifetime. Doing family history is a way to investigate its powers, to take control of personal history. It provides a distinct type of self-knowledge, which is timely and even indispensable in this age of abstractions, ideological battles, and mass culture. As we set off on this quest for truth, variety, and individuality, family history shows us the specific historical creatures who shaped our parents and their parents, making us see ourselves, too, as actors in an immediate, lived history—and this is worthy of reflection.

In this book I seek out fresh themes and approaches for rethinking family history. I do this by example, exploring these ideas while writing a history of a typical multi-ethnic, undistinguished, and poor North American family—my own, through seven generations. Though I concentrate on migrations and settlements, individual circumstances and fates, I find myself also recounting a national story of the poor, of the shift of the nation's population from land to town to industrial city, and of the unprecedented transformation of material conditions, which took the majority of Americans from scarcity and necessity to abundance, leisure, and choice.

Jacob's Well: A Case for Rethinking Family History is a companion work to my recent *Rethinking Home: A Case for Writing Local History*. In the latter I proposed fresh approaches to local history, which has been largely left in the hands of its amateur practitioners. In this book, I seek to expand the historical imagination of those who wish to write family histories that have significance for national, economic, and social history.

There are challenges, of course. A family history can be limited by narrowness of subject, distorted by gaps of information and evidence, and constricted by the interests and imagination of its creator. Furthermore, family historians must take care that their ideals don't distort their histories. The family we live by today, placed at the heart of our values and sentiment, increasingly becomes synonymous with the nuclear family. We forget that families were not always composed of two parents and their children, they did not always exist in the same household, and they were dedicated to reproduction and economic survival rather than fostering individual emotions and happiness. Until roughly a century ago, the household was a work unit, necessary for survival in both countryside and town. And even with this in mind, it is easy to forget, when contending with sentiment and nostalgia, that variations in circumstances, environment, and institutions determined the stability and form of the family.

Only over the course of centuries, starting with the wealthy, has the family been transformed into a social institution that fostered the individual and the intimate person. Correspondingly, in contradiction to Christian faith and theology, the family evolved in popular belief and sensibility to become the principal unit of the afterlife. We once identified ourselves locally in terms of a specific place on earth and collectively "in the Great Chain of Being," which vertically linked being from God, creator, to the smallest mite. But in the last hundred and fifty years or so, we have come to define ourselves not in place but in time, in what historian John Gillis calls "the Great Line of Progress."[1] As a consequence of this revolution in worldview, the family has its meaning not in a defining origin but in its democratic and progressive advance across time.

So as we discard the regressive search for noble origins and pure lineages, we come to know ourselves literally as the makers of our family and the definers of family tradition. We recognize that history is an active craft. The historian learns and makes as he proceeds. Moving back and forth between memory and research, fashioning and refashioning connections and contexts, and weighing and judging events, the historian simultaneously shapes narratives and deepens explanations. And as much as history serves as a medium for discovering the past, it also is, we confess, a means to invent it.

The academic study of the family, which took form in the last decades of the twentieth century, also rebuts mythic and stereotypic histories of the family. The discipline offers the family historian a comprehensive approach to the Western family. With a felicitous metaphor, historian David Levine, who traces the origin of the modern Western family to the Middle Ages, identifies the three composing strands of the family: the biological, the cultural, and the political. He argues that this "triple helix of family," historically bonded in space and time in the Middle Ages, was thereafter subject as a form to historical contingency, variation, and mutation.[2] While affirming the fundamental place of the family in human experience, those who study its development through time confirm that family is forever subject to societal, cultural, and political revolutions around it—including those surrounding the contemporary American family.

Even though considerations of family history turn up throughout this book, its principal quest takes us on a different path. Its subject is the ineffable individual, the singular family, distinct and even opposing generations, specific locales, myriad conditions, and particular locales. As suggested by each chapter's introductory head notes, I start my inquiry with questions and themes rather than theoretical problems and extended arguments. The first two chapters, which ask after the fate of one of my grandmothers and the source of the restlessness of the other, demonstrate both the role of grandparents as our main conduits to the past and the importance of using psychology when writing family history. Chapter 3 debates how far back the family historian should go in seeking origins as I query the meaning of the arrival of my Acadian family in a new land as prisoners and wards of the state. Chapters 4 and 5 show that families can be more about migration than settlement and that documents in obscure archives can help a historian narrate a family's search for home—specifically, up the slopes of Maine, on the poor land of New York, or on to the farms and towns of Wisconsin. Treasured family stories are the focus of Chapters 6 and 7, in which I seek to fathom one great-grandfather's death by rabies and contemplate the rise and fall of another immigrant great-grandfather, a man of relative prominence. In Chapter 8, the cousins stretch the story and form the cusp between family and society as I explore lives and cultures of mill-town immigrants who move to urban industrial Detroit. In the last chapter, I explore the union of my parents as urban villagers and their strong allegiance to family, city, consumption, and progress.

Questions of this sort require research that solicits explanations that call for metaphors, which invite narratives and define chapters. So I catch the fish that fit my nets. With curiosity calling and nostalgia beckoning, I am pulled most by the star of childhood, which emitted the first and thus most lasting impressions and memories. Here, on the ponds of first experience (now removed by sixty years and more than two generations), like an early winter skater on a singular course, I hesitantly cross the season's first ice. The open water, the absence of all and any evidence, imperils all around. But I must do more than evade it. I must pick an axis that joins individual lives, singular deaths, and unique stories to defining conditions, trends, and movements, regions, groups, and nations, and the shifting course of economies, commerce, and technologies. All this sets me on a curving path of historical explanation and reaching metaphors—and I write a mix of comedy, pathos, and tragedy as I give life to the mash and mingle of things that make the turning arc of a family's history.

While the change and variation that characterize all family history prove its historical pedigree, they do not remove the objections that individual family histories, unless of the mighty and influential, are unworthy of the historian's attention. In part, transforming the individual family into a microcosm of some greater and more significant whole meets this criticism. I specifically do this by joining my family story to a 250-year history of the American poor and its movement from farm and village to town and city. However, as abstractions do not furnish good legs for human understanding, so concepts and generalizations deliver us, I would contend, to a vacant landscape of disembodied people and ghostly movements. Justification for the writing of an individual family history lies elsewhere. It is found in the power of one family to represent another—and the value of presenting a single life from the past to the living present.

Beyond satisfying our curiosity about, as Rabelais joked, "the kings and thieves" that alternately bejeweled our past, family history truly does provide detailed and concrete ways to talk about society and ourselves. It confirms our family's stories, testifies to duties and indignities borne, and validates individual acts of wrong and evil and the price of risk, loyalty, and sacrifice. Likewise, this same history joins us to other histories, as we discover that we are not of pure heart or certain lineage, of single class or race or ethnicity, or of definite origins or fixed causes. Chances weigh heavy, they are in fact preponderant, that we are of mixed breed, an incalculable and perhaps unfathomable result of diverse combinations and unexplained but indisputable mutations. Woven of fad and fancy, commerce and technology, war and revolution, freedom and necessity, our individual histories testify to the singular but crooked paths along which we traveled to the present. We are of the fleshy, spirited, contradictory stuff democratic poet Whitman sang. When we write family history, we join that song.

Acknowledgments

My wife Cathy shared, supported, and encouraged the making of *Jacob's Well*, as did our children, Felice, Anthony, Adam, and Elizabeth. Friends Jeffrey Russell, Leon Rappoport, Jim Rodgers, Richard Davies, David Pichaske, and especially Michael Kopp offered friendly and constructive criticism. David Levine of the University of Toronto, who offered many useful suggestions, warned me at an important point in my study that I had not reached "the beginning of the end" as I presumed, but, alas, only "the end of the beginning." I was encouraged by the promises of Donald Yerxa and Joseph Lucas of the journal *Historically Speaking and of Anne Kaplan of Minnesota History* to publish excerpts of this work. Many conversations with friends Thaddeus Radzilowski and Rudolph Vecoli on the topics of migration, assimilation, class, and, most importantly, the formation and continuity of ethnicity in industrial America, have advanced my understandings of these crucial themes.

I found for each of my families an indispensable genealogist, a crucial family historian, or a vital supplier of information. I could not have written on either the Amato or Notaro families without the multi-dimensional genealogical and historical work of my double first cousin, once removed,

John Notaro. His work in Sicilian church and public records and U.S. and Detroit immigration, census, and legal records, coupled with his scouring of family memories and his mother's attic, his evolving genealogies, and website, Sicilian Family Research Home Page, made him a true companion of this work. Contributions to understanding the Sicilian half of the family were also made by my cousins, Jennie Grant, Rosemarie (Rizzuto) Fazekas, Angela (Messina) Evans, Francesca Di Blasi and family of Cerda, and Salvatore Notaro and family of Montamaggiore Belsito. Donna Gabbacia of the University of Minnesota's Immigration History Research Center provided helpful comments on Sicilian history.

For all-important census work on the Boodrys, Sayerses, and Linsdaus, I am indebted to local southwestern Minnesota genealogist Jerry Engesser of the Prairieland Genealogical Society. I am also particularly indebted to the imaginative and professional genealogical work of Kris Beisser Matthies, who provided a foundation for identifying the Linsdau and O'Brien families and for understanding the history of the Lake Winnebago, Wisconsin, region from 1850 to 1900.

Frederick Boyle, a professional genealogist in New England, truly paved the way for identifying the Acadian origins of the Boudrot (Boodry) family in Nova Scotia and Massachusetts. Wisconsin cousins Ray Boodry and Delores Johnson, and researcher Diane O'Brien of Tecumseh, Michigan, supplied vital information on the Boodrys.

Kansas cousin Irene Kolman set the basis for my understanding of the Sayers family and its moves. Genealogist Don Burke and local historian Gary Bushaw made important additions to my work on the Sayerses, as did genealogists Earl Cody, Anne Cady, Jan Godfrey, and Mary Zanoni of the St. Lawrence County Historical Association. Janet Timmerman and Professor Geof Cunfer helped me understand south central Kansas.

For the Linsdau and O'Brien families, I acknowledge the help of Linsdau cousin Elaine Campbell Dantoin of Green Bay, who invited me to a first family reunion almost fifteen years ago and furnished me with her research and a manuscript of a play written by Great-uncle Emmett Linsdau. Four cousins—the "Linsdau sisters" Helen, Gerty, and Corrine of Menasha, Wisconsin, and Pat Walker of Mt. Clemens, Michigan—all added pertinent family, church, and cemetery records and valuable photographs. My mother's first cousin Vernon Linsdau, another "talker," furnished a journal filling ten or so small loose-leaf notebooks with his keen and poignantly confessional reflections on his youth, education, career, marriage, family, and religious beliefs. His son Robert, daughter Nancy, and wife Phyllis generously provided family records and photographs.

A family's history depends on local history, and that brings a long train of indebtedness to state historical societies, local and county museums, and courthouses, which contained all-important property and probate records. The many institutions cited in the footnotes provided diverse and valuable genealogical and historical research materials. Some individuals provided particular help: Stephen White at the University of Moncton's *Centre d'études acadiennes* in New Brunswick; local historian Paul Surette, who led my wife and me on a day-long regional tour of New Brunswick marshland; formidable local genealogist Shirley Adams of Rangely, Maine; Anne Cady, author of diverse work on St. Lawrence County, New York; local journalist Peter Adams of the Lake Winnebago region; researcher Winifred Pawlowski of the Menasha Historical Association; Mike Thomas of the Neenah Public Library; Mara Munroe, who provided skilled research assistance at the Oshkosh Public Library. In Sicily I had the help of Antonino Impallaci of the Biblioteca Regionale, Palermo.

I am especially grateful to the whole electronic kingdom, which has so enhanced the reach of genealogist and local historians. Reference Specialist Duane Swanson at the Minnesota Historical Society pointed out to me "the best beginning point": CyndisList.com, which now contains about 250,000 links to electronic resources in the United States and Europe.

Writing family history augments and differentiates one's gratitude. As I increasingly felt my debt reach to distant scholars, archives and institutions, so the making of a book turned my gratitude toward home. Special thanks to Jan Louwagie of the Southwest Minnesota University History Center; Cy Molitor of the Prairieland Genealogical Society; and local university librarians and staff: Mary Jane Striegel, Mara Wiggins, Joann Robasse, Connie Sten-

srud, and Shawn Hedman. I relied on the critical help of three keen university students and friends, Jody Grismer, Donata DeBruyckere, and Melissa
Kleindal. Finally, my thanks go to professionals of the Minnesota Historical
Society: reference librarian Deborah Miller was, as always, responsive to my
designs and requests; press director Gregory Britton took the risk to accept
the work at its first maturation; and intelligent, vigilant, and empathetic
editor-in-chief Ann Regan, grasped, improved, and guided the work to its
completion.

I conclude by exonerating all herein mentioned of all errors herein found.
I ask special forgiveness from all my relatives and ancestors, whose everyday
lives I have probed, but whose inner hearts I have in no way fathomed.

JACOB'S WELL

Putting on the Coat of the Past

I put on the tattered but many-colored coat of my mongrel family past. Formed on North American shores for more than 250 years, my family was woven out of strands of Sicilian mountaineers, French Acadian swamp dwellers, English Midlanders, West Prussian farmers, and pre-famine Irish Protestants and Catholics. My family's past was composed on the largest looms of North American history, with its laws, economic transformations, industrialization, migrations, and wars, yet it can only be re-created in the spirit of the long and patient handcraft of quilting, by joining bits and pieces from church, work, and cemetery records; ship manifests, censuses, and property titles; excerpts of newspaper articles, personal letters, and notes; and one extensive journal. In the process of reconstructing the family past, I found myself juxtaposing distinct paths of migration, studying numerous localities, examining individual marriages, and pondering the meaning of many stories and singular fates.

Like the family histories of many, if not most Americans, *Jacob's Well* is a history of mixed ancestry, which has proved, contrary to common prejudice, to be rich in information and filled with surprise. Formed of rural and pre-national peoples, of no single literate or national culture, my family surely was more a creation of nature, environment, and local conditions than any pure ethnicity. Although some of its members served, even died, in almost all the nation's wars, including in the military ranks of colonial Massachusetts during the Revolution, the family never made a soldier's claims to the national tradition of military glory. More than anything, our story is coincidental with the history of the American poor. In their first century in this nation, my poor forbears, perpetual migrants, simply tried to eke out a living on barren lands and in small mill towns. At the turn of the twentieth century, they joined the emerging urban industrial working class and, over time, became wage earners, consumers, and members of national, popular, and mass culture.

Having once found some comfort and, thus, a kind of therapy in the idea that I was a combination, perhaps an alloy, of my stoic father, Joe, and my vivacious mother, Ethel, I extended this embrace of opposites to my Sicilian grandmother, Rosalia, and my American grandmother, Frances. With the most ancient Mediterranean sense of fate, and with a modern sense of discontent and restlessness, Rosalia and Frances joined in me the contrasting worlds and ages of ethnic and Yankee ways. The very difference between them led me to understand their controdictory lives and times—and how one life is many lives, one time, multiple times.

Family has any definitions. Recognizing family as either a matter of those who live together in the present or those who, independent of place and age, are related over generations, the law defines family as both a matter of household and a relation of consanguinity. Anthropology and sociology explore family as rooted in tribe, society, ethnicity, and class. The formal academic study of family history, which flourished in the last decades of the twentieth century, looks at family through the prism of environmental, social, economic, and cultural changes. Having harvested a veritable forest of distinctions and comparisons, insights and debates, and theoretical and quantitative findings, it requires skill to use cuttings from the history of a family in the building of a family history.[1]

Yet, beyond macro-historical and social science approaches, it must be remembered that family is the terrain of elemental and abiding human experience. Family awakes primal feelings, core senses, primary metaphors, and the first experiences surrounding biological events, daily circumstances, indissoluble attachments, and rites of passages. Family largely determines, at least for the great majority, how we experience, know, idealize, and remember life. Both nest and fortress, and the bed of our sleep and the pillow of our dreams, family equally forms our necessary and intimate lives.

As memoirs and biographies attest, moving and compelling stories arise out of the family, which both nurture and stifle. Family provides a first knowledge of and first steps into the world around us. It is where we are born, nurse, learn to love, grow up, marry, reproduce, work, and die. An object of nostalgia, a source of inner discord and bitter feelings, the family fills hearts to brims. We scour it for true stories and self-discovery. Source of love, gratitude, hate, remorse, and more, it is the subject of many of those first and elemental memories, which we cannot and should not forget. The living and the dead mingle around the family hearth in the classic world; in the special west room holding the heirlooms in old rural Ireland; in the "colorful" corner centered on an icon in a Russian peasant's hut; or, as on the dresser top of Grandmother Rosalia, before the photograph of a husband, a statue of the Infant of Prague, and a few candles. There we catch a sense of James Joyce's words: "The now, the here, through which all the future plunges into the past."

Keeper of the Graves, Writer of Family History

As the only surviving son and the oldest sibling, accepting his natural obligation, my father tended the family graves. Starting around 1960, when I was twenty-two and soon to be out of university, he sometimes brought me along. In one way, it was just another duty that he performed with unquestionable certitude and regularity, almost as he might shovel the snow or water the grass. Yet it seemed a destined mission, carrying with it all the momentum he had internalized as the son of Sicilian peasants: he had started to work, selling fruit, at seven years old, and then spent his life in step with the industrial discipline of Motor City Detroit. There he learned to go to work, take a bus, read a newspaper folded into small squares, wear white shoes, dance the fox-trot, drive, shop for and purchase his own car, root for the Tigers, save for and buy a home, and acquire and use tools to do his own repairs. His life merges there with the stereotypes of the nation's middle decades: the play and blind pigs of the 1920s, the grim days and unionizing of the 1930s, the war years of the 1940s, and the improved wages and abundance of the 1950s.

On a Saturday morning each spring my dad and I would set out, with my father driving slightly above the speed limit and going as directly as possi-

My parents, Joseph Amato and Ethel Linsdeau Amato, early 1950s. The photo
was an unintentional double exposure; an image of the two of them with me
looms behind them.

ble to Mount Olivet Cemetery on the east side of Detroit. He parked and retrieved from the trunk his little aluminum bucket, which held a trowel, a short three-pronged hoe, and a brown collapsible army trench shovel. Then my father first headed to the graves of his family. At the top of a knoll covered by mainly Polish gravesites was a row of four graves that held his mother Rosalia and father Antonino, both of whom came to the United States in the first decade of the twentieth century from towns in the Madonie Mountains of Sicily; his sister Fina, who died young, expecting her first child; and Fina's much-older husband Phil Trupiano, who also came from western Sicily and remarried after Fina's death. After watering the graves' grass and removing the excess grass that had grown up around and over the edges of the small flat tombstones, my father knelt, made a hurried Sign of the Cross, recited an Our Father. Then we briskly set out for the newer section of the cemetery, where my mother's parents were buried. Again we cleaned up, prayed, and promptly left, making it home in time for lunch.

Shortly after my father died in 1989, my mother moved to Minnesota to live with my wife and me. I became the keeper of the family graves. My annual pilgrimages to the dead involve a good deal of talking to myself (which serves as my principal internal gyroscope) and increasingly confirm that the older I get the more the dead take hold of me. I like the notion that my heart is a temple of memory in which they intermittently reside. I feel compelled, in some way or other, to complete their lives, to honor their gifts and sacrifices. With no brothers and sisters to help remember and revere my parents and grandparents, and as the oldest male on both sides of the family, I must take up the pail and shovel and tend the family's graves as my father did.

My father's tombstone, like most contemporary stones, economically offers the onlooker only a name and two dates: "Beloved Husband and Father 1912–1989." Only my memory rescues him from anonymity. His stone does not say, as somehow it should, that he was a good man who gave his life for work and family and who, on matters of principle, stood his ground. His parents were impoverished Sicilian immigrants, and he was only three years old when his father died. When his stepfather was imprisoned, my father took full responsibility for the family. After graduating from high school at sixteen, he found employment with Western Union, where, advancing from clerk to management, he missed only two days in more than forty-three years of work.

Thoughts of my father also evoke sharp regrets for him. I wish, for example, that he had found a way to defy my mother and the duties that tethered him to a staid life. But he was a quintessential family man; such a rebellion would never have fit him. He was sequestered by the life he and my mother had chosen to live. He subdued her, an intelligent, and spirited woman, by not letting her work and not supporting her wish to adopt additional children, when they realized I was the only child she would bear. She, in turn, domesticated him by not allowing him to stray too far from home, which he had no interest in doing anyway. As a couple, they resisted distraction and change, embracing the limits they set.

Most of all, I wish that my father had lent his imagination and energy to his own future. He could have harbored a distinguishing passion, fashioned a notable skill, been something unto himself. He could easily have been a lawyer, an accountant, a political leader, or a labor mediator. I wanted him to shirk his duty—to spend weekends fishing, hunting, or golfing. But that was not his way. Over time I came to realize he simply was other than my wishes. A sense of necessity and obligation ruled his experience, as abundance and choice gifted mine. Shrewd, calculating, and loyal, he was an old Sicilian peasant. There was a grim Spartan integrity about his life that he only once contradicted, by telling me, "Have a good time. Life goes by quickly." I do well if I can imitate him and his kind.

At his graveside, I no longer feel a need to argue with him about his choices. I regret that our hearts did not draw closer—but he was not a talker, rarely expressed his feelings, and more, we were of different worlds and ages. Nevertheless, we did share good times. I enjoyed his laugh. We drank an occasional beer together, played bocce ball, went to Detroit Tigers games together, prayed shoulder to shoulder in church, agreed that Republicans are not our kind of people, and argued over our shared Democratic Party. We each knew and conceded—and there is a dignity in knowing this—that in some way fathers and sons are not meant to be soul mates.

Yet ideas, impulses, sentiments, hopes, and this study of family history unify us. I know we are joined in a tradition of loyalty to work and family and in a high estimation of honesty and truth. I hope heaven's promise includes our reunification. And when I visit his father Antonino's and his mother Rosalia's home in the mountains of Sicily, a place he never saw, I draw close to understanding him.

With an active memory for story and detail and a quicksilver spirit in command of a well-exercised tongue, my mother delivered me to a different past. She made talking and being as close as they could possibly be. In contrast to my father's parents, who came from identifiable villages and families, her family's long and complex American background is one of incomplete family trees, incongruous details, and grounds rife for speculation. This difference between the families was magnified for me by the polarity of my stolid, repressed, and predictable father and my energetic and protean mother. While he was steady, reliable, and laconic, she was volatile and highstrung. What he made emphatic by repetition of his fixed daily regime, she spontaneously invented while talking with strange words, novel ideas, and enthusiastic repetitions of past stories. In this way she held attention, and her childhood was ever alive and present. With her tongue she lashed the world into what she took to be its proper place or what she willed it at any given moment. Her constant stream of anecdotes and memories provoked my father's mounting plaint in his retirement years, "She remembers everything, and I can't recall anything."

Mount Olivet, an old and large Catholic cemetery, holds the remains of Joe and of Ethel, who died in 2002. It seems a small piece of green to hold their once-brimming lives. The cemetery knolls and flats are rich in mute clusters of oddly shaped stones. Italian, Polish, German, and Irish names form a microcosm of the city's east side Catholic and ethnic neighborhoods, which Ethel and Joe once knew like the backs of their hands. However, the cemetery says little about the dead and their relations to the living. Its grassy green and many trees, whispering but faint wishes, form a frail wrapper around past lives and histories. I must ponder the dead to hold oblivion at bay—to keep them, the family, and me alive.

"Let the dead bury the dead!" Discard the memories and stories that chain you to them. Dispatch the dead to their reward—or leave them undisturbed in their long sleep. Do not interrupt their journeys to God or spoil their peace in ever-ending forgetfulness. We must not, the present cautions, seek the long and losing way between the here and now, the once that was, and the here-after. But I dissent from this emptying philosophy. It cuts too deeply into the tissue of memory and hope of sparking wakefulness. I prefer a jumble of his-tories to an empty void. For the course of this work, I will let the dead parade within me, and I will fashion their story into mine and mine into theirs.

The Trinity of Family History

While this spirit and philosophy moved me to write this book, a select set of premises, themes, and tools shaped its form. First, I acknowledge my work is experimental insofar as it seeks to unify what is normally left apart. It joins a personal quest for a type of self-knowledge with a professional historian's concern for appropriate narrative and proper context. While stressing the importance of local and regional history for family history, I do not overlook the mounting and universal power of national and inter-national history. Seeking to define a major revolution in everyday American and family life, I contrast the place of necessity in shaping the lives of earlier generations with the improved well-being and greater choice enjoyed by later generations.

On this count, *Jacob's Well* traces the ascent of the American rural poor at the end of the nineteenth and the start of the twentieth century. In the con-text of the developing mill towns of Wisconsin's Fox River Valley and emer-gent industrial and commercial society, I see the family, for the first time, structured around regular work, steady wages, and house ownership. This world—that of my great-grandfather, Prussian immigrant Jacob Linsdau, and my Wisconsin forbears—began to afford sufficient means and adequate public space for the development of individual careers, personal choice, and the hope of happiness.

Beyond this, the family here is made a microcosm of the social and cultural mutation of the modern world. Though embedded in locality and traditional culture at the start of their sojourns in North America, in the last two centuries my families have never been isolated from the effects of expanding markets, encroaching government policies, the opening of new lands, and the building of canals and railroads. Though moved by the perennial desire to find a place on the land, the family's migration was energized and driven by the mounting and increasingly paramount modern need for money. The various branches of the family followed the Great Lakes and new canal system to frontiers of the old Northwest. Starting from the impoverished countryside of mountainous Maine, the freshly settled regions of northern and western New York (known as the "burned-over district" because revivals of the 1820s and 1830s had so thoroughly evangelized the people), and the developing Canadian and American shores of Lake Ontario, as well as rural Ireland and West Prussia, the family joined in settling east-central Wisconsin in the 1850s and 1860s. By the end of the nineteenth century, their stories expressed the national shift from countryside to town, where both as families and newly born democratic individuals, they were transformed by mass, commercial, industrial, and national society into wage earners, soldiers, citizens, entrepreneurs, entertainers, and everyone else of whom an era's Whitman may have sung.

Finally, I must mention in brief the tools I used to create this work. Utilizing what I call the trinity of family history—genealogy, history, and storytelling—I first turned to genealogy, the indispensable starting point and official scorecard of family history: You can't tell the players without a program! Profoundly improved in its resources, methodologies, and popularity in the last few decades, genealogy proved essential to establish not just names, dates, relations, and origins, but immigration, military service, the sale and purchase of property, and so much more that provides a family with coherence and detail. Aside from a patient and imaginative search for new evidence, it requires a detective's concern for detail and connections.

Just as crucial as genealogy, local and micro-regional history provided an all-important understanding of the many small and defining worlds my family inhabited since their arrival in North America. As articulated in my

study *Rethinking Home*, local history and regional history offer ways to reconstitute the substance of everyday family life as abstract and general theories
never can. At the same time, I had to make use of national, macro-regional,
and even international histories, which explain how outside forces and
ideas penetrated and shaped farm and village lives at accelerating rates in
the nineteenth-century North American countryside. American democracy, as French visitor Alexis de Tocqueville observed in his 1831 trip across
the United States, was individualistic, mobile, and dynamic. As I observed
in my family, one consequence of this was, in the words of twentieth-cen-
tury French commentator Paul Valery, a mass society characterized by "inter-
changeability, interdependence, and uniformity in customs, manners, and
even in dreams."[2]

Yet no matter how keen the use of genealogy and how ample and critical
my application of local, regional, state, and national histories, this project
required more, if I were to put an individual and human face on the family. I could not treat the family as mere molecules in the flow of a great river,
nor portable mannequins for my reaching generalizations. While paying
attention to all sorts of vital family matters, I also had to look inward and, in
measure, reconstitute the emotions, sensibilities, motives, beliefs, and metaphors that moved and guided family members. In effect, I had to discover
and invent them, remember and resurrect them, and yet beyond the cultivation of their meaning, give them control over their own lives. Anthropologist
Greg Dening pertinently wrote,

> *History . . . is not an artificial curiosity at all. History, by common sense, is the*
> *past itself. It is independent of our knowing, as wild as reality, controlled and*
> *ordered like life, perhaps, but not by us.*[3]

Moving between exterior and interior worlds and on alert at all times for
the interplay between family and place, nature, environment, and society at
large, family history scavenges the past for every scrap of evidence. In reconstructing a family, all counts. This includes school, church, company, and
military records; photographs; productions of crafts and tools and their orga-
nization; gardens, foods, and recipes; and so on. We must strain our memo-

ries and those of our relatives and friends to recall the actions, gestures, and interactions, and the words, anecdotes, and stories of the family. My family comes to life today when we think about the wine they made, the chickens they slaughtered, the gardens they staked out, the songs they sang, and the food they made. The telling fact, indeed, can be how they prayed or cursed, took notes, wrote letters, or even kept score at cards. My grandmother Rosalia revealed her understanding of life when she took the optimistic proverb, "Every dog has his day," and twisted it to say, "Every day has its dog." We adopt new methods, to quote cultural historian Carlo Ginzburg, "to bring to light those forms of knowledge or understanding of the world which have been suppressed or lost."[4]

Family stories, which can be considered the richest wells but often are the most ambiguous gems of all evidence, are always to be sought and to be deciphered, sometimes anew by each generation What does it mean, for instance, that my mother said her grandfather worked as a veterinarian at the end of his life, when in fact he worked as a hostler? What significance is found in Prussian Catholic great-grandfather Jacob's battle against the local temperance league? And yet what do I make of his son's, my grandfather William's, instructions on how to take the curse off a white horse, or spit under a chip of wood to make a wish come true? In this tradition, his daughter Ethel, my mother, was a well of stories from which I continue to draw insights into Jacob's tribe.

Stories, deciphered and retold, are the third and last member of the trinity of family history. They provide the richest clues and deepest enigmas in the family's past. Enticing, baffling, revealing, and enlightening, stories constitute a family's heirloom seeds. More than an inherited pocket watch that quit ticking a century ago, a barely worn family rosary, or a grandmother's recipe for dill pickles, stories reanimate the spirit and set it dancing across time and space. They reveal original conditions, consuming situations, fixed attitudes, as well as mixed feeling and ambiguous motives. A tiny story can sum up a horrific life. It can synthesize the individual and the universal, while making the ironic, paradoxical, contradictory, and tragic stand forth. Stories prove the best bait for hooking the impressionable minds of grandchildren.

Whether in the form of Shakespearean drama or simply a short bawdy tale, stories call the present into the past and invite—when records are lost, forgotten, and still—their retelling in the future.

The family historian must master the art of storytelling. What, after all, is truth without anecdote, history without events, explanation without narration—or yet life itself without a story? Stories are not just the wells from which we drink most deeply but at the same time the golden threads that hold and bind—Ariadne's precious string that leads us through the labyrinth that connects living present and the living past. And then, *once upon time*, there is the story of my Italian grandmother Rosalia and that of my American grandmother Frances, who came together in the family of Joe, Ethel, and grandson Joey, from worlds away and worlds apart to give us their lives, tell us their stories, and in some way make us them.

I

Rosalia, a Misery as Ancient as Sicily

We who were fortunate enough to know our grandparents well knew them with the direct-
ness and fullness of our youthful senses and the wonderful openness of impressionable minds.
In contrast to our disciplining and guiding parents, grandparents provided us a gentle and less
confrontational encounter with the past. Grandparents themselves were the children of genera-
tions whose individual traits and ways have been irretrievably lost to the body of deep time,
transformed into archetypical myths of distant origin, epochal migrations to and primitive
settlements in primordial lands. Without grandparents' stories, photographs, and documents,
their childhoods are lost to the great gulf of time, and we are ignorant of their family and every-
day life. Knowledge of their diets, manners, gestures, habits, thoughts, emotions, sensibilities,
and beliefs vanish, and we must reconstruct them. They are the most "familiar strangers" from
the past we know, and they prove the right spot to begin our work on the family past.

Grandmother Amato has been since I can remember my first way into a different time,
mind, and world. My Italian grandmother, she constituted a first contact with a past that no
longer existed and a place to which the family once belonged. I knew her home and the table
she set. I saw her once dance the tarantella and more than once walk the narrow lanes of family
graves. I cuddled close to her at bedtime, took in distinct body smells, and learned a peculiar
pattern of breathing. Short and heavy, but filled with energy and grace, she connected me to
another form of mortal flesh and keen spirit. When angry and cursing, mourning and moan-
ing in Sicilian, she took me as close to that distant island and place as I could have ever been.
Out of Rosalia's life I fashioned a history, tradition, and self. In calling her forth I enter into a
land where past and present are one.

The ethnicity or class we claim as ours, either reflexively or by conscious
choice, provides us an identity, a past, and an inheritance. It can also distort
our writing and rob us of a living past. We must forever take care lest, in our
desire to magnify and monumentalize, we trade real persons for abstractions

and clichés, which empty the family of true individuals and make of it a canister of hollow servants and callow ideologies. Selves and families are not entities frozen in time that can be known and preserved simply as names.

My father, who liked grand arias, especially as sung by Caruso and Lanza, was an Italian who couldn't sing a note. In fact, he was Sicilian, and though Sicilian—a language distinct from Italian—was the only language my father spoke before going to school, he rarely used it, and then only with Grandmother Amato. Our family knew nothing of Italian high culture; the glories of Rome, the paintings and sculptures of Michelangelo, and even the romantic gondolas of Venice did not float in our minds, even though my father took a vague pride in all things Italian. At the same time, we were without any relation to and had not even an iota of knowledge about the Mafia. Our thing—*Cosa Nostra*, so to speak—was food, jobs, home, a car, and our own family. The family was preoccupied with making it through the Depression, getting home alive from World War II, deciding how long a strike would last. Living on Detroit's lower east side, we were peasants huddled under the shadows of Chrysler Motors. Our Sicilian world, though not lost entirely in mind and manner, folkways and food ways, was an ocean and a third of a continent away from the mountain towns of Sicily that grandparents Rosalia and Antonino left in their youth in the first decade of the twentieth century.

Our surname Amato—"the loved one"—announced and identified us to the outside world as Italians, even though we were Sicilians to the mixed ethnic neighborhood of Germans, Irish, Canadians, and older Americans.[1] The two "a's" and the "o" at the end joined us to relatives with vowel-studded names like Notaro, Bomegna, and DeCarlo and gave us our own heroes and champions like Rocky Marciano, Frank Sinatra, and Guglielmo Marconi, whose development of wireless telegraphy made him special to my father, who worked more than forty years at Western Union. Stereotypes about us as Italians and Sicilians abounded, but my family, like most immigrants to this country, had more important affairs to attend to than the ignorance of others. Almost all my relatives swapped their Italian first names for American names, so Cruciano became John; Vicenzu, Jimmy;

Rosalia, Rose; Epifenia, Fina; Carmela, Mildred; and so on. Although some of our relatives looked like the tan and dark-eyed Arabs who conquered Sicily, Rosalia and Antonino's families looked more like the fair conquering Normans who displaced the Arabs. While some considered Italians dark and sinister, of another race, skin color and prejudice did not prevent my dad and his cousins from marrying Irish and German girls, place them in segregated units in the armed services, or cause them to identify with Detroit's radically increasing groups of blacks, whom they increasingly associated with poverty, crime, and disordered living.

My own childhood generally spared me overt expressions of anti-Italianism. However, I do remember the mild taunting that I suffered in elementary school every St. Patrick's Day. "Amato—that's Italian, right? What are you doing wearing green today?" I was always left speechless. I couldn't say my mother made me wear green—and, in fact, she was every bit as much German as Irish.

Only at the university did I start to examine my relation to Rosalia and my Italian-Sicilian-American identity, which I preferred to all other identities. Aside from joining my name and ethnicity, it clearly separated me from the mass of American society. It afforded me a tie to peasants and the poor rural people, an identity I particularly cherished and increasingly valued. A range of European and Italian rural writers like Giuseppe Verga, Ignazio Silone, Emile Guillaumin, and Pierre-Jakez Hélas broadened my identity with the plight of the peasant, which I consider the painful heart of the great transformation from the tradition to the modern and contemporary worlds. I linked this profound mutation with the fate of my Sicilian grandmother and grandfather.

In the last fifteen years, I have gone to Sicily several times to establish and renew my acquaintance with their villages and families. My trips only further pressed on me my role as keeper of dead, while joining me to the spirit of Sicilian writer Giuseppe di Lampedusa. In his melancholy book, *The Leopard*, Lampedusa describes how Sicily, that cherished Mediterranean garden that lured the peoples of more than twenty civilizations to its shores, sentences history to oblivion with the most ancient law of the stars and intractable human nature. "Nowhere," he contends, "has truth so short a life as in Sicily; a fact scarcely happened five minutes before its genuine kernel has vanished, been camouflaged, embellished, disfigured, annihilated by imagination and self-interest, shame, fear, generosity, malice, opportunism, charity, all the passions, good as well as evil, fling themselves on the fact and tear it to pieces; very soon it has vanished altogether." In this Lampedusa only says what comes to every practitioner of family history with the ripening sorrow of old age: death not only undoes the body but steals memory, the mind's most precious fruit. Approaching the serious age of seventy, the only son of an only son, I ponder the lives of Rosalia and Antonino. I hereby testify that with their whole lives they tried to find their way out of the labyrinth of poverty.

The Sicily They Left Behind

Rosalia was singular and unique. In her wedding photograph she is that petite four-foot, seven-inch bride, freshly arrived from Sicily. She became the mother of my father, his sister, Fina, and three stepsisters, Josephine, Mildred, and Pauline. In later age, she more and more resembled all those typical older Italian women whom I remember as short and stocky widows dressed in black. Unfalteringly in her affection for my father and me, she is a gyre of my reflections on the past. Nevertheless, Rosalia's great crossing was anything but hers alone. It belonged to Sicily, to Europe, and to a century that witnessed one of the greatest movements of peoples in all history. Her decision was the irreducible part of that unprecedented exodus of southern and eastern Europeans to the New World in the last decades of the nineteenth century and the first of the twentieth century.

The same is true of Antonino. He was born in 1881 to Giuseppe Amato, my father's namesake, and his wife, Epifania Rizzo, namesake of my father's sister. In his wedding photograph he appears as a short, solid, square-jawed man, of even features, light complexion, and large shoulders. He stands at least a head taller than Rosalia. His individuality and determination is not be discounted, yet we know that his fate, like those of all young men who are participants in

Rosalia Notaro and Joseph Amato at their wedding, 1907

great causes, depends on the acts of states and markets—and their lives are compounded and quantified along with millions of others.

In fact, my grandparents, who count so much to me individually, tally as only two of the 3.5 million Italians who left their homes for the New World between 1901 and 1910; only two human beings of the 7 million Italians who emigrated to the New World between 1871 and 1914; only two of the 30 million European immigrants who arrived in the United States between 1870 and 1914. Their epochal journey belongs to the phenomenal expansion of cheap steamship and railroad travel. It was a consequence of the promise of a new life, the opportunity to work and make money, which scoured the most remote corners of Europe for immigrants to work in mines, forests, and the booming factories of the United States and Canada, the interiors of Brazil and Argentina.[2]

Their narrative by birth, condition, and class belonged to that of the landless poor. They were members of Europe's largest family, the peasantry, which, in fact, has been in constant mutation since European feudalism, the Catholic Church, and the emerging trans-regional markets formed them into a class around the year 1000. I have found that I cannot read the rich history of European peasantry, in all its variation of place and time, without harvesting insights or yet compounding questions I have about their lives.[3]

Surely at the time of emigration they and their families were not the archetypical peasants who, in the words of Romantic historian Michelet, "loved only the land. That is the sum of their religion! They worship only the manure on their fields."[4] Rather, my grandparents were extra children in a community of landless day laborers and surplus humans. Sicily had been in decline for a century and half, since the time this agricultural island exported wheat and animal products to the world and celebrated its surpluses with the bountiful baroque churches found across the island.[5] If Rosalia and Antonino clung to the hope of having a place on the land until the eve of their emigration, it was because it was the only hope they had and could imagine. Even when parceled into the smallest gardens, attained only on the condition of paying increasingly prohibitive rent, the land was the known way to survive, unless one emigrated to the cities along the coast. The land was their lot and their destiny—a frail life raft, which put them on a sea of vicissitudes of droughts, mudslides, and crop failures. Currents from a growing European and world market steadily pushed rural Sicilians toward a world in which money alone mattered. Their little piece of land, or hope of having it, lashed them to a lifetime of hard work, misery, and inferiority in a delineated rural hierarchy. Steadfastness, prayer, and resignation drawing short of despair were the only answers, aside from the all-important dignity.

Attachment to the land subjected my peasant family to man-made calamities. They came incarnate in the guise of a tax collector, the steward of an absentee landlord, along with packs of shrewd and swindling merchants, dishonest bankers, greedy priests, ambitious politicians, and yes, in many places, even the tentacular Mafia, which enforced the will of the distant owners of the island. Certainly, my family suffered the common plight of the rural poor everywhere. Classified a rank lower than peasants who were small landholders, Rosalia, Antonino, and their families were day laborers without a secure niche on the land, without money, overtaxed, and too populous. If they were to marry and to have a home, to have something and be somebody, they had to leave. By migrating and emigrating, organizing, and even revolting, the poor proved that they were anything but "potatoes in a sack."[6]

Rosalia's and Antonino's homes were in the neighboring agro-hill towns of Montemaggiore Belsito and Cerda along the River Torto. Hundreds of feet above the sea and to the south of the port town of Termine Imerese, one bay away to the east from Palermo, these towns enjoyed *aria fresca;* that is, they were upland refuges from the malaria (*mal aria*) that had ravaged the Italian seaside lands since Roman times. Without good roads or animals and carts to haul them, the towns' poor were isolated. Their condition and status was local and particular. The common measure throughout the island was whether they had land, a dwelling, a good garden, a mule or donkey, and whether they had friends, a good godfather, who formed a vital system of support and protection, and a decent landlord who stuck with them in bad times. In mountain towns like Cerda and Montemaggiore Belsito they were identified by which end of town they inhabited and their destinations when they left: The better off went to work their own fields, gardens, and olive trees, while the poor—the gatherers, shepherds, and day laborers, including young Rosalia Notaro and her family—went to work land owned by others, guide others' animals, pick greens, or forage in forests.

Church and municipal records sparsely identify the Notaro family in Montemaggiore as early as 1750 and an Amato family, which, however is probably not ours, in Cerda as early as 1815.[7] Both families inhabited rural Sicily as *contadino, coltivatore,* and *compagnolo,* terms that designated the *villici,* that class of landless and land-poor peasants who lived outside the village center and in remote communes near the fields they tended.[8] If my Amato family owned a home, which the children of Antonino's sisters doubt, it probably consisted of a single room with an earthen floor. Furnishings would have been sparse— a table, a bench, candles, perhaps a chair, a saint's statue, an oven or stove, a large bed for the parents, and a cradle, along with some utensils for cooking, needles and thread for sewing and crocheting, and a small collection of tools, among which were tongs, shears, a shovel, a saw, an axe, and an adze. Children would have slept on straw mattresses, crowded together in a small loft. Animals surely shared their residence at certain times. A photograph of Antonino's father, Giuseppe Amato, taken when he was in his late forties or early fifties, tells the toll life took on poor Sicilian peasants in the late nineteenth century. A prominent nose, reminding me of my father's, forlorn eyes, and large ears, distinguish his thin, creased, and unshaven face. He wears a cravat around his scrawny neck, a tattered coat, a collarless shirt, and a worn vest missing one of its four buttons.

Pressing poverty dominated the families of Antonino and Rosalia. Working scanty and rocky uplands, which at most served as biological incubators for richer and prospering valleys and town below, my Sicilian ancestors' lives resembled the vast majority of rural folk in modern times.[9] Caught in the pervasive draft of downward mobility, they were steadily transformed from peasants to agricultural laborers and small craftsmen into day laborers, *giornalieri,* the poorest and largest part of south Italy's work force.[10] It was inevitable that they, as the whole population of the island, calculate the costs and advantages of the most distant migrations—to mainland Italy, northern Europe, Argentina, Brazil, Canada, and America. In one way, they, as a large

Antonino's father, Giuseppe Amato, about 1900

family, were compelled at least to consider the choice. In another way, they
and their kind were mere twigs carried by a mighty spring torrent, down out
of the mountains of Sicily onto waiting ships that carried them across the
ocean to the shores of another world.

Their descent truly began before they were born. Elemental forces,
including improved health and nutrition, had set Sicily's population multiplying and migrating in the course of the nineteenth century. Conforming
to regional, Italian, European, and transatlantic patterns, the Sicilian population grew from 1.5 million inhabitants in 1800 to 3.5 million inhabitants in
1900, with population density tripling in western Sicily. It is estimated that at
the beginning of Italian unification in 1860, only one in six peasants owned
land in Sicily—and farm plots were uniformly too small to produce a subsistence cash income. (Absentee landlords—gentry, nobility, and the church—
did not invest in modernizing their lands.) It appeared that only the new central government could carry on the development that the preceding regime,
the Bourbons, had neglected, but Rome consciously chose to do otherwise.
It adopted policies of free trade and an open economy to industrialize the
nation rather than reform its agricultural society.[11]

For western Sicily, economic decline was accelerated by a diminished
export of its principal crop, wheat, due to competition from Russian and
expanding North and South American grain production. At the same time,
free trade brought a mounting import of mass-produced goods, which displaced workers in indigenous crafts such as textile manufacture, candle- and
tile-making, ceramics, hide-tanning, fish conservation, boat building, and
coral polishing. Intensifying an overall loss of local power, swelling emigration coincided with the rise of the Mafia, which functioned as rural entrepreneurs who bridged gaps between the superstructure of government and
outside markets and local infrastructures and populations.[12]

According to an 1886 Italian government report on agricultural conditions in the Sicilian countryside, unemployment ravaged the peasant class *(la
classe dei contadini)*.[13] The frequency of poor harvests in this period worsened
the deteriorating condition of the rural poor, who lacked cash to rent or
buy land, to purchase essential goods, to defray the rising costs of services

such as milling, or to pay the ever-increasing taxes remorselessly imposed by church and state. Small holders found themselves forced to mortgage their homes and to sell their donkeys and mules to make it through the winter and prepare spring planting. Sharecroppers were thrown more and more on the mercy of the landholder or his agent, while day laborers, living hand to mouth, lacked even the means to emigrate.[14] This disastrous situation reached its nadir at end of the century, when, as Sicilian historian Giuseppe De Felice observed, "The little proprietors melt[ed] like the snow before the sun."[15] Among them were Rosalia and Antonino and their families. Their emigration, like that of Sicilians and millions of others in Europe and North America, shows simultaneously how local, migratory, economic, and international family history is.

My paternal grandparents were siphoned off the impoverished hill towns of Sicily and formed droplets in the flood of emigrants that poured in swelling streams to the coastal port below and into the holds of cheap-fared transatlantic ships. To find work, to earn money, to take a mate, to establish a family and home of one's own—the singularly desirable, only imagined, and truly honorable things to do—commanded their exit. Forsaking the country and the land of your birth, made easier by the prior emigration of uncle, brother, husband, or neighbor, made departure seem both a necessity and a choice for those who could scrap together the means to do so. In 1900, the decade of the greatest Sicilian exodus and Antonino's and Rosalia's emigration, 70 percent of the Sicilian population clustered in communities of ten thousand or more, which were closer to the sea, where work was a little more available, cash attainable, and ships for the New World stood at anchor.

Antonino's Story

In 1904 *Nunnu* Antonino left the island's enduring poverty behind, but he did not taste in full the happiness of golden America. Almost a century later, at the home of Antonino's grandniece Francesca and her husband, Francesco, in Cerda, I learned how descendants of the Amato family continued to suf-

St. Joseph's Table, set by an earlier generation of Francesca Di Blasi's family, late 1940s
(*Overleaf*)

fer long after, through the Depression and after World War II, having barely a penny to their name and owning no property. Francesco tells me that he only acquired their small, less-than-two-acre garden, on which his household so depends and tenaciously clings, by gathering and selling as scrap metal the shell cases that Patton's army left behind on his drive through Madonie Mountains to Palermo. Three letters received from Cerda in post–World War II, dating between 1949 and 1951, written by Antonino's sister Francesca to her older sister Margherita in Detroit, express the family's impoverished condition. In a first letter, Francesca gives thanks for the modest sums of money and package of clothes she has received from Margherita and sends prayers, greetings, and best wishes to Rosalia. A second letter lists penny for penny all the ingredients bought to prepare *un tavola di San Giuseppe*, a modest dinner without meat served to neighbors and their children in honor of St. Joseph and dedicated to seeking his help in curing Margherita's son, Sam. Demonstrating that the wolf still stood at the family door, the third letter reports that the family was simultaneously being sued by the town doctor and butcher and was waiting for the outcome of a judicial hearing to determine whom they should pay first.

The April 1904 manifest for the steamship *Marco Minghetti* (a slow ship of twelve knots service speed) lists third-class steerage passenger Antonino as a workman who, significantly, could read and write. After a long, three-week voyage from Palermo, he arrived in New York City with $4 and a train ticket.[16] His next destination was the tiny northeastern Pennsylvania coal-mining town of Kelayres, located in Klein Township, one of the last township settlements platted in Schuylkill County in 1872. It was a mere patch of a town, a company settlement, named for early Irish residents Kelly and Ayres, who were construction supervisors for the Leigh Valley Railroad in the 1890s. There he would join his uncle Giuseppe Rizzo, who had reached the New World a year earlier. The risks of migration were somewhat offset by the promise of financial reward for unskilled workers, like Antonino and Giuseppe. Working as so-called pick men in the mines, they might earn as much as $500 a year, which could be five or even ten times what they could have made in Sicily.

Such Sicilian names as Sacco, Capriotti, Nazzareno, Tornabene, Malatesta, and Jumpeter (Gian Pietro) filled Kelayres's directory and the tombstones of the Catholic cemetery, while testifying to a chain migration linking the mountains of Sicily to this Pennsylvania mountain village and to the city of Detroit. I frequently visited Kelayres, which shares a border with my wife's hometown, McAdoo, a larger coal town of a few thousand inhabitants directly to the east, to which her father's parents immigrated prior to its incorporation as borough in 1896. In Kelayres, where I still had Amato and Notaro cousins and had even visited once as a boy, I had several conversations in the 1970s with a ninety-year-old retired local teacher, Tony DiMaria, who actually remembered Antonino. Tony whetted my interest about Kelayres by telling me of the 1934 Kelayres Massacre and other vivid stories of its Sicilian settlers, many of whom left Kelayres before World War I for industrial jobs in Buffalo, Rochester, and Detroit.[17] Unfortunately, Tony could add nothing about Antonino other than he had worked in a small local grocery store, which, I conjecture, paid at most $1.25 a day. He preferred it, family stories confirm, to the darkness and danger of the mine, the world below in which he worked only one day.

Beyond this, we know only few things about Antonino in Kelayres. He came when he was twenty-three years old with the help of his maternal uncle, and he, in his turn, assisted the immigration of two of his younger sisters, my great-aunts Margherita and Carmela, respectively in 1909 and 1912. Unfortunately, Antonino never had the comfort and luxury of retirement to sit on his front porch and tell his grandson about the old country, or how his garden fared, or his first days in Kelayres and Detroit. As for thousands of thousands of immigrants, destiny overran his dreams.

Rosalia, La Destinata

Fate also wrote the life of *Nunna* Rosalia. Choice was not her rudder; dreams were not her life-catching sails; and ambition did not transport her to desired shores. Instead, she rode out life on the vessel of family. Her companion was misery, a misery as old as Sicily, that same old misery that was so openly keened in the Old World and so real but unrecognized in the New World.

In 1906, at age nineteen, Rosalia left Sicily, never to return. But she offered glimpses into that past. Once she told me that she encountered a big black snake in an olive orchard. She attended school for two years before being sent to the fields to work as girl of seven or eight, where she received two crusts of bread for a day of gleaning a farmer's field on a nearby hillside. On our autumn trips through southern Michigan, *Nunna* Rosalia declared that our rich fruit harvest was inferior to those of verdant and fertile Sicily, never explaining why she did not share in its bounty or have the slightest wish to return to her *bel paese*. However, she once related an anecdote that revealed the answer to these questions. One day as she stood at the side of the road, the passing local prince threw coins from his carriage, and she and her companions—greedily, "like chickens"—rushed and scrapped to gather them up from between the cobblestones. The proverb about her mountain hometown, "*Muntimajurisi, mangiaghiènnari*" (The people from Montemaggiore eat acorns), suggests the scarcity of the country that failed to nurture Rosalia and accounts why she left her *paese per l' America*.

The young husbands and single men left first for the New World. While traditional mores forbad young women who were not the heads of families to travel without husbands or chaperones, the desire to couple and marry set the women's hearts on travel. A song of the era reveals the dilemma of the young women, equally forbidden to travel yet determined to have a man and family. She calls out and her mother responds:

> *Mother, mother, give me a hundred lire.*
> *For to America I want to go,*
>
> *I won't give you the hundred lire.*
> *And to America, no, no, no!*
>
> *If you don't let me go to America*
> *Out of the window I shall jump.*
>
> *I won't let you go to America.*
> *Better dead than dishonored.* [18]

Rosalia got her hundred lire and went to America. Her two older brothers, Pietro and Cruciano, were waiting for her, as was her prospective husband, Antonino, the man with whom she had exchanged photographs. His photograph and the accompanying letter from Pennsylvania convinced her that Antonino, who came from Cerda, a small town only five miles down the mountain from her Montemaggiore Belsito, was solid, good looking, and well-intentioned. Antonino, in his turn, on the basis of a photograph and what her brothers said, took Rosalia to be a handsome and fitting countrywoman, of good family—all and all, a fitting bride. Antonino would bring her to Kelyares, where she would find other *paesani* and her oldest brother, Pietro, and his family, with whom she lived until she married. The 1906 manifest for the steamship *Lazio* recorded Rosalia as being a nineteen-year-old "workwoman." Like Antonino, she arrived with $4 to her name. She indicated on the manifest that her destination was the home of Cruciano, who lived in the nearby but larger town of Hazelton, and who, showing the intermarriage of *paesani*, villages, and families, married Antonino's sister, Margherita, in 1909. Rosalia and Antonino wed in spring 1907, six months after her arrival in America.

Antonino, with Rosalia and their infant son, the first to be called Joseph, moved to Detroit, Michigan, in 1911. The news of good-paying factory jobs in the burgeoning auto industry had gone out to the nation, and workers from across the Upper Midwest responded, making Detroit the new century's fastest-growing American city. (In 1913, a year before Henry Ford offered to pay all of his workers $5.00 dollars a day, basic daily pay for a laborer was $2.34 a day, or 26 cents an hour, a much better wage than the $1.00 or $1.25 made by a farmhand or a mill worker.)[19] Detroit, which had 285,000 inhabitants in 1900, grew to 466,000 in 1910; between 1900 and 1920, it received more immigrants than any other American city, with the exception of New York and Chicago.

Antonino and Rosalia joined approximately ten thousand other Italians, who found their principal sources of employment at the city waterworks, the Michigan Central Railroad, the Pingree and Smith Shoe Factory, and various auto and stove manufacturers. Among them also were entrepreneurs who owned small stores, saloons, and produce stands. The young couple settled on Russell Street in a downtown Italian neighborhood composed of residents from Lombardy, Genoa, and Sicily. The city's large produce market, Eastern Market, where my father worked as very young boy, was close by, as was the parish of Santa Familigia, which the Sicilians, who were the dominant group of provincial Italians in Detroit, made their own.[20]

Antonino and Rosalia arrived, as the poor usually do to a city, too late. They missed the boom of Detroit's industry, which peaked in 1909, arriving instead amid the mini-depression of 1910–12. Antonino scoured the immense industrial landscape for work along with tens of thousands of other job-seeking newcomers. On one occasion, he followed a rumor of available work at the new Ford plant in nearby Highland Park, which in 1909 had pioneered the assembly line with production of the Model T, joining a large, unruly crowd that pushed against the fences. Plant security police drove the job seekers off the property by spraying them away with powerful fire hoses. Rosalia told how Antonino returned home wet and dejected. As things were difficult on the streets, so tragedy struck within their home. Shortly after their arrival in Detroit their first son, Joseph, suffered fatal burns when he overturned the scalding waters from Rosalia's scrub bucket on himself.

However, Antonino and Rosalia, buffered and nurtured by a Sicilian community and the first sketches of network of *paesani* and extended family, made progress in Detroit.[21] Already by 1912, living in the Congress area, a downtown Italian neighborhood, Antonino was able to sponsor the immigration of his younger sister Carmela. By 1915 Antonino and Rosalia were making headway in Detroit. He had obtained a day-laborer job at the Anderson Forge Company. They even had earned sufficient funds to put a down payment on a house on the east side's Beniteau Street, two miles east from the point of the original Sicilian settlement. There, sheltered from the prejudice and harshness of the new industrial order, they found themselves in a community where they could speak their own tongue, buy and grow their own foods, and pray in their own church. There was much to pray about.

My father, Joseph, was born in 1912, and his sister Epifania (Fina) was born two years later. Then, on a horrible October day in 1915, fate struck again and harder. Antonino, only thirty-four years old, came home from work, complained of feeling sick, and collapsed into Rosalia's arms. He died the next morning from a burst appendix. Rosalia could have no doubt that *la miseria*, the companion and ever-present shadow of the Sicilian poor, had followed across the great blue seas to America. In an instant, she was doomed to an unhappy life. "The bad," an old proverb runs, "arrives on horseback, and departs on foot." The young widow put on the traditional Mediterranean black mourning dress—and rarely ever took it off thereafter.

A twenty-seven-old immigrant with two young children, Rosalia remarried the year after she was widowed. Her new husband, Samuel Marziano, was in no way the equal of her beloved Antonino. Married before, Samuel was a thirty-four-year-old Sicilian peddler, who owned his own horse and cart. He had been naturalized as an American citizen in New York. He lacked Antonino's broad shoulders, square jaw, regular features, fair skin, and alert eyes. A short man, around five foot two, of slender build, olive complexion, with an artificial left eye, he had an erratic temper. When intense and sharp-tongued Rosalia scolded him for touching other women in her presence, he retaliated by hitting her and accusing her of having illicit affairs. One of his errant blows aimed at Rosalia sent their youngest daughter, Pauline, to the hospital after she tried protecting her mother from him.

Rosalia's thirteen-year marriage to Samuel, which produced three daughters—Josephine (b. 1918), Carmella, known as Milly (b. 1921), and Pauline (b. 1922)—ended abruptly one morning in August 1929. Under Rosalia's questioning, Fina, then fifteen years old, acknowledged that her stepfather had forced himself on her the night before. Breaking the stereotype that Sicilian women endure abuse in silence and never make their complaints public, and defying all the premises of the notorious Sicilian code of honor, Rosalia went directly to the nearest police station and accused Samuel of raping her daughter. He was formally charged. Before the trial, a court official working through an Italian translator concluded that Samuel Marziano possessed only borderline intelligence. This useful though painful document noted, "Mental Age 5, Intelligence Quotient 31"; "unstable and impulsive, with certain neurotic tendencies"; "Likewise, he appears rather lacking in insight, simple and childish in his judgments and in basic make-up, seems definitely primitive or elemental." At the conclusion of a brief trial, he was found guilty of sexually abusing Fina over the course of a year. He served approximately fifteen years of a seven- to twenty-five-year prison sentence.[22]

I saw my step-grandfather, of whom we never spoke, only twice. The first time, when I was about ten years old and he was just recently released from prison, he came for a short visit to my Aunt Pauline's house, where the family was celebrating a baptism. I was with my dad when Samuel approached me in the backyard. After a brief greeting, he gave me a large hunting knife with a long scary blade and a hideous purple plastic handle. It was nothing like the leather-handled Boy Scout knife I coveted, and even then, I recognized it as something ugly and out of place. On Memorial Day a few years later, I saw him through the car window as my father, mother, and I went to visit family graves at Mount Olivet Cemetery. He was standing on the edge of the road at one corner of the cemetery, selling small American flags, pinwheels, and other grave decorations. We didn't stop or wave—and he didn't see us.

My Aunt Fina, Samuel's hapless victim, was born in 1914, the first year of World War I, and died in 1945, the last year of World War II, suggesting (as perhaps every family historian must acknowledge) how both the most intimate and global interpenetrate family history. Denigrated by Samuel's crime, Fina could not marry someone of her own age and choosing. Her husband was Philip Trupiano, a Sicilian seventeen years her senior. A longtime employee at Chrysler, Phil had an energetic crackly voice, an effusive kindness, and cunning as a card player. (To my delight, in three-hand pinochle he arrayed his fifteen cards in an intricate peacock-like fan.) Fina died unexpectedly during her first pregnancy from a blood clot that traveled to her brain. Superstitions surrounded her death. Advance notice, as mother contended, was given in three ways. A month before her death, a reader of tea leaves, at a ladies' tea party, could not decipher a future in the dregs of Fina's cup. A few weeks before her death, my mother, while examining her and her stepsisters' palms as they gathered around on Rosalia's big armchair, announced that she found only the shortest lifeline on Fina's palm. And on the day Fina died there occurred another bad omen: a bird flew into her and Phil's home.

But at the end of 1929, on the eve of the Great Depression, Rosalia, now

Aunt Fina, Uncle Phil, and Rosalia, about 1937

My father, Joseph Amato, at high school graduation, 1928

forty years old, was a divorced widow with five children. She found support with the families of her brother John and sister Paulina, who lived nearby, and one of her neighbors on Beniteau Avenue, whom she always respectfully addressed as *cummare* (godmother) Rosalia Brucato. However, if she and the family were to survive, Rosalia had to count on her seventeen-year-old son, Joe, my father. She recognized his crucial role as the principal wage earner of the family, in effect the man of the house. She gave him his own room and sometimes served him meat, while his four sisters ate the standard fare of pasta, beans, potatoes, and greens. Because Rosalia had always favored her only surviving son, she honored his wish to keep the family together and not put the younger girls in an orphanage, despite the urging of relatives. Rosalia also worked hard to bring in money—as a laundress, a midwife, and landlady for boarders.

Even though she had completed only two years of schooling in Sicily, Rosalia valued education. She taught herself to read English by poring over the daily newspaper, and she proudly signed her own name on her naturalization papers, instead of scrawling an "X" on the document, as did her brother Cruciano and many other immigrants. At one time, in the early 1920s, she even found money to pay for violin lessons for Joe. A few years later, Rosalia expressed her protectiveness of her Joe, who had just been removed from public school to attend Ford's trade school, which they hoped would lead to the all-important good job. When he reported to her that a fellow student at his new school had lost his hand in a machine, Rosalia had opposed Samuel and insisted that her son be immediately withdrawn and returned to Southeastern High. Rosalia would not sacrifice him to industry and family need. Joe rewarded Rosalia's trust by skipping a year and a half of secondary school and graduating with honors at age sixteen. Although some of his own high school teachers offered to help pay his first year expenses at college, he immediately went to work as a white-collar clerk at Western Union, where he remained as a hard-working and advancing employee for the next forty-three years.

Dad never disappointed my grandmother. Like the eldest child in many immigrant families, he did not shirk the immense responsibility that life

had foisted upon him. He embraced his role as breadwinner, making sure
the family was fed and housed and that the girls always received at least one
Christmas gift. He was adamant that they, too, finish high school. Dedicat-
ing a large portion of his salary to the family, he put off getting married
until he was twenty-five years old and knew Rosalia was secure and the girls
were mature. In the mid-1930s, in order to secure Rosalia in a house she
could afford, he had purchased a duplex for the family on Hillger Street two
blocks east of Beniteau, and after World War II sold it for a modest sum to
Milly and her husband, Sam, stipulating that Rosalia would live with them
until she died.

Once her daughters were raised, Rosalia began working as a janitor at
nearby Foch Elementary School and remained there for a decade. By the
time she retired from that job and began collecting Social Security benefits,
she was worn out and suffering from emphysema. Her cough grew longer
and worse, and sometimes amid a bout of coughing she would wet herself.
Increasingly, she called on God to spare her any further days here, down
below. Teasingly, my mother, who invented and half-believed myths as fast as
she could talk, cautioned Rosalia that each such entreaty would add a year
to her life, but Rosalia continued her supplication. Misery had remained
her companion, and complaint, which echoed so discordantly in a 1950s
and 1960s America of opportunity, hope, and progress, had been become
her lifelong habit.

In such profound contrast to my restless maternal American grandmother Frances, *Nunna* Rosalia never questioned who she was, where she had
been, and what she could become. Life, for her, was about fate, not choice.
And unlike Frances, who moved so frequently that I remember her in a
dozen different houses, I associate Rosalia with the Hillger house. There she
reigned supreme from my first memories, around the start of the war in 1941,
until a year or two before I graduated from high school in 1956.

La cucina—food, its preparation and consumption—centered *nunna's casa*.
At her dining-room table we celebrated all the holidays and gave proof of our
well-being and her cooking. The kitchen was at the back of the house, which
had a small porch where the family sat and ate watermelon as a favorite sum-

mer treat. On one side of the kitchen, there were built-in cupboards and an icebox, beside which my dad and my young uncles rolled up their sleeves, got down on their knees, and "shot craps," calling out the names of the combinations they wanted ("Little Joe," "Box Cars," and the like) as they rolled the dice. On the opposing wall, the oven and a metal cooling window box protruded out into the tight shaded walkway that separated grandma's house from the neighbor's. Running along the front wall was the sink, from which, to my and my cousin Angela's glee, the unattended snails once escaped and slithered their way up the wall and across the ceiling. The rest of the house fed the kitchen. Beans frequently soaked in the bathtub and in pots in the closets, which got in the way of grandchildren's games of hide-and-seek; a two-foot-long box of spaghetti was stored under *nunna's* bed, which Angie and I turned into "swords," then ate after they snapped off in battle. In the musty basement was a wine barrel and cages for the chickens, whose necks Rosalia wrung with a quick twirl. Like many other immigrants to America, Grandma Amato had a small and crammed garden of greens, herbs, tomatoes, and vegetables along one side of the backyard. At its back stood a garage, with the horse stall that once held Samuel's house and cart. Rosalia delighted in recounting how once in the backyard my father caught a wild rabbit, a gift of nature under the shadows of Chrysler, that they turned into a small feast.

My grandmother animated the household, and we cringed in the face of her stern defense of the living room and its furniture. But after every scolding, she compensated me—her only grandson, the only child of her only surviving son, born of her first husband—with hugs and money. During the nights I stayed at her house, I snuggled up next to her to sleep. She recounted in the morning, to my joy, how I tossed and turned and kicked all night long, proving that I was really strong.

Nunna seemed most happy when she accompanied my parents and me on our Sunday excursions into the Michigan countryside, which provided opportunities to buy fresh fruit and reminisce about the bountiful harvests of Sicily. She also enjoyed trips with us to northern Michigan. Sometimes she became as giddy as a child. Once, when my parents hired a buggy to tour Mackinaw Island, my grandmother and I sat up front, directly behind the

Christmas at Grandma Amato's house, 1939.
Rosalia holds me; my father's sisters join us, Millie at left and Josephine, right.

driver and his farting horse. With each step, there was a fart; with each fart, a giggle, which turned into steady chuckle that cascaded into contagious and uncontrollable laughter. Fort Mackinaw and the Grand Hotel—it seemed the whole island itself shook with hilarity.

Near the end of her life, a brief trip to the Italian grocery store sufficed to reinvigorate Rosalia. It was as if she had returned to her first true love and ultimate necessity of her life, food. But for all the times I saw her happy, I more often saw her sad. I remember her happily bustling about in her kitchen, but I also recall her walking slowly and painfully out of Foch Elementary School. (One day, by chance, she happened to board a bus I was riding, but she did not see me; it was several minutes before I recognized the short, worn-down woman as my grandmother.) She complained how difficult it was to climb a ladder and clean the windows, but she relished telling me how a big snake escaped from its case in the science classroom and how all day long she and a fellow janitor worked in fear lest the snake reappear. I recall her, especially now that I approach my own seventies, sitting in the back row of Italian De Santis's Funeral Home for hours, huddled with the other old women dressed in black—talking, remembering, reviewing lives and the deaths of her Fina, Milly's Sam, Pauline's first child, her baby Joseph, and her beloved Antonino. And there was the story of his sister Carmela who arrived in Detroit in 1912, the year my dad was born, soon married Giacomo Bomegna, had five children, and died in 1921 from a miscarriage, which relatives suspect was the result of a botched abortion.

The Measure of Life, the Memory of a Person

Nunna Rosalia's life forms my memory. Her life convinces me of a not-too-distant time when work, pain, and death ruled the lives of the many. As close as I once was to her in flesh, we remained worlds apart in experience. I, who spent so much time at play and sport, truly belonged to another generation. Freedom, optimism, and choice went with my life, whereas hers was encased in necessity and fate. While my kind knows, even presumes, comfort and pleasure, her kind, across the chafe of the ages, pulled great blocks for pharaoh, plowed fields without horse or mule, and bore the travail of children that nature freely gave them. Alternately and in combination, they suffered the weather, famine, scarcity, disease, and the landlord. I began to sense the tragic nature of her life when I was old enough to recognize the tragic nature of life itself. She contradicted the facile consolation of faith and optimism. Knowing her immunized me from visions of long and happy life. Long before she died, death had chewed on her and the graveyard (*il camposanto*) had submitted its claim on her. Beyond it, Antonino stood, waiting, holding open the gate.

When Rosalia was seventy-seven years old, in 1964, death finally kept its rendezvous with her. Daughter Milly and her second husband, Dale, had moved Rosalia from the old neighborhood to the far east side, within a few blocks of the city limits. Wearied by age, her breath stolen by emphysema, sequestered in a non-Italian neighborhood, and weighed down by heavy memories, Rosalia, truly, was ready to die. She often bruised the feelings of gentle, good-natured Aunt Milly with Mount Etna–like emotional explosions. Visits from the relatives and trips to the Italian grocery weren't enough to suppress her constant petitions to God for a prompt death. In her final hours in the hospital, when I stood vigil down the hall into the early morning hours, I, too, prayed that her belabored breathing would stop. She had journeyed far from her ancient Sicily, in a mutating and imperiled family across a changing America, and now she stood on the threshold of Heaven. It was time for her load to be eased, to pass her breath on to the family that would follow. She deserved a refreshing sleep that would erase *la miseria* and reunite her, dancing, dressed in white, with her Antonino.

2

"Forty Acres, and All Mine"

Since the members of your family are human, there is no way to write of family and its relationships as simply a matter of home and household. You cannot reduce family and its members to being a mere sum of circumstances—much less make them a simple expression of gender, race, class, or ethnicity. As its self-appointed chronicler, your due to family is greater than an account of time, change, situations, conditions, stages, and events. You must also learn to speak of its interior worlds. You need to probe vices and virtues, emotions and passions, ambiguities and contradictions, the inner stuff of humans. You must classify them in terms of commanding moods, compelling ideas, eradicable passions, singular obsessions, and yet an underlying will despite no number of peculiar ticks, strange senses of humor and odd foibles. As little as you might take yourself to be a psychologist, you nevertheless find yourself in the thick of psychology when you write family history.

I found this to be the case in writing about my American grandmother Frances, as well as my Sicilian grandmother Rosalia. As Rosalia lived by passion and fate, Frances lived by ephemeral wishes and an insatiable hunger for happiness. So profoundly American in her restlessness, Frances is but one of a whole cast of characters here.

Of the multitude of homes my grandmother Frances Boodry Linsdeau owned during my youth, she showed her greatest enthusiasm for the forty-acre place she owned "up north." This phrase held for southern Michiganders living in Detroit all the magic of the woods, and it resonated for Grandmother Frances with all the happiness she associated with the simple life of her childhood home in rural Wisconsin. In contrast to my Italian grandmother Rosalia, whose fate pinned her to a place and yet in another sense put her beyond any place, my American grandmother Frances, over the entirety of her adult life, linked her happiness to being in the right place, if only she could find it.

Her up-north home was a rough and unfinished two-story house that lacked indoor plumbing and was supplied water by a hand pump on a small and flimsy back porch. Probably not at all insulated, it was without sufficient heating until Grandpa Bill, with the help of Frances's deaf and mute brother, Tom, built a great stone chimney on its back. The house was set back less than a hundred feet from the major north-south State Highway 27. On it Spikes, my favorite dog, a black and white border collie, was run over. One winter the snow was stacked so high on the highway that when my grandfather stood on it, he could reach the telephone wires that ran in front of the house—and I have seen the family photo that proves it. Behind the house stood a small log cabin where Grandma did some of her cooking and I slept when visiting her. Thin slices of flat pastureland along the north and south sides of the house ran back to a great impenetrable swampy woodland, which comprised the great majority of the forty acres she bought. It was just a few miles north of Vanderbilt, Michigan, and sixty miles south of the Straits of Mackinaw that separate Michigan's Upper and Lower peninsulas. Frances and husband William, whom she (and she alone) called Will, acquired the land after World War II, when they were in their late fifties and their three children—my mother, Ethel, her younger sister, Mabel, and "baby" Bill Jr.—were already grown, married, and raising families of their own.

When Frances first spoke of her Vanderbilt place, she told of her heaven on earth. My parents could not entirely fathom why she had given up a perfectly fine two-story house on Springle Avenue, close to her children and grandchildren on the east side of Detroit, to live more than two hundred fifty miles away. It was even less comprehensible why my grandfather should leave a good and secure job with a pension at thriving Hudson Motor Car Company (which would remain in business until 1957) for minimal wages at a local box- and pallet-making yard. Despite the loss of pay and security, Frances touted the virtues of her new place "in the woods." She declared the neighbors decent folk, found fishing nearby—and, trumping everything else, could affirm at last, "Forty acres, and all mine." This phrase, which had echoed throughout the course of the history of the American rural poor, professed a minimal, precarious, toilsome, but cherished hold on a place in the countryside—and it sarcastically initiated and ended family conversations about Frances's move north. "Forty acres, and all mine" was heard in my house whenever Frances summoned her children to drive north to visit her. The family complaint ran, she had left Detroit to live in a run-down house in the woods, far from towns, stores, and doctors, where one pumped water and had to use outdoor toilets, which "stank to high heaven," contained nasty wasps, and could have their interiors chewed out by salt-craving porcupines. Frances, her children agreed, had chosen to go backward in time and was, in effect, contradicting all the progress the family had made in the Motor City.

The phrase "Forty acres, and all mine" proved as revelatory as the most telling artifact or photograph. In sharp contrast to my parents' tenacious bid for a good and mortgage-free home, as the lynch pin of their security, Frances sacrificed houses and my grandfather's jobs to try to be at home with herself and in the world. The phrase also voiced, although unbeknownst to her, a profound rural impulse that derived from both sides of her family, both the Boodrys from Massachusetts and Maine and the Sayerses from western New York, whose lives were fashioned around the conviction that better lands lay elsewhere and beyond. As Grandmother Rosalia had a definite fate, so Grandmother Frances had a wish. As Rosalia ceaselessly called on God to end her sufferings, so Frances continually rallied herself, until late in life, with hope of a new home in a fresh place. Even though Frances knew hard times, prayed, knew how deep family quarrels go, and had suffered the deaths of her infant child Ellen and her father, she hungered for happiness in the here and now. Even in the closing years of her life, when high blood pressure and arteriosclerosis had caused two strokes and whittled her down to a ghost of her former self, she still summoned enough energy to defy her family's wish to put her in a nursing home.

Games and Things To Do

As a boy I loved Frances and Grandpa Bill's home. There were games and things to do. Frances always had a candy dish filled with my favorite, candy corn, and hers, maple candies. Besides all of the games I played with my grandfather, she involved me in continuous paper and pencil games such as tic-tac-toe, cootie, and hangman, and as far back as I can remember there was always a lot of card playing. By the time I was five or six, I was already good at rummy. By ten or so I became the fourth at pinochle and joined in entertaining Frances with cards, an expected and yet a minimal way to pay her back for her extraordinary Sunday meals, crowned by a choice of pies. Once in a while we also played poker in one of its countless variations, including what I took to be the obscenely named "Spit in the Ocean." Grandma concocted her own games, too, which drove my father crazy and tested his respect for her—none as much as the absurd "three-of-kind-or-better-to-open, nothing-wild, five-card poker." For a while in the early 1950s Frances insisted on playing fashionable double-decked canasta, which required her to buy a machine to shuffle the deck and challenged me to hold more cards than my clumsy hands could manage in a game I considered rummy run amuck. When cards at home didn't satisfy Frances, her daughters and her husband were pressed into service hauling her off to church basements across the east side for entire afternoons and whole evenings of bingo. She played five or six bingo cards at a time, etching such numbers as numbers "B 7" and "O 69" indelibly on her memory.

More to my taste than the bingo outings, at which I was too young to play, were Frances's fishing expeditions to my Aunt Mabel's small cottage on nearby Lake St. Clair. It was a two-room, lackluster cottage, from whose ceiling draped coils of flypaper, on a shallow waterfront invaded by reeds and lily pads. Nearby war-activated Selfridge Field Air Base sent its planes zooming overhead, practicing bombing runs by dropping sandbags on targets placed in the lake. At Aunt Mabel's I had fun. I shot my BB gun at birds (to Frances's dismay), fought snakes whose heads darted in and out from the wood pile under the porch, tried to stand upright in Mabel's old hammock, and swam and dived at the neighbor's boathouses. I also went with Grandma out on the lake in the rowboat in pursuit of pan fish. By the time I was ten or eleven I could row and swim, which made me an ideal companion for Frances, who couldn't swim and barely could row. Her fear of water did not deter her from fishing, however. Though never far from shore, she would fish for hours on

Dinner at Grandma Linsdeau's in about 1953.

From left: Frances, myself, young Cousin Billy, Aunt Margaret (married to Uncle Bill),

William, my dad, and my mother.

end until her stringer was filled with perch or no worms were left for bait. A single bite, or even nibble, which Frances always seem to get just as we ready to pull up anchor, would postpone our departure for shore by what seemed like yet another eternity.

Each of Frances's houses added to my youthful education. There was a house on a creek where I skated, a cottage on a lake with a weedy shore-line, along which I hunted frogs with a bow and arrow. There was her 40-acre place up north, where she and Grandpa Bill filled me with fear with horrific tales of a wolverine's revenge and a story of a baby thrown to pursuing wolves so that the family could escape. With Grandma Linsdeau's houses came the adventures of water and woods that made me an all-American boy, a Tom Sawyer. She lived where a boy might encounter a bear, could surely hunt a squirrel or rabbit, and definitely learned to put oars in the water, let arrows fly, or simply whittle a stick. With her and good Grandpa Bill I did all the country things of which city boys dream.

My grandparents tied me to them with their stories. They told Gothic tales: Their local dead priest became a revenant. When the lights in the church went on in the middle of the night, he had returned to say Masses for the Dead, for which he had taken money but had never performed. Aunt Sadie periodically hid in her house for months at a time, but inevitably tracks in the snow from the house to the outhouse betrayed her presence. A young girl from Frances's rural township got pregnant, and when her beau refused to marry her, she committed suicide. Worse, there was the case of the bizarre vendetta. A husband ran away, abandoning wife and children. He returned years later and asked to be taken back. After much hesitation, his wife reluc-tantly relented and let him back in the house. She discovered the next morn-ing that he had fled again, leaving a single-word note: "Vendetta!"

By the time I became a university student, I acknowledged my grand-mother as a kindred spirit. Her restless moves from place to place matched the inner tumult that moved me from book to book, idea to idea, and identity to identity, hoping that they would somehow quiet my mind and secure me a place in the world. Frances, for her part, confessed to being concerned about life's deeper issues and expressed regret that she had not had a chance to go to college. A year of business school had not been enough to fill her soul with the books and learning she craved. She contended that she should have become a poet or lawyer and insisted, almost as if offering herself a consolation prize for an education not received, that one day she would write a book of her own recollections. Five or so years before she died she gave me two books. One was a collection of romantic poetry, the other an anthology of writings entitled *The Great Hereafter, or Glimpses of the Coming World; Golden Gems Gathered from the Great Historians, Orators, Philosophers.*[1] I had no doubt she was asking me to remember that she, too, puzzled over the meanings of things.

As I grew older, I grasped the anguish of my American grandmother. Though she had lived a life as a traditional woman, fulfilling the roles of mother, homemaker, and cook, her spirit roiled like that of a modern woman caught in the whirlpool of having too many selves. Her mind belonged to a free and individualistic American democracy, the changing countryside, turbulent mill towns, and that emerging mass popular culture that defined the possible other selves of adolescence. Melodramatic by proclivity, her moods were many and changing. She both belonged to her childhood along the Wolf River in rural Wisconsin, and to her teen years in the developing mill town of Appleton, Wisconsin, where wealth, education, and leisure were on tantalizing display. Lending herself to the era's soupy romanticism, she identified with local poet and songwriter Eban Rexford, who though born in New York in 1848, was raised in the small mill town of Shioctin, Wisconsin, which bordered Maine Township, her birthplace. She sang his sentimental "Silver Threads Among the Gold."

> Darling, I am growing old,
> Silver threads among the gold
> Shine upon my brow today,
> Life is fading fast away.
>
> But, my darling, you will be, will be,
> Always young and fair to me,
> Yes, my darling, you will be,
> Always young and fair to me.

Feelings and dreams made my American grandmother modern. Inside this devoted wife and mother, who could sew, cook, and bake with the best of her country cousins and loved and took great pride in being the wife of husband Will, existed a restless woman who suffered her moods and thoughts over a lifetime. In her ambivalence about society, she resembled no one other than the romantic father of modernism, Jean Jacques Rousseau: Like Rousseau she had a desire to shine in the eyes of others and an equally strong wish to remove herself from judging society. Chained to a cycle of expectation from and disappointment with others, Frances alternately judged the world as being for and against her. This wheel of emotions, which turned within her, formed a rut in her and shaped a common family path. Therein, at her worst times, she played sibling against sibling, rotating each in and out of her good graces. In the last years, having suffered strokes, she multiplied accusations against my grandfather for having an affair behind her back.

Her restlessness, I am forced to conclude, grew out of her painful inner discontent. Her inner logic surely moved on the premise, a new house, a new self. Sometimes my grandmother would enact this cycle, which proceeded from infatuation and purchase to disenchantment and sale, in a matter of a several months, and other times within a few years. From the time I was two, in 1940, until her death in 1966, I recall a dozen homes my grandmother owned. When I was three, her home was in Roseville in the neighborhood of Gratiot and Ten Mile Road. There my grandparents had a two-story home with a large front porch that ran the length of the house and two acres or so of land on the south side that my grandfather intently gardened. They lived next door to a family of twelve or so, who, much to our amusement, using the running boards of their car, went to town one and all on the same trip. Grandma and Grandpa left that house for a two-story house on the east side of Detroit on Springle Avenue. From that house, which had an ample open front porch and small backyard, we went as a whole family in at least two cars to see my uncle Bill off to military service. To my grandfather's pride, Bill had enlisted in the Navy just after Pearl Harbor. A service star hung on the front window of the house until the war was over and Bill returned. In the backyard of the Springle house I learned to shoot a single-shot, bolt-action .22

caliber rifle. My first shot, my grandfather delighted to tell, went thorough a bottle of linseed oil and ricocheted off my older cousin Sally's doll buggy.

Frances and her Will remained up north at the Vanderbilt place for three years after the war before returning to the east side. Then, between about 1949 and 1956, the year I graduated from high school, they moved first to Rohns Street, then to Bellevue Street, and to a small house on Ashland Street, which backed directly onto Fox Creek. From a very small back porch off the kitchen, precariously mounted on stilts, she fished. After owning a cottage on Mud Lake near Pontiac, Michigan, she took up residence in St. Clair Shores, near Nine Mile and Mack. Then, in 1956 or 1957, if my memory serves me, Frances returned up north to Omer, "Michigan's smallest town," where on the banks of the nearby Rifle River she found good fishing and on the side of the house Grandpa sat up his croquet court. There she remained until Grandpa had a heart attack, returning them yet again to the east side of Detroit, where they lived in a small wood-frame house on Belvedere in a mixed neighborhood, shadowed by crime and racial tensions. It was there that Frances died in 1966, and then William in 1969.

My grandmother never found happiness, and her family consequently never took root in a neighborhood or parish. The children were moved from school to school, and my mother never completed high school. Grandpa, in turn, never tasted the full fruits of his labor. His retirement was a modicum of what it could have been and his homes were invariably smaller and in poorer neighborhoods than his lifetime of factory work entitled him. Rather than accumulating wealth in their home, a principal goal of the working class, the properties they bought from 1940 to 1956 remained in the $3,000 to $5,000 range, while the average value of similar homes in Detroit, including those of their two daughters, at least tripled in the same period.

To a Different Tune

When I was young, I wanted to have large-veined, knowing hands like my grandfather's. With them, he hoed gardens, built rock chimneys, worked wood like his father and sister May, and once cut, deflated, and took por-

William and Frances Linsdeau on their fiftieth wedding anniversary.

cupine quills out of my dog's face. My adoring eyes didn't see that he had a glass eye (lost when a boy, playing at rolling hoops by the mill) until my mother told me. And, though he prayed at the foot of the bed every night, I didn't know just how sensitive he was until my mother told me that when her three-year-old baby sister Ellen Frances died in the 1932, Grandpa Bill was inconsolable to the point that they thought he would lose his mind. Every day for a period of months, he trudged three miles to her grave in Mount Olivet Cemetery.

I never attributed a mean side to my grandfather, even though he shot dogs from his porch with a slingshot, put fishhooks on a line in his pea patch to catch sparrows and starlings, and near the end of his life harshly criticized black rioters and war protesters during the 1960s. To the boss, bully, or somebody who just rubbed him wrong, he was quick to use his favorite phrase: "Kiss my ass!" However, he was kind to most people. To those he knew best he was lovable, though at times a damnable tease, with his constant clowning, telling jokes, donning his daughters' Easter bonnets, striking up a tune on his harmonica and dancing an odd jig when the music was right, and tickling more than one person without warning. He nicknamed Mabel's husband, a high school track star, "drag ass," claiming that his short legs and low-slung behind allowed him to spark himself into high speed running, and no doubt my father qualified as one of those Italian "Tonys."

On stage and off my grandfather was a jokester. His old-time use of nicknames and practical jokes showed no reverence for today's sacrosanct borders of individual privacy and ethnic propriety. Once, when my mother was dating, he took a pair of his shoes and a pair of hers and pressed them toe-to-toe in the snow on the front porch so that they would resemble the tracks of embracing lovers. Then he took my mother out to inspect and explain the footprints before upbraiding her for such carrying on. He transformed some of his standing jokes into family traditions. He taught every one of his grandchildren how to skip the wrong way, making it a forward hop with one stiff, trailing leg. This caused his daughters no end of grief with their children's kindergarten teachers, who had to enforce the public requirement that a child know how to skip before being allowed into the first grade. His imitations and improvisations, subtle and coarse, went on and on. Expected and part of the family tradition, they stopped just short of his own father's outrageous trick of sending grandchildren chasing after farts with bags, offering a nickel for each one they captured.

Grandpa Bill marched to a different tune. In his world little things mattered a lot. The simplicity of walking a dog, playing a harmonica, listening to a ball game, or gazing on the striking colors of his favorite zinnias satisfied him. At least, so it seemed to me, the grandson whom he taught to shoot a slingshot, walk on stilts—even up and down stairs—and for whom he always had a fresh joke. Grandpa Bill was big in my childhood. He took me on short car trips in his '37 forest-green Chevrolet convertible, with a rumble seat. He put birdseed in his thinning white hair and had a canary sit on his head. During my university years, before I could cross the threshold from his porch into his living room, he insisted that I say "Hello" to his dog Skippy, and I had to wait until Skippy replied with a moaning, yelping bark, resembling "Hello." He always asked whether the college teachers had me reading "Snakeshit" (Shakespeare) before I downed a necessary shot and beer and we went to the basement for a three-out-of-five game of pool.

The armor of his humor did not crack until the last years of life. When Frances died and his health faltered, he was terribly lonely, and he lived only by daily telephone calls from his children and recently popularized TV dinners. Sometimes, he cried openly and bitterly over the loss of his beloved Frances and the condition that life had delivered him. During my very last visit with him at his house, he tried terribly hard to make my new bride, Cathy, and me laugh. One day, shortly thereafter, he forgot to light the oven and filled the house with gas, causing him to suffer another and final stroke. After two days in a coma, he awoke only to find he could not speak any more. Turning his back to us, he sank back into a coma and breathed heavily until he died. I still stand at his graveside knowing that our boyhoods crossed and that we intertwined, like his beloved bougainvillea, through the lattice of generations. I pray that he and Frances be healed, together again, and I can visit their fully sufficing home.

Grandpa Linsdeau and Skippy, 1966

A Poor Country Girl

I approach the seventh decade of life, when whatever lies ahead becomes more certain and insistent and what lies behind requires more and more understanding. My grandparents stretch back in time before 1900. I speculate that my grandchildren may actually be alive after 2,100. With two centuries in play, I find myself becoming my parents' parent, and then my grandparents' grandfather. With my own life lived out in ever more fixed time and completed relationships, time and family relationship become liquid, even dizzying, as I take up the humbling business of writing about exploring the lives of William and Frances.

With a sense of impudence, I can ask about William. How much was he in a state of inequality in his marriage to Frances? Did he turn himself into comic to disguise the fact that her changing whims denied him the right to cast himself as a serious person, at least to be half-master of his home? Or did he simply follow a common male role in the modern family, that of increasing subservience? On this subject, his father and mother had instructed him. Surely, his mannered Irish mother, Mary Jane O'Brien, with her refined home on the second floor above the family saloon, imposed order on her Prussian barkeep husband Jacob. Nevertheless, however much my grandfather inherited his comic cue from his clowning father Jacob, there is little doubt that he incorporated humor, a well-practiced family art, as a dodge and a shield against Frances's shifting, serious, and demanding moods. He was doing nothing unusual in tiptoeing around a wife's anger, or, as he commonly did, rationalizing her irrationality and insisting that his children respect their mother. What finally requires explanation, in fact, is not William's surrender to Frances's constant desire to change homes, but the depth and strength of that desire.

The power of Frances's itinerancy is best measured by the degree to which it undercut her husband's ability to get good steady work and to attain and keep a good house. Family historian Richard Bushman insightfully wrote of the importance of family ownership to the working class:

[It] served as a flywheel to stabilize a family against the fits and starts of the urban economy and the vicissitudes of personal health. Its importance was partially measured by the exertions city workers made to acquire a house. [American historian] Stephan Thernstrom found that two-thirds to three-quarters of the working-class men who [in the mid-nineteenth century] remained in Newburyport [Massachusetts] for twenty years owned town property, usually house and lot. To acquire a house they sacrificed other amenities, including education for their children, and often entered into burdensome mortgages.[2]

Doubtless, grandmother's need of mind overruled the drive of class. The inner pathology of her restlessness requires a biographical explanation, and this is not to be separated from her background as a poor Yankee girl, of country extraction.

Frances was a bright, handsome girl. She spent her self-conscious teen years as an attractive young dressmaker in one of the department stores of the emerging and rich mill town of Appleton, Wisconsin. A photograph of her at about sixteen, provided to me by a Kansas relative, captures an attractive young woman. Dressed in white and wearing a white brimmed hat, with intelligent eyes and a generous lower lip, there is no doubt that young Frances already knew something about fashion and expected the world to gaze at her.

But she looked outward from an insecure social foundation: Her family had recently arrived in the town from a poor farm in an impoverished countryside. Her father made his living as a stable keeper, a hosteller; they lived in rented places, and not a single older brother or sister escaped rural poverty. Frances had to find her place in a flourishing world in which her well-off peers, an emerging smart set, consumed goods, wore the dresses she made, and went to the local private college, Lawrence. They drove new cars, rowed on the river, and took vacations to far-away places like New York and even Europe. Her year at business school in Clintonville did not elevate her status or negate theirs. Her origins simply lay on a poor farm to the north and on equally poor lands in rural northwestern New York and mountainous Maine.

Of certain poverty and obscure lineage, Frances took, I surmise, the family of her future husband to be a cut above hers. Of course she belonged with him to the same new and self-conscious generation of the turn of the century. Unquestionably, she could sing the popular songs of the hour with her Will and even take a bit part in acting out one of his older brother Emmett's own vaudeville skits, which were performed on his tours at venues as far away as Green Bay. But, in the end, Frances could not join her in-laws as an equal. That her parents spoke English as their first language and had recently joined the Appleton Presbyterian Church and were not foreign like Will's did not cancel one overriding and paramount truth. His family had money and prestige, and hers did not. Will's father, who worked as a foreman at Menasha's main mill, owned a bar on the first floor of their two-story brick house on Broad Street, had held public office for almost a decade, and was considered in the book commemorating the town's fiftieth anniversary as one its "prominent men." Will's mother ran the family's well-appointed home on the second floor.

Their marriage in June 1909 did not make twenty-year-old Frances confident. The young bride only discovered that her new husband had a glass eye—which they had custom made in Chicago, according to my mother— when her new mother-in-law asked her whether he was taking care of his eye each night, as he should. Two months after the wedding, her father, James Boodry, died what might have been considered a degrading death, from a rabid dog's bite. Though never a drinker, Frances took to cards, including poker, which she enthusiastically played the rest of her life. However, she suffered throughout her life intermittent bouts of guilt for having converted to Catholicism.

Other things worked on Frances and frayed her inner sinews. A sense of inferiority seeded in Appleton blossomed in William's hometown Menasha and its sister town Neenah, where he worked in a paper mill. According to my mother, Frances never felt at home in working-class, Catholic Menasha or in richer Scandinavian, English, and Protestant Neenah. In fact, life in these growing Fox River towns only deepened her sense of inferiority as a rustic country girl among prospering urbanites. As a young bride she clung tight to her Will and considered herself in rivalry with Emmett's new wife, Marie, over proving herself a good wife and daughter-in-law. All the while she feared the loss of her husband to the flirtations of Will's female fellow mill workers. Indeed, this fear, according to my mother, might have spurred their migration to Detroit in 1919.

A Long Way from Home

Frances and William did not come to booming Detroit entirely unprepared. Both believed themselves, as youth generally does, ready for new things. William was a smart and willing worker with knowledge of millwork. Like his father Jacob, he was a natural foreman. He understood precision work and factory discipline. Aside from having a friendly personality, he knew his mathematics well and thought through things on his own. William brought supplemental economic skills to their new life in Detroit. He knew how to grow vegetables and raise chickens. William also was committed to the old Catholic discipline of work and prayer, which meant regular attendance at Mass and evening prayers.

Frances also brought useful skills to the emerging industrial city. She was an exceptionably hard worker. She had training in business, and at least on one occasion in their early days in Detroit, she performed in a sales display for cooking with Carnation milk. However, with two young girls, both born prematurely—Ethel in 1912 and Mabel in 1914—Frances had her hands full. Her style of homemaking centered on cooking and sewing and did not involve the accumulation of goods or fancy decoration. She only had a handful of knick-knacks and doilies; in her Springle bathroom, next to the toilet, was a print of a young boy proudly urinating into a pond with a smiling frog sitting on a lily pad. Frances excelled at sewing, knitting, and crocheting and was an enthusiastic and marvelous cook, taking special pride in her sauerkraut with pork ribs and her wonderful pies, which on Thanksgiving included the required pumpkin and apple, and my grandfather's favorite, mincemeat.

Many of the arts and skills they brought from rural Wisconsin, such as pan fishing, squirrel hunting, berry picking, and even gardening to supply food, became superfluous in the city. They soon shed extended family, which had already grown attenuated in Wisconsin. Relationships with the two older married brothers, John and Emmett, who had come to Detroit before the death of their mother in 1919, fell apart fairly soon after William and Frances's arrival, while contact with unmarried sister May remained fragile and mediated through May's love of my mother. John and Emmett did not find good work and were in no position to help William. Moreover, Emmett's wife Marie and Frances profoundly disliked each other, and May, a public health nurse, didn't care for either of them, even though she loved Ethel and Mabel and Emmett's son Vernon. Without the drama of single and decisive confrontation, at least one that could be remembered as the great dividing point, the Linsdeau family dissolved in decade-long quarrels and grudges with origins that outlasted the memories of all involved.

Frances and William brought no ethnicity to serve as a social compass and direct them to preferred neighborhoods and churches. Frances's ethnicity, a mixture of English, old American, and Acadian, had long been erased by a succession of migrations, intermarriages, and isolations in the remote countryside. William's ethnic identity, conversely, was bifurcated at its core between his mother's Irish Catholic working-class inheritance and his father's immigrant West Prussian–Polish Catholic ancestry. While his father, Jacob, affirmed his German identity by use of the German language and German club affiliation and activities, William was assimilated from youth into emerging American national and mass cultures. The one-hundred-percent Americanism preached during World War I and its aftermath scoured all of German identities and foreign allegiance of every sort.[3] Simultaneously with their migration to Detroit, William and his siblings had in fact changed their last name from Linsdau to Linsdeau in order to disguise their German ancestry. And it was Linsdeau I knew as my mother's name until I became curious about family history and the German part of the family.

Because of their constant moves, the family also lacked any sustaining neighborhood identity. By the time their children became engaged and married, they had no grounds to object to Ethel's wishes to marry east sider Joe Amato, a Sicilian; Mabel's wishes to marry east sider Jimmy Williams, a son of white southerners; or Bill's marriage to Margaret Kaleel, a Lebanese Christian from North Carolina, at the end of World War II. Contact, class, and romance nullified all divisions on the east side, excepting those of black and white.

Frances and William entered their fifties without community or public identity. They looked almost exclusively to their children for entertainment, social interaction, care, and guidance. Even though William had found a steady union job at Hudson Motors and by the eve of World War II they had bought two decent houses of their own, Frances was never at home in Detroit. Her heart increasingly sought escape. In fact, as the war ended, she inwardly was in full flight from Motor City. Aside from what little relief she found fishing at my aunt Mabel's cottage, she began scouring northern woods and nearby lake areas for the farm, cabin, cottage that would give her the peace she sought. Her imagined flights never explicitly returned her to Neenah, Menasha, Appleton, or even her childhood rustic Town of Maine. Instead they led toward an idealized countryside, where she would be one with herself, could fish to her heart's content on the undisturbed banks of a quiet river, and fill her life with Will and her womanly chores.

Frances was a country girl who didn't take, a hayseed that didn't germinate in Detroit's oily soil. Good wages and a home and short stints away did not outweigh her discontent. Nothing kept her inner fulcrum in balance. This yearning, however distinctly hers, also belonged to whole generations of rural Americans, who envisioned happiness free of the complexity of advancing commercial and mass society, and the industrial society to which want and need delivered them.

With her phrase "Forty acres, and all mine," Frances bugled her dissatisfaction with town and city and called for a return to the land, which alone would free her of the inferiority and dissatisfaction that came with Appleton, Menasha, and Detroit. The phrase carried essentially a psychological significance, resonant with many meanings. Forty counted the days of the Flood, the years of Moses and his people in the wilderness, and the days Christ spent fasting on the desert preparing himself for being tested by the Devil. For the poor, forty acres was the promise of westward expansion. In such profound contrast to the land speculators who, counting in tens and tens of thousands of acres, shaped North American colonial history and that of the new Republic, forty acres was the basic modular unit and common denominator of the new democracy's advance west. Six hundred and forty acres or one square mile made up a section, but forty acres, a fourth of a quarter of a section, was the primary unit of the surveyors' grid of the 1787 Northwest Ordinance.[4]

By the time Frances hitched her hope to "Forty acres, and all mine," she was poking for flames among the long-darkened embers of American expansion. Farms of forty acres, perhaps never viable when measured by income rather than self-sufficiency, were by then for all purposes extinct—only a memory of a past wish. Nevertheless, Frances's call aroused not just her soul but the entire family's North American past. She echoed her Arcadian Boodry ancestors' attempts to restore themselves in homes in Massachusetts and then Maine after their eviction from their farms in Nova Scotia. She resonated with her grandfather Sylvester's settling of forty acres in the Town of Maine and her own father James's decade-long and losing struggle to keep a forty-acre place there on the banks of the Wolf River. Frances's restlessness expressed her maternal family's search for land: Grandfather Leonard Sayers, defeated by grim poverty first in St. Lawrence County, New York, and then on a plot of less than twenty acres south of Neenah, Wisconsin, finally succeeded on his third parcel of land in south-central Kansas.

Frances's restlessness joined her to the nation's rural poor, people in quest of land. In the course of the nineteenth century the search metamorphosed, mutating from field to factory, from remote rural communities to mill towns, and finally to great urban places. Along the way, the poor became wage earners, consumers, practitioners of birth control, and national citizens. Living in ever-greater numbers in smaller and self-isolating nuclear families in towns and cities, family members mutated into distinct emotional individuals who prized choice, career, and personal happiness over land and family itself. The need to have land eventually turned into a nostalgia to return to it. Frances was not all that different from my friends who seek wholeness and rebirth in a place up north. This quest, in all its forms, that so shaped the American mind, justifies me in calling my beloved Frances my American grandmother.

3

Banished from Acadia,
Exiled in Plymouth Colony

The quest for origins bedevils the family historian. Lured by the connectivity of blood and the persistence of name, the historian in quest of a golden lineage succumbs to the futile process of ceaseless regression. As the search for cousins can dissipate the historian's efforts in a crablike, sideways movement in time, so the quest for first ancestors impels the historian deeper and deeper into the vanishing and ultimately unknowable past. In the end, no child of Adam can trace his lineage to our first father. Nevertheless, the search for origin cannot be entirely forsaken, as long as we need starting points to tell a family story.

The discovery of the Acadian origins of the Boodry (Boudrot) family, Frances's ancestors, gave birth to this book, joining my family to one of the earliest settlements of North America and identifying Frances's homelessness with a poor people, long in exile and deep in exodus. Pierre Boudrot numbered among those tragic Acadians who, in 1755, were uprooted en masse from their homeland in Nova Scotia. The subjects of Longfellow's Evangeline, *the Acadians were taken captive by guile, then cruelly dispersed to the seas, and in the case of Pierre's family, delivered to inland Massachusetts where they were held as wards of the state until the American Revolution.*

The Boudrot history in North America was more than a century older than the United States. My people were French and Catholic, and—further thwarting the colonial designs of London and Boston—they were allied to the Mi'kmaq (Micmac) Indians. They were victims of the great French-English rivalry for North America and they began their great journey in America in bondage in colonial Massachusetts. They are the beginning of the story of my American family.

Genealogy holds wonderful surprises. Defying those who seek pure racial, ethnic, and moral identities as rulers or victims, it makes us a wonderfully mixed breed. A search for roots delights those who like surprise and enjoy irony. The obscure occasionally discover that they are the descendants of the great and famous, while those who pride themselves on aesthetics commonly find their ancestors to have been coarse or principally skilled at counting money. The pacifist, in turn, may find he was the great-grandson of a murderous general, the anti-Semite discovers that his mother was half Jewish, the American Indian that he has an educated Norman lineage. The delightful incongruities of past make us all, as Rabelais long ago knew, the children of kings and bastards, princesses and prostitutes, tycoons and martyr saints, zealots and cynics, and surely people of many places and groups rather than single races, ethnicities, and nations. Indeed, the past is filled with individual surprises that force one to rethink his family's history. This happened to me when I discovered, with the help of a professional genealogist, that my grandmother Frances's family was Acadian.

This single fact placed my poor, local, and largely obscure family at the heart of North American history and made it inseparable from one of its most tragic events: the *Grand Dérangement*, that singular and great uprooting and disbursement of an entire North American people. With a single bold and cruel stroke in the fall of 1755, Britain, in concert with the town of Halifax and the colony of Massachusetts, banished approximately seven thousand Acadians to the colonies and Europe. Occurring on the threshold of the Seven Years War (1756–1763)—known in North America as the French and Indian War—the *Grand Dérangement* initiated the history of my family in the United States. They, like so many North American Indian peoples, were victims of what we now define as ethnic cleansing: violent, forced removal from their land.[1] Indisputably the Boodrys entered North American colonial history as an uprooted and captive people before the Revolutionary War, and they made their search for a lost home and land a dominant theme of the first Boudrot in the United States.

If the individual descendant's mind somehow carries within itself the defining traces of ancestor experiences, November 1755 profoundly entered the roots of my grandmother Frances's consciousness. In that month and year, when the aftershock of the Lisbon earthquake was recorded as far as along the eastern seaboard of North America, Frances's ancestors were exiled from their Acadian garden and banished to the very heart of old Plymouth Colony.[2]

The Acadian Garden

Frances's ancestors had been a local country people for more than a century before being uprooted. With ingenuity and toil, Acadians had tamed the swamplands of present-day Nova Scotia and New Brunswick. By fencing out the rising sea and, at the same time, draining bayside marshes, they transformed a wild and agriculturally barren land into cultivated farmland. In remarkable accord and continuing cooperation and intermarriage with the native peoples, the Mi'kmaq Indians, they shaped the Acadian environment into a comparatively prosperous land. The inhabitants sailed and fished its coasts, bays, and rivers, farmed its rich meadows bordering the Annapolis and other rivers, grew crops, and raised many cattle.[3] The Acadians raised gardens and sought out wild plants and game; made clothing of the flax and wool they grew and made their shoes and moccasins of moose and seal skin; and built modest wood-frame homes, which often housed more than a single family. Through marriage, the learning of the native language and ways, and the practice of trade and alliances, the Acadians made themselves the trusted neighbors of the Mi'kmaq peoples who had helped teach Acadians how to live off the land like *les vrais peuples du pays*.[4]

The fundamental activity that characterized them as agriculturists in Acadia was diking and draining. The collectively created and maintained dikes joined families and communities in a single and ongoing project to hold back rising tides, the highest in the entire world, and drain abundant unwanted water from interior marshes, streams, creeks, and rivers. Bumper wheat crops and large populations of all-important cattle, in addition to pigs, sheep, and poultry, measured their success. In their rich and varied gardens they grew cabbages, turnips, peas, beans, onions, corn, and apple trees. Their prospering lands supported a flourishing human population, which had dramatically grown since its founding in the Annapolis Valley in the 1630s. In fact,

these successful wetland dwellers (whose origins lie among established farmers and professions such as blacksmiths, surgeons, boat makers, tool makers,
and tailors from the regions of Poitou–Charente in central France and Perche
in the north) thrived, multiplied, and spread. Resembling in reproduction
and diffusion a thriving muskrat population, each successive generation,
larger in number, evicted its progeny and forced it to find and tame a part of
the extensive marshlands for its own. Without significant immigration after
the founding generation from 1610 to 1640, the original Acadian population
multiplied many times over between 1650 and 1750, spreading out from the
Bay of Fundy, throughout present-day Nova Scotia and New Brunswick, and
beyond to Prince Edward Island.[5]

The growth of the Boodry family itself illustrates a subject of considerable interest to the historian, the fertility of the Acadian population. This
history begins with Michel Boudrot, the founding patriarch of all the Boudrot in Acadia.[6] Born in France in 1601, he arrived in Acadia sometime before
1639, at which time he, known as a settled farmer, was designated as the civil
magistrate at Port Royal (now Annapolis Royal, Nova Scotia).[7] A Canadian
historian found evidence of his continued activity as "general representative
of the King and civil court in 1648."[8] In 1663, at age sixty-two, he was listed
as first administrator of Port Royal at a baptism.[9] In 1671 he was identified as
lieutenant-général de la jurisdiction à Port Royal et juge du lieu (lieutenant-general of
law at Port Royal and local judge).[10] In 1685, King Louis XIV named him, at the
advanced age of eighty-five, *lieutenant-général civil et criminel du Roy au pays et côte
del' Acadie.* He was dismissed from this office in 1688 by an order of the king,
which remarked that Boudrot was "not in a condition to carry out the functions of his post because of his great age."[11]

By the standard measure of the old order, Frances's Acadian founding
father, Michel Boudrot, had lived a full and good life. In a rural world in
which success was measured, as it had been in medieval France and Europe,
by the number of children, land, and animals one possessed, he was truly
a successful patriarch.[12] At age seventy, as described by the 1671 census, he
had triumphed over scarcity and impecuniousness. With his wife, Michelle
Aucoin, 53, he had three married daughters, Françoise, 29, Jeanne, 25, Mar-

guerite, 20; and eight unmarried sons, Charles 22, Marie, 18, Jean, 16, Abraham, 14, Michel 12, Olivier, 10, Claude, 8, and François, 5.[13] Michel also had five cattle and twelve sheep.[14] A different but unidentified inventory listed his wealth at a certain point in time as twenty cattle (*bête à cornes*), twelve sheep (*brebis*), and eight *arpents* of land, which is probably less than five acres.[15] Michel's son Claude (1663–1740) established himself in the Grand Pré (Great Meadow) region, the heart of Acadian settlement, on Minas Bay at the mouth of the Avon River. There Claude had nineteen children.[16] One of his sons, Joseph (c. 1687–1763) and his wife Françoise Comeau, who are present in a 1755 census of Grand Pré, had fourteen children, four cattle, eight cows, fifteen calves, fifty sheep, twenty-six pigs, and three horses.[17] One of their sons is Pierre—one of the "three Pierres" listed by British Lt. Col. John Winslow's on his classic list of Acadians expelled from Grand Pré and the most likely of three to be our relative—had in his household, according to the expulsion census, a wife, two sons, four daughters, four bullocks, ten cows, thirteen calves, fifty-five sheep, thirteen hogs, and three horses.[18]

Revealing how the genealogical enterprise turns on argument, conjecture, and hypothesis, and results in imponderable details and irresolvable uncertainty—or, put more simply, more shells than pearls—contemporary Acadian genealogist and scholar Stephen White, a critic of Father Bona Arsenault's classic work of Acadian genealogy, identifies Frances's direct ancestor not to be any of the Pierres from historic and celebrated Grand Pré but yet another Pierre of nearby Pisiquid.[19] Located on the Avon River on the site of today's Windsor and later Fort Edward, Pisiquid (founded around 1700) was a growing settlement in the Minas Basin region, second in size only to Grand Pré. With its hub focused on two parishes, St. Assumption on the right bank of the Avon and *Ste. Famille,* the Boodry's church, on the left bank, Pisiquid, parallel to the Boodry family itself, manifested a true population explosion. The settlement grew from a single parish in 1714 with 351 residents, composing 56 families, to approximately 1,400 inhabitants around 1750 and home to two parishes.[20] However, during the subsequent five years on the eve of the *Dérangement,* the inhabitants of Pisiquid, among whom numbered numerous local relatives of Pierre and Marguerite, had begun to emigrate to escape the increasing English intrusion from nearby and newly established Halifax into their lives.[21]

Last Days and the Exile

The stubbornly independent, largely isolated, and comparatively prosperous Acadians, so difficult not to depict as innocent and secure dwellers in a garden of their own, did not collectively grasp the ominous English threat of removal. Without a local government, a land registry, or courts of justice, and with all but the most exceptional and intractable matters determined by Port Royal and, after 1713, the English governor, the Acadians were a rural, local, and pre-national people caught up in a western world of emerging national societies.[22] Made up of relatively self-sufficient farms, amidst a tight network of cousins and fellow village-marsh-dwellers, the parish proved the first and often sole point of contact between Acadians and the outside world. Travel for the majority rarely exceeded the distance they could walk, ride (in a cart), paddle, or sail along the coastline (*caboter*) between sun up and sun down. Isolated, they received news most commonly from itinerant priests, passing merchants, and friendly natives. After more than a century of intermarriage, Acadian society amounted to a life in a community of cousins. But under the closing strictures of British rule, Acadians were increasingly denied access to priests and schools. Consequently, they relied ever more on traditional dance, song, language, and stories to express themselves. Free of the influence of Paris and Québec, it was as if the world and mentality of Rabelais's *Gargantua and Pantagruel* had been transported nearly intact to Acadia.[23]

But it is important to contradict the common genealogical and family history temptation to allow nostalgia to populate the past with static communities and unchanging tradition. In truth, Acadians were not isolated from the intrusive forces and ideas of the outside world. Census takers and tax collectors, who were one and the same, regularly appeared. Unexpected visits by conscripting officials, passing armies, or outside raiders even more rudely dispelled the Acadians of the illusion that they were alone and free in a garden village of their own. Living on the edges of streams, creeks, and rivers, bay and sea—all affording seasonal water roadways—and with almost each family equipped with a boat of some sort, the Acadians encountered the outside world on the waters around them.

Of greater importance, Acadian communities were never free from the pull of distant markets, which by the eighteenth century infiltrated settlements near and far across North America. Acadians gathered wool and saved their best meat and grain to obtain money, which procured a growing list of necessary commodities: clothing, shoes, thread, combs, fishhooks, lines, kettles, dishes, spices, molasses, knives, axes, guns, and other goods. They not only welcomed a chance to trade with English, French, and New England merchants and Indians, but the boldest of them made themselves middlemen in distant transactions, which brought highly prized local Indian furs to New England markets. One successful Acadian merchant, a son of Michel Boudrot and a great-uncle of Pierre, was Abraham Boudrot. With both French and English passports, Abraham moved goods regularly between Port Royal and Boston, where on at least one occasion he received a consignment of goods to take home for sale in Port Royal.[24]

Although priests, to whom Acadians adhered with a particular tenacity, had their activities constricted by English laws, they brought ideas, fashions, and rules from France and Québec. Despite restrictions, in fact perhaps because of restrictions, the priests' intellectual hold increased under English control, as the Acadian population became less and less educated and literate. The population's heightened allegiance to the church and its preachers of course compounded and in measure confirmed the suspicions of some Englishmen that in the inevitable war to come, the Acadians would prove to be allies of the Pope, Québec, France, and the Acadians' long-standing allies, the Mi'kmaq.

The *Grand Dérangement*

The narrative of my family becomes inseparable from the *Grand Dérangement*. Janus-faced, the expulsion points back in time to the cruel colonial practices of planting and removal of ancient empires and forward in time to modern

nations' insistence that peoples, cultures, and faiths must be transplanted
and made contiguous within national borders. The *Grand Dérangement* came
in the context of England's attempt to resolve once and for all what Francis Parkman described as "the most momentous and far-reaching question
ever brought to issue on this continent: Shall France remain here or shall she
not?"[25] The expulsion of the Acadians and their replacement by English stock
(many sons and daughters of Scots evicted from their native Highlands) satisfied a military desire to eliminate a threat and secure a contested zone, while
fulfilling a colonial vision of incorporating rich and fertile Acadian lands
into the burgeoning English economy in North America.

Lying along the fault line of two empires and without the advantage of
having a government of their own, the Acadians ended up doing exactly what
Machiavelli advised against in his *Prince:* They tried to follow a middle course
of alternately appeasing and temporizing the demands of two great neighbors, the French and the English. Because they considered taking an oath
to the English throne to be equal to committing a religious sacrilege, they
did not offer unquestionable adherence to the new ruler. But after the 1713
Treaty of Utrecht, they equally did not migrate to Québec at French request
or shape their conduct to conform to Québec's interest. By 1730, the Acadian middle course had won them the title "Neutrals." But when the British
founded Halifax in 1749, they increased the throne's domination over Nova
Scotia, Grand Pré, and nearby Pisiquid. Peace and prosperity, combined with
a sense of independence and a condition of disbursement, encouraged the
Acadians in their folly of pursuing a middle course at a time when they were
already gripped by the talons of their most dangerous foe, England.[26]

Pisiquid had reasons to suspect that bad times lay ahead. A few years
before 1755, marriages and fraternization between them and the English
had been stopped. Soldiers from a nearby garrison began to regulate villagers' everyday movements, demanding that locals have travel passes and per-
mits to transport limited crops and goods. Additionally, the inhabitants of
Pisiquid, which lay along the principal route from Halifax west to the Bay of
Fundy, were frequently conscripted to work on roads and bridges and were
subject to frequent requisitions for food and wood. One incident augured

days ahead. In 1754, the local and outspoken priest Henri Daudin encouraged the Pisiquid community not to comply with an order to supply wood for the local garrison. On being informed of Pisiquid's refusal, Halifax ominously instructed its troops to respond by burning homes one at time, from the garrison outward, until the village complied with the order or nothing was left. Only apologies by a delegation from Pisiquid spared the burning, and only an apology by the priest saved him from banishment.[27]

In the fall of 1755 the great catastrophe occurred. Furious with the Acadians' intractability and their disingenuousness in refusing to pledge unconditional loyalty to the throne, Halifax's new governor, Charles Lawrence, determined to end the Acadian problem with a single blow.[28]

Attempting to mitigate mounting British aggressiveness, the Acadians in Nova Scotia voluntarily disarmed. But disarmament came too late. In late May of 1755 Lawrence, with English and Massachusetts troops, began dismantling Acadian forts. Lawrence instructed the troops: "If you find that fair means will not do with them, you must proceed by the most vigorous measures possible, not only in compelling them to embark, but in depriving those who escape of all means of shelter or support, by burning their houses, and by destroying everything that may afford them the means of subsistence in the country."[29]

In the summer of 1755 he assembled two thousands troops from Massachusetts Bay, which had its own territorial ambitions to the north, joined them to a much smaller contingent of 250 English regulars, and placed them at Acadian population centers in Annapolis, Beaubassin, Cobiquid, Grand Pré, and Pisiquid. Then in near-simultaneous operations started in early September, Acadian men were lured into forts for informational meetings, taken hostage, and held until deportation. Troops swooped down upon other Acadian settlements and rounded up the men. In the most hideous instance, following Lawrence's most severe instructions, officers carried out a scorched-earth policy. They torched homes, burned crops, and slaughtered cattle. Their intention was to deny food and shelter to renegades who had fled rather than being taken hostage and were living off the land. The fall offensive alone netted as many as five thousand Acadians, while thousands of others escaped into the woods—finding refuge with Mi'kmaq friends and relatives, setting out on foot for Québec, or yet forming an armed and long-lived resistance movement.[30]

Even a stern judge of the Acadians like Massachusetts historian Francis Parkman, who held the Acadians largely responsible for their own doom, conceded, "The plain realities of their condition and fate are touching enough."[31] Between 1755 and 1766, 6,050 Acadians were captured and deported from the Bay of Fundy, with 1,664 coming from Annapolis (Port Royal); 1,100 from Beaubassin; 2,182 from Grand Pré; and 1,100 from Pisiquid.[32] Of an estimated eight thousand Acadians deported between 1755 and 1778, twelve hundred drowned at sea and an estimated one-third died en route from their first exposures to smallpox, typhoid, and yellow fever.[33] In two decades of migrations from 1766 to 1785, several thousand Acadians made varied and torturous journeys from Nova Scotia, New York, Maryland, Virginia, South Carolina, England, and France to Louisiana, where survivors reformed themselves in the Louisiana wetlands to establish the Cajun community.[34]

The report of Massachusetts Lieutenant Colonel John Winslow, serving under colonial Governor William Shirley as commander of His Majesty's troops at Grand Pré, reveals the impact of the *Grand Dérangement* on the Acadians of Grand Pré and a significant portion of the Boudrot clan. On September 15, 1755, Winslow inventoried what his army had done: It had imprisoned 1,923 Acadians and confiscated 1,269 oxen, 1,557 cows, 2,181 young calves, 8,690 sheep, 4,197 hogs, and 493 horses. Among his list of deportees there numbered twenty-six Boudrots, including five named Joseph, three Jean, and three Pierre, one of whom might possibly have been the Pierre Boudrot of Pisiquid.[35] Beyond the tragic enumeration of his deeds, Winslow confided his strong personal distaste for what he done, writing to fellow officer Captain Alexander Murray, "I am in hopes our affairs will soon put another face, and we get transports, and I [am] rid of the worst piece of service that ever I was in."[36] Captain Murray had conducted a similar and simultaneous operation at Pisiquid, using Fort Edwards as his base.

But it is the details of the evictions that make even a reader with only the slightest empathy shudder. On September 5, the men of Grand Pré were summoned to a meeting at the church and told they would be held as prisoners until transport was available for their expulsion. The only concessions were the assurances that their families would not be split apart in transport and they would be able to take their money and all the goods that they could fit on the ships. A week later the men of Pisiquid were similarly summoned to hear an important announcement. They were taken prisoner and told that they and their families were to be deported. As in the case of Grand Pré, while not told when, how, or where they would be exiled, they were assured that their families would not be split apart and that they could take the valuables and necessities that the limited space on the ship permitted.

Fear, anxiety, terror, and horror swirled throughout Pierre's Acadian community. They were stunned by the speed, thoroughness, and ruthlessness with which they were being evicted onto dangerous autumn seas. In a single blow, they suffered the worst thing a people and a family could. They were taken from homes and places on their land, made prisoners, and sent as unwanted cargo, precariously across the ocean, to an unidentified inhospitable world. They could not imagine what would happen to them.

Exiled in Plymouth Colony

If Pierre and his family came from Pisiquid, there is a good chance they arrived on the 81-ton ship the *Sea Flower*. Under the charter of Charles Apthorp and Thomas Hancock of the Boston Mercantile Company, the ship set sail from Pisiquid on October 27 and cast anchor in Boston on November 19.[37] Pierre belonged to one of the early groups of five thousand Acadians initially banished and sent south to New England and were among Massachusetts' "first permanent Acadian residents." Now known as "French Neutrals," the Acadians entered a Massachusetts where popular opinion judged them to be heretical Catholics, dangerous Frenchmen, and allies of the perfidious Indians. Without the economic value of slaves or indentured people, the Acadians, much like the contemporary world's boat people, literally brought boatloads of problems and were seen as both a potential threat to colonial society and an unwanted tax burden. In an age when human misery was awash on

the shores of every port and at the doors of every community, the Acadians comprised a cargo of human wretchedness and woe. Mixed among the
almost uniformly debilitated, grieving, and depressed, there were widowed
and pregnant women, sick children, impaired elderly, and the dying.

Having expediently denied the Acadians the status of being prisoners
of war, evictors Halifax and Great Britain exempted themselves from incur-
ring costs for the care and keep of the people they had discharged to distant
ports. Individual New England colonies responded in their own ways. Reli-
giously tolerant and Catholic Maryland, for instance, explicitly repudiated
any charge of responsibility, humane or otherwise, for this act of empire. In
Virginia, eleven hundred Acadians were denied permission to disembark
and sent as prisoners of war to England, where they remained until the Treaty
of Paris in 1763.[38] Other colonies did allow Acadians to disembark but refused
them all aid once they were ashore. Left to their own wits and resources,
some purchased flimsy boats and perished in attempts to return north.

Massachusetts, the colony most complicit in the expulsion, was the most
humane in the treatment of the Acadians. After a November storm cleared,
the most northern colonial port, Boston, received the first ships of expulsion,
six transports, which included Pierre and his family. The unconscionable
condition of the ships forced the colony's port authorities to prohibit them
to sail farther. The Massachusetts House and Council, acting in the absence
of Governor Shirley, wrote to Halifax and declared that the colony would
admit more Acadians but expected indemnification for all costs. Without
the hint of a response to its claim for reimbursement, Massachusetts continued to receive hosts of these unwanted strangers. Between fall 1755 and
August 1756, Massachusetts received 1,189 Acadians.[39]

In exigent circumstances, the Acadians were driven to cajole, petition,
and beg their new and openly anti-Catholic hosts for relief. Nevertheless,
they were fortunate to have come ashore in Massachusetts, whose citizenry
was by comparison distinguished by its virtues of justice, piety, and sobri-
ety. The colonial government oversaw the seaworthiness the ships in which
the Acadians arrived and surveyed and ministered to the health of those on
board. They provided rum, sugar, raisins, and white flour to the sick; milk

for the children; "physicians" to attend the births of children; and coffins for the considerable numbers of dead. New arrivals were provisioned with food, clothing, shelter, and even tools for working the land.[40]

The colony's government did even more. As the case of Pierre's family testifies, it opened itself to complaint and petitions for redress by allowing Acadians to directly address the Committee of the Great and General Court, which existed when the governor, the House of Representatives, and the Governor's Council were assembled.[41] Beyond this, members of the House inspected the conditions of the Acadian old, infirm, sick, and orphans in the respective towns to which they were assigned. Such prominent Bostonians as Governor Thomas Hutchinson, Councilor James Bowdoin, and Representative Jeremy Gridley established themselves as an Acadian lobby, arguing that the colony shared responsibility for the plight of the Neutrals. They lent their considerable skills to assuaging Acadian suffering and assuring them basic rights by bringing forward their appeals and complaints in well-crafted petitions that were addressed to the highest level of government.

Unannounced boatloads of Acadians dispatched from the north and returning from southern ports, where they had been refused disembarkation, formed a growing economic, political, and moral problem for the colony and increased the general populace's concern about colonial security, authority, and a dangerously high and mounting debt.[42] Distributing the Acadians throughout the colony did nothing to solve safety and housing shortages or to clarify the matter of who would host these uninvited guests. Fearful of the Acadians escaping by ship or "caballing" and forming themselves into an internal enemy, the colonists banned Acadian travel. They passed laws against travel on Sunday, lest these aliens steal from their hosts who were absent at church. Desperate to know the fates of family and friends, Acadians violated the Sunday ban, which made the matter of wandering Neutrals a source of colony-wide anxiety. Only in 1760, with the threat to security finally allayed, did the Massachusetts Court drop its bans against travel and give the Neutrals who supported themselves permission to live wherever they chose."[43]

Individual Massachusetts towns resented the imposition of groups of

French Neutrals for their keep and care. Though townspeople were accustomed to keeping indentured servants, slaves, and redemptioners (bonded servants who worked to pay for their voyage to the colony), the Acadians promised little in return for their keep. Without initial colonial guarantees of indemnification, and with a tradition of "warning out" strangers to keep them off local tax rolls, localities were nevertheless ordered to take in at one time as many as ten or twenty Neutrals, many of whom who were too old, sick, young, or involved in the care of their own to work for others.[44] This imposition came when towns already festered with anger over increasing taxes, and some communities had taken the drastic act of moving, lock, stock, and barrel, out of the colony. Towns ultimately could only trust that they would eventually receive indemnification for having welcomed these costly strangers into their midst. [45]

Family by family, the Acadians were settled into individual towns along the coast and inland. Their experiences varied widely, depending on the townships and individuals to whom they were assigned. Defying generalization, some keepers and employers of Acadians displayed exceptional charity, while others exploited the newcomers and their children as cheap labor, and yet others capitalized on the Acadians' skills as farmers, carpenters, and boat builders.

As we will see in the case of Pierre's family, the Acadians were exploited and abused in many ways. Without local recourse to appeal, they were driven to petition the colonial government itself for relief from and redress of wrongs, which included unpaid or underpaid wages and the separation of older children from families for forced work in other communities. Hope itself was attacked in this Protestant wilderness, which forbade priests under the ban of perpetual imprisonment, offered no fixed tenure, and refused the possibility of return to one's homeland.[46]

The Wilderness of Plymouth Colony

Sometime in winter or early spring of 1756, after a few months' stay in Boston, Pierre, his wife Marguerite, and their five children,[47] along with approximately thirty-five other Neutrals (many of whom, if not all, came from Grand

Pré), were sent by ship south down the coast to Scituate, Massachusetts.[48] Midway between Boston and Plymouth, Scituate appeared at least a decade before the town's incorporation in 1636. Though established at a port with a good harbor, Scituate, like New England townships of old, sprawled out into the countryside in all directions. Composed of small farms, linked by winding cow trails, paths, and narrow roads that circled swamps and thickets, Scituate reached ten miles inland.[49] Rich in timber, especially white pine, for shipbuilding, the environment also afforded abundant water in the forms of streams, a river for transport, and ponds, which drove the all-important small mills of pre-industrial North America.

At Scituate a first group of seventeen Acadians was put under the care of mill owner Joseph Clap. They lived in a small hut at the western end of town, north of Black Pond and east of Mount Blue, at the end of a cart path called Cuffee's Lane. Ten other Neutrals were sent to live under the guidance of Dr. Joseph Jacob of Assinippi in inland western Scituate, on the northern border of Hanover. There, in a town incorporated in 1727, he and his brother, Joshua, ran a sawmill and gristmill located on the banks of what became known as Jacob's Pond. Later, nine Neutrals from one of the two groups were taken to nearby western Hanover and were eventually lodged in an isolated house in Cricket Hole.[50]

Pierre and his family lived in a town that explicitly opposed assuming the economic burden of housing what local government called "the people from Nova Scotia."[51] The individual citizens who took them in—fed, clothed, sheltered, and even gave them a little money—were owed compensation by the town, which in turn justly looked for payment from the colony, which since 1755 had asked reimbursement from Halifax.[52]

Clues about the everyday conditions of Pierre and his family at Scituate can be extrapolated from those of the Acadians living directly to the north of Scituate, at nearby Hingham, in what was called "The Acadian House." The house was built into the side of a hill. The Neutrals were lodged in its cellar, which on one side stood above the ground. Occupants of the Acadian House included a family of eight, composed of father and mother, five small children, and one single woman. Although the Acadians were set to work husking corn and doing other jobs, their upkeep was costly. The town paid for tools and provisions, from June 1 to November 10, 1760, 12 pounds, 14 shillings, and 4 pence, a sum sufficient to build a house or a small church. Thirty-eight pounds of salted beef were to be charged to the old Frenchmen Joseph Brow, Alexander Brow, Charles Trawhaw, Peter Trawhaw, and John Trawhaw; the latter surname, spelled as "Trahan," was a common name at Grand Pré and Pisiquid and appeared along with the surname Boudrot among the earliest founders of Port Royal. The anonymous late nineteenth-century author of a local history comments that near the Acadian House was a field in which "these poor unfortunates were in the habit of meeting, to hold, in quiet and peace, religious services in the faith of their youth and homes"; he remarks that on a small pane of glass recovered from the Acadian House, "exiles had scratched their names … with a ring," leaving a trace of "the fate of those families lost in the obscurity of history."[53]

Their Petitions

Unsolved local grievances and complaints led Acadians to appeal and petition directly to the colonial government twenty-three times between 1755 and June 1766, to which the Council responded favorably in eighteen cases. For instance, disagreement sprung up between the "Trawhaw" and the town selectmen of Scituate. The former's wish to keep their family together conflicted with the latter's drive to extract maximum work from those in their keep or to export them. In a letter originating in Boston, May 4, 1756, suggesting reliance on sophisticated colonial advocates, brothers Peter and John Trawhaw of Scituate petitioned the Honorable His Majesty's Council of Massachusetts Bay: "That your petitioners the said John, aged twenty-six, the said Peter, twenty-four, are threatened to be separated from their parents by the Selectman of Scituate in which town they are placed, and where indeed they endure many hardships, and have been denied any provisions for fifteen days past, which makes them more unwilling to be separated from their parents, since they are desirous to do what they can for their relief."[54]

Their neighbor and my grandmother Frances's ancestor, Pierre Boudrot, filed a similar petition on March 21, 1756. Identified in this instance as "Peter Boudreau," he addressed the highest colonial authority, "To his Honour the Lieutenant Governor and to the Honourable his Majesty's Council of the Province of Massachusetts Bay House of Representatives." "The Petition of Peter Boudreau," it started:

> *humbly sheweth that he being formerly an inhabitant of Nova Scotia with his Wife and Family being Seven in Number were ordered to Scituate, where they have above enduring numberless Hardships still now and being unable to live there any longer they are comes up here to Boston to implore your Honour's Protection. They have taken two of his children from him and forced them to work like Horses, and after two or three months have given them nothing but a few Rags. That your Petitioner would gladly work and his children work, if they could be paid for it, but when they are paid little or nothing for their Work, not understanding the English Language and Customs, they know not where to apply for Redress and the Country People do just what they will with them.*

"Your Petitioner," Pierre's petition continued,

> *this winter was employed to cut wood for . . . Jirad Randall [and] cut about twenty four Cord of which he has been paid only for eight Cord in necessary's which he took up for his wife who lay in, the other remains unpaid for to this Day nor doth he know how to come at what is justly due to him, but by applying for your Honours: He is refused Subsistance and can't be p'd for his Work, when he is fortunate enough to find work to do and this Week they were to come and take his Children from him, which he can't bear to think of wherefore he comes to your Honours for Protection and begs your Honours would afford him such Relief as in your great Wisdom you shall think proper; and your petitioner shall ever pray.*
>
> The mark
>
> X
>
> of Peter Boudreau[55]

Pierre's petition, no doubt written and executed with the help of the Acadian advocates in Boston, opens a window onto the distress of a poor family, which historians of common people, like mine, must seek to capture. The head of a family that had fallen on the worst of times, his list of complaints is woeful indeed. His children abused, his wife incapacitated by pregnancy, his wages withheld, unable to speak the language or get suitable employment, he has no recourse. The rest of his large and many-branched family, the natural source of his and his family's strength and identity, had been scattered across Massachusetts and the world.[56] He found himself with no other option than to throw himself on the goodness of strangers in distant Boston and appeal to the highest authority of this alien place.

The Council of the House of Representatives took up Pierre's case on April 1, 1757; on April 19, it removed Peter "Bodroitt" and his wife Margaret and five children from the care of Scituate, assigned them to the town of Dudley, approximately sixty miles inland, and provided for their transportation.[57] While it is unclear whether or not the family actually went to Dudley, Pierre reentered Massachusetts records in 1760 when he joined Acadians who, in increasing numbers, gathered in Boston in search of work, medical care, or assignment to a new place in the countryside. In this same period, Pierre signed a petition of Neutrals, which stated their dissatisfaction with life in Plymouth Colony and the rest of the Massachusetts Bay Colony and requested that they be allowed to leave Massachusetts for old France. The Acadians voiced an illusion common to the rural peoples of the old European order that the king of France, like God in Heaven, cared about them on this earth; Boston demurred. They had no evidence or reason to believe that king of France cared a single iota about Neutrals as his subjects or that he would lift a finger to help them in their journey toward a new home. The colonial government rejected the petition. Then, as if to resolve the nagging Acadian problem once and for all, in April, 1760. it reassigned all the Acadians, ever troublesome, pleading, and litigious, to new towns, issuing a fresh set of orders and directives about both their care and their behavior.[58]

On June 8, 1760, the Committee of the General Court moved Pierre's family inland to Raynham, in Bristol County, formerly known as the New Plymouth Colony. The Committee empowered Misters Lazarus Bowker and John Bowker "to take Peter Boodroitt and Magarett his wife & their two children, who named as Francis & Peter, with their baggage and convey them in as cheap a manner & as soon as you can to Raynham in the County of Bristol, and Deliver them to the Selectmen of said Town; and make Return to me of your Doing & Charges."[59]

Well into mid-life and entering the fifth year of the Diaspora, Pierre arrived with his family in Raynham, a small village adjacent to Taunton, thirty-six miles south of Boston. His unrelieved preoccupation as head of the family remained the same: Keep his family together in this alien colony until such time as they could find their way to a new home.

Pierre and his family came to Raynham under the auspices one of the town's most important citizens, Selectman Colonel Zephaniah Leonard. Born in 1736, Colonel Leonard, one of fourteen children of Major Zephaniah and Hannah King and a graduate of Yale University, had held the office of High Sheriff of Bristol County for thirty-two years, while pursuing the affairs of court and government and assisting his brother in the manufacture of domestic metal articles. There is no way to know precisely what motivated Selectman Leonard, who proved a helpful sponsor to the Boudrots. He was aware that a 1756 Massachusetts provincial law directed selectmen to provide at the province's expense a house, rent free, to each Acadian household whose head undertook to support his family, while continuing to obligate selectmen to care for those incapable of supporting themselves.[60] Leonard himself already was experienced in having Neutrals under his direct control, making use of their labor, and being reimbursed by the town for their care. In 1756 the town compensated Colonel Leonard 8 pounds, 12 shillings, 4 pence for outfitting two middle-age Neutral brothers, whom he praised for their industriousness. His bill, similar to those of other Acadian sponsors, counted all done in pounds, shillings, and pence, proving that goods and services, including transportation, were measured and compensated for by money.[61] It also allows the family historian to grasp the cost of everyday life in colonial Massachusetts.

Before the Massachusetts Bay Legislature formally voted to compensate towns for the support of poor persons who were "cast upon the town," Colonel Leonard joined fellow selectmen in voting to build a "small house for

the French family." Town records show that building Pierre's family a house
was a community project that advanced individual economic interests. Cutting and hauling the wood, making bricks, hauling and setting stone, carpentry, in addition to the maintenance cost of the family—all supplied diverse
members of the town with work and income. The total cost was about 20
pounds, not including an additional expenditure of approximately 6 pounds
for transport, installation, and maintaining the family with food, shelter
and wood, and providing medical care of a surgeon (physician) during the
house's construction. This sum of 25 pounds exceeded the sum dedicated to
the town school in 1763 and was almost half of what Raynham citizens collectively paid to its Harvard-educated, Brown University doctor; property-rich
Reverend Peres Fobes, the Congregational minister, managed by preaching,
lending, and rent to have an impressive income of seventy pounds a year.[62]

If the new house in Raynham proved a port in the terrible sea of exile
for Pierre and his family, it was no so for the majority of other Acadians in
Massachusetts, who refused provincial land grants for settlement, and in
one case in 1759 declined to accept the colonial offer to take over the abandoned town of Oxford. The only thing the colony required was that they
leave the dole.[63]

In 1763, with the conclusion of the Seven Years War, expectations ran
high among the Acadians that they would soon be free to strike out on their
own. In 1764, 406 Neutrals requested that the colony provided for them free
transportation to the West Indies.[64] An irresponsible letter by St. Domingo's
governor, promising all—transportation, hospitality, and land—aroused
Acadians' expectations, which grew throughout the fall of that year.[65] As if
deliverance were at hand, Acadians disposed of family goods and encum-
brances and reported to Boston in hopes of transport to the West Indies.
However, no ship appeared. Disappointment grew; their hopes of friendly,
warming shores did not brace them against the closing teeth of winter. Again
the Acadians appealed, as they had on arrival, for direct and urgent relief.
However, the urge to exodus was irrepressible. On January 1, 1765—a decade
after their banishment and exile to Massachusetts—the Acadians assembled
another petition to be set free and allowed to travel to the French Colony

of San Domingo (Hispaniola), where they could practice their own religion and be among their own kind. Possibly, though unlikely, our very own Pierre, who was on the verge of becoming a landowner in Raynham, was one of 400 fellow Acadians who petitioned the governor (under the name "Pete Bowdry") to be allowed to go to San Domingo.[66]

Their desperate and fantastical petition was declined on grounds that this was an expedition certain of a disastrous end. The Council, in turn, dispatched money to the Boston Overseers of the Poor for their immediate relief, and at the same time, it called for an investigation into the condition of the Acadians, which by their own admission in their New Year's Day petition (signed prominently by Jean Trahan among others) confessed: "There are some of your people that think we [are] rich. This has never been [the] case with us since we have been in this country, but less so at the present than ever, for the riches which remain to us are Poverty and Misery."[67]

Acadian discontent intensified in the turbulent years of 1765 and 1766 when Massachusetts, whose deeds and plans were beyond its income, was embroiled in protest against the imposition of new taxes in the form of England's Stamp Act and agitated by original ideas of national independence. In a collective petition in 1766, the Acadians, hoping to take advantage of a March 1765 proclamation by the governor of Canada welcoming settlers, urged Massachusetts to encourage him to provide them with support and land in order to be settled in Canada.[68] In the very summer of 1766, 890 petitioning Acadians, of approximately 1,100 in Massachusetts, acknowledged their willingness to take the oath to the throne and were given permission, but not transportation, to return to the regions of Arcadia or Quebec—but not to their ancestral homes or lands.[69] In a subsequent petition in the late fall of 1766, 89 families, composed of 491 people, repeated what they had done two years before: They came to Boston in order to seek transport to return to Canada, and again they found themselves stranded in Boston, without money or work as winter arrived.[70] While the government authorized relief, given the Acadians' "necessitous circumstances," it ordered them to return to their assigned town or run the risk of losing rent and housing provisions.[71]

Pierre had not joined the group of 890. The question why reveals vividly the frustrating situation that historians of individual families face. Wanting a narrative and an explanation turning on facts and details, they often have to construct lives and events out of airy suppositions and complex conjectures. Nevertheless, this story has a certain terra firma: a decade after their banishment and ten years before the Declaration of Independence, Pierre and Marguerite renounced hope of returning north to Acadia or Catholic Québec. I have no clear knowledge of their inner arithmetic, but surely they knew the dangers of sea travel, which included storms, sinking, contagions, and even piracy, recently illustrated by the fate of eighty young Acadians taken and pressed into the service of privateers. They knew that they retained no place or residual rights in Nova Scotia. Moreover, old age, the very ache of their fifty-year-old bones, reminded them how difficult it would be to scratch out a new place on leftover and, thus difficult, lands. Just perhaps, they still resisted taking an oath to the throne.

However, there is another, and I believe stronger, line of explanation. Just possibly they and their children began to envision rural Massachusetts as home. Pierre and Marguerite's children had no doubt learned English and accustomed themselves to the ways of these strangers. Time had *not* resulted in their isolation, and familiarity with Protestants and colonial law had *not* bred contempt. Just possibly, they calculated that they would be better off in Raynham with the Leonards than starting another exodus. That very year, Pierre took a decisive step, one that lends weight to this line of reasoning, when he publicly avowed his intention of taking up full membership in Raynham, Massachusetts. With colony Court Officer and Selectman Zephaniah Leonard vouching for his credit, on December 17, 1766, when other Acadians again waited in the Port of Boston, Peter made himself a colonial landholder, thus citizen and taxpayers. He bought approximately 20 acres, his first parcel of land, for 13 pounds, 6 shillings, 8 pence—about the cost of the "small French house." The deed on the family's first ownership of American land reads, "Peter Boudrott," a "French neutral." [72] On this wooded, swampy, rocky, and pond-filled Massachusetts soil, Pierre planted a Boudrot home. As a landholder, freeman, and citizen, he joined fellow colonists in paying taxes to care for the poor and support a school, a government, and a church.

Although we have no evidence that Pierre and Marguerite joined the town's dominant Congregational faith, they must have made occasional use of the church building, which doubled as a city hall. Indeed, a dispute over the church's location accounted for Raynham's split from Taunton in the 1720s and its subsequent incorporation as an independent town. In 1769, Pierre witnessed fellow landholders of Raynham fall into a terrible row over the building and location of a new church in the northern end of the town.[73]

Aside from such a telling sign of integration as the use of anglicized name "Boodry," which echoed the common New England name "Boodry," Pierre and Marguerite had the common experience of immigrant parents of watching their children boldly enter and take irreversible steps in joining the new community. In 1773, in neighboring Taunton, Pierre's son Joseph—my Frances's great-great-grandfather—married Hannah Leonard, the daughter of a prominent landowner.[74] Peter Jr. matched brother Joseph in 1779 by marrying colonial daughter Lovina Andrew.[75] Peter had already done more than that in enrolling the Boodrys in the very formation of the American nation. He joined a Massachusetts regiment to fight the English, in what Acadians called *cette guerre de folles*, "this war of fools," that incomprehensible fray of Englishmen fighting Englishmen and colonists battling colonists. Peter Jr. served as a private from August 8 to October 31, 1780, in a company raised to reinforce the Continental Army.[76] Indeed, Boodry assimilation into the nation coincided with the American Revolution and the very birth of the Republic.

Debt, exaggerated by the Revolution, abounded within the colonies and drove the people's movement into the frontier. The poor, the widows, and the sick were still auctioned off for care in community *Vendues* (public auctions), as they were known before the Revolution. Neither the land nor the houses of the smallest and humblest holders was exempt from legal action to recover debt. The Revolution, which magnified federal and state debts and left the majority with useless currency and no means to repay, turned newly ordained national citizens into ordinary migrants and squatters. The battle raged between creditors and debtors, the financial and mercantile coast against the farmers of the inland countryside. Nowhere was it as intense as in Massachusetts, with Shay's Rebellion, a revolt of the indebted. In August 1786 the legislature raised taxes to satisfy the speedy repayment of speculators who purchased state debt certificates, but adjourned without hearing the petitions of debt-ridden farmers to issue paper money or stay the mounting number of farm and home foreclosures.[77] Led by veterans of the Revolutionary War, scattered groups across rural western Massachusetts sought to shut down courts intent on collecting debt. The rebellion, a terrible shock to the new nation, ended in 1787, having achieved little, except lowering court fees and exempting clothes, household goods, and tools from seizure for debt.

Debt only further set in motion the majority, sending them to emigrate back to the larger coastal cities, where there was a chance to find work and make money, or initiating the great trek inward toward the frontiers. The Boodrys, losing memory that they were Acadians but never able to escape the reality of their poverty, first went north to Massachusetts's frontier, Maine and its mountains, and then, a generation or two later, joined great streams of New Englanders for the Old Northwest lands in southern Michigan and central Wisconsin.

4

Up and Down the Hills of Maine, and Off to Wisconsin

The conflict of the empires cast the Boudrots like alien seed in remote and Protestant Scituate, Massachusetts. Their material condition, which presents a challenge for the local historian to construct, came not to differ from the great majority of poor colonists. With only a tenuous hold on place, they lived impecuniously in a freshly established and indebted society, rich only in the promise of land. Home did not guarantee subsistence or security; locality provided less of community and support and more of deprivation, insult, rejection, and even expulsion. Spare a friendly neighbor, a helpful church, a benign landlord, and a begrudging, parsimonious town dole, the family was only one bill away from the road. For their children to have something, anything, they had to choose migration.

It is of this common plight, so rich in variation yet scarce in detail, that family historians must learn to research and write. They must seek their subjects not by membership in century-long communities, towns, and cities, but in the context of obscure rural places. Without uplifting narrative themes of the certain advance of prospering democracy or the sure entitlements of moving west, they must trace individual migration from small and thin-soiled valleys to non-commercial patches of land on the infertile slopes of mountains.

Family historians of the migrant poor also use histories of national expansion, government policy, and industrial growth. They can supplement their work with studies of the changing American family, environments, and economic life. At least, I found much of this to be true in the case of grandmother Frances's family. From Massachusetts to several parts of Maine to Wisconsin, in a succession of moves over three generations, the Boodrys sought a place where they could succeed. Their migrations, unique to them, were typical of hundreds of thousands of poor American families who had their hopes and sought their place in the interior of the new and expanding republic.

In colonial America, as was the case in Pierre's Acadia or Rosalia's Sicily, the family household functioned as a commonwealth unto itself. The

family braided together human biology and culture. Ever subject to matters of reproduction, nutrition, shelter, and care, the household dictated a
person's well-being and conduct. As the hub of local mutuality and at the
heart of traditional morality, the family household dominated social life in
the countryside and city until recent times, when the abstract state and distant markets came to dominate. American colonial historian James Henretta
concluded that "family life could not be divorced from economic considerations; indeed the basic question of power and authority within the family
hinged primarily on legal control over the land and—indirectly—over the
labor needed to work it." On this count, the early American family, patriar-
chal and conservative by tradition, was not that different from its European
counterpart.[1]

The individual without family and the family without land belonged
nowhere, and they were unwelcome everywhere in times of scarcity, judged
by others as a public burden. Barely casting a shadow on the landscape, the
family without land has no rights, no basis to borrow money, no patrimony
to marry off its children. A bad season, an unexpected accident, or any significant shift in circumstances could render the American poor homeless—
perpetual migrants and illegal squatters; they traveled on the broken trail of
crushing necessity and unexpected opportunity. This fragile and mutative
condition shaped the destiny of the majority in the early American Republic,
including the Boodrys of Acadia and Massachusetts, who migrated to and
within Maine and then to and within Wisconsin.

As with other large families who did not have a hold on the land, the
Boodrys' fertility caused them to slosh over the brim of the stingy soils of
Raynham, Taunton, and New England. At the same time, the Atlantic economy produced the indebted new Republic that pushed the Boodrys and others like them to migrate. The patriarch Pierre's meager patrimony did not
provide his family with a firm platform in Raynham and Taunton society.
Multiplying at rates of ten, fifteen, and twenty children per family, which
described Acadian and Yankee patterns equally, the Boodrys' reproduction
outstripped local impoverished lands and scarce jobs, leaving emigration
their answer.

The disjuncture between high fertility and low mortality and the equal disjuncture between "belly and womb," to use an expression of anthropologist Marvin Harris, impinged on the Boodrys and their kind. Excessive population for the land, according to historian James Henretta, afforded a dynamic quality to New England rural life from the seventeenth century until the middle and late nineteenth century, when mass industrial and individual society displaced it. American historian David Danbom explains the dynamics: there were six live births per woman, only one in ten children would die before they were twenty years old, and normal life expectation reached seventy years.[2]

This mismatch between a fertile population and a parsimonious land had a long history in New England, which was characterized by a harsh climate and thin soils with limited yields, averaging fifteen bushels of wheat per acre. At the same time, long, harsh winters accounted for intense timber use, estimated to be from three-fifths to three-quarters of an acre of timber for an average New England family per year. Shortages of land had appeared in the oldest New England towns by 1700, and lands and forests were degraded prior to the Revolution. By the time of the Revolution, thousands of colonial Massachusetts farmers were trying to survive on less than forty acres, which was a unit only a third of the size that first-generation colonial farmers worked. Consequently, New Englanders were driven to seek nearby seasonal employment on large farms and in waxing and waning mill towns or larger seaside cities and towns. American historian Kenneth Lockridge concludes that until 1800 settlement remained clustered near the eastern coastline on small tracks of land, reduced from approximately 150 acres to 40 acres. Though never autonomous, these farms became less and less self-sufficient and more and more subject to debt, causing each generation to look toward the interior for new land. The standard division of lands with two shares for the eldest son and one for the younger reduced land size by a third, leaving once yeoman farmers increasingly resembling in poverty and scarcity of land Old World European peasantry. By 1790, Lockridge concludes, the poor were not only increasingly present but even posed a threat to the young Republic. Only a mass exodus to the frontier, not the Constitution, Lockridge concludes, "may [have] rescued

America as the land of mobility and opportunity at a time when it was beginning to lack both."[3] The Boodrys joined this exodus.

Joseph Is "Warned Out"

Pierre and Marguerite, like the populous rural poor, did not have a secure
grip on their land. In fact, like small landholders throughout American history, no sooner did they obtain land than they began mortgaging it. Among
property records, indispensable for reading the economic plight of a family, on July 7, 1768, "Peter Boudrott," still calling himself "one of said neutral
French" conveyed his land in mortgage to Seth Crossman of Raynham for
39 pounds.[4] Crossman conveyed the land back to "Peter Boodrott" on October 15, 1768.[5] A few months later, on February 21, 1769, "Peter Boodree," now
called a "Raynham husbandman," again conveyed the same parcel of land,
which can be estimated to be anywhere from five to thirteen acres, to Crossman. Boodry did the same in 1774 and 1778 with a certain John King, whose
property is shown on an indispensable 1830 map of Raynham to be on the
south end of the pond near Leonard's Old Iron Works. In this transaction, the
value of the property value had depreciated to thirteen pounds.[6] In his last
recorded transaction, Peter—notably no longer distinguished as yeoman but
considered a "labourer"—sold his twenty-two acres of land to Josiah Dean.[7]
Although there is a tax list for Massachusetts Colony in 1771, Peter Boodry's
name does not appear on it.

Pierre and Marguerite, thereafter, vanished into obscurity. Most likely,
he was buried on a small patch of Boodry or neighboring land in Raynham, where his wife Marguerite died in 1803. It is altogether unlikely he ever
made a final return to his homeland in Nova Scotia, where the name Boodry
(Boudrot, Boudreau) lived on as inhabitants and prominent enemies of English control.[8]

The 1790 census described Pierre's son "Joseph Boudre" of Raynham as
head of a household consisting of daughters Trifena, Lucinda, and Hannah,
and sons John, Nathan, Sylvester, and Joseph Jr. The latter was Frances's great-
grandfather. Father Joseph (perhaps named after Pierre's father) was born

around 1745 in Acadia, making him approximately ten years old at the time of the *Grand Dérangement.*[9] He entered fully into English Protestant colonial society, in August 1773, when in Taunton he married seventeen-year-old Hannah Leonard. She was the daughter of Bethiah (Drake) Leonard and Benjamin Leonard, a well-off landowner who amassed enough cash to leave the immense sum of ten thousand dollars in his will, of which Hannah and Joseph would, in 1818, receive five hundred dollars.[10] Coming from typical large families, whether they were Protestant or Catholic, the young couple proved more fertile than rich, having produced at least seven identified children and returning to live as non-land-owning laborers in Raynham sometime prior to 1790.[11]

As if to get the welfare rolls in order for the New Year and the newly formed state and national governments, on January 12, 1790, the Raynham's town selectmen "warned out" twenty-one local families, Joseph's among them. His eviction notice read:

> *Bristol ss. To the Constable of the Town of Raynham within Said County. Greeting*
> *In the Name of the Common-wealth of Massachusetts you are hereby directed to*
> *notify and warn Joseph Boodrott Labourer now residing in Raynham within the*
> *said County of Bristol, who have lately come into this Town for the purpose of*
> *abiding therein, not having obtained the Town's consent therefore that they, and*
> *each of them above mentioned, their Wives Children, and all others under their*
> *care, (if such they have) depart the limits thereof within fifteen Days, and of this*
> *Precept, with your doings theron you are to make return into the Office of the*
> *Clerk of this Town within Twenty Days next coming that such further proceed-*
> *ings may be had in the premises as the law directs Given under our Hands and*
> *Seals, at Raynham aforesaid this Twelfth Day of January in the Year of our Lord*
> *Seventeen Hundred & Ninety.*[12]

Warning out was an established colonial instrument for localities to coerce the newly arrived poor to leave town, thus transferring the cost of their maintenance to the colony, and now it was being applied to longer-term residents. Town selectmen across New England made particular use of it against the mounting numbers of costly landless poor generated by the

American Revolution.[13] Local communities still measured all goods and services not just in pounds and shillings but single pence, and they considered
all tax increases highly onerous. In 1791, for instance, the Raynham church's
"Bellfery Subscriptions," its largest annual contributions of three and four
pounds, fell on only a handful of households; the rest paid in shillings and
pence. The very building of the church was calculated in small denominations: 10 shillings, 6 pence for nails; 1 pound, 5 shillings for 210 feet of pine
planks; and 4 shillings, 6 pence for 250 long shingles.[14]

Money was scarce; goods were precious; personal property, however
shabby, was of utmost importance. Theft warranted execution. It was the
worthy subject of the preaching skills of the local minister, Peres Fobes, who
himself had amassed a small fortune over a lifetime of preaching, teaching,
administering, and lending money.[15] In April of 1790, the year Joseph's family
and twenty others were warned out, the neighboring small Town of Middle-
borough held its annual Vendue (Auction Sale) of the Poor. For the almost
staggering sum of 69 pounds, 10 shillings, the successful low bidder promised
to provide provisions—clothing, housing, all "necessaries" excepting doctor's
bills—for eight auctioned poor families. The town also paid approximately
half that sum for short-term boarding for local families, widows, and children, including their medical bills, the apprehension of fugitive poor, and a
few 6-shilling coffins for the burial of those permanently off the tax rolls.

Given such costs for the poor, Raynham understandably greeted the
arrival of impoverished newcomers with notification of their eviction.
"Warning them out," rather than initiating immediate removal, served as a
community disclaimer of responsibility. It immunized it against any and all
future costs associated with the strangers. In addition, warning out in 1790
may have carried a degree of urgency in light of what the new and indebted
Republic might portend for state support.

While the revolution had won political independence, it had not secured
solvency. In fact, it had further impoverished Massachusetts, whose very
attempts to use general taxes to remedy its situation helped provoke Shay's
Rebellion in 1786–87, which gave the disgruntled English hope the Revolution was coming unraveled.[16] Almost two hundred insurgents marched on

the court in Taunton, where only troops and well-spoken words successfully dispersed them.[17] Whether or not the Boodry family participated, the movement belonged to those lacking that minimal twenty or so pounds a year of income required for a family of six. In other words, a dearth of assets spurred their migration to the interior.

The frontier promised land. Hopes, real and mythic, stirring need, fantasy, and greed, led colonial people inland. Decades before the Revolution, Massachusetts settlers had already started to move to the colony's frontier, Maine. Starting in the 1820s, migrants from Maine, New York, and all of New England pushed in a succession of waves toward the opening Northwest. Bobbing corks in the shoals of New England poverty, the Boodrys joined in the westward migration.

To the Maine Frontier

The great migration from the coast inland was the second American Revolution, and over the course of a few generations formed a new society, commented on by Toqueville in his 1835 *Democracy in America*.[18] Pierre's grandson Joseph led the family in a new exodus north to Maine. As the poor usually do, Joseph arrived at least two generations late to find a fortune. He followed speculators, often housed in England, who originally dealt in tens of thousands of acres, and he came after land companies, small speculators, settlers, and squatters had already quarreled and gone to court to establish their claims. Joseph arrived in the central valleys of Maine with the mass of landless poor. His highest hopes were to deal in tens of acres and join that common abject Yankee immigrant group, which, in the words Maine traveler Timothy Dwight, had "large families and small farms."[19]

Joseph was not the only Boodry to try to improve his lot on the frontier. His older brother Sylvester from Taunton and Sylvester's two sons tested their fortunes in Maine, before seeking a new footing in distant southern Michigan in 1834, three years before Michigan became a state.[20] With no money to buy a place in a central valley, Joseph's search led him to the finger-narrow and thin-soiled valleys of the Adirondack Mountains in southwestern Maine, incised by glaciers and covered with woods. Joseph first appeared there in the 1810 census living with his old sister, Trifena, in Livermore Falls, on the southwestern edge of Kennebec River Valley. Two years later he had moved twenty miles north to Farmington, incorporated in 1794 and made seat of Franklin County in 1834, which occupied the head of a small valley created by the shallow and steep Sandy River. In Farmington, Joseph, of the nearby small upland village Avon, married Catherine Riant on November 30, 1811. Born in 1789 or 1791, she was fifth child and fifth daughter of poor Revolutionary War veteran Joseph and Sally (Powers) Riant, of Dorchester, Massachusetts, who had thirteen recorded children.[21]

When the poor married the poor, misery was never far off. In the parsimonious Sandy Valley, Sally's father Joseph, born in Connecticut, spent the last decades of his life, until his death in 1843, deeply impoverished, ill, and continuing to petition the state government for aid as a Revolutionary War veteran.[22] In 1816, he described his and his wife's meager circumstances, which included a house full of children, estimated property worth $400, animals (oxen, a horse, 3 cows, and so forth) valued at $200, $10 worth personal property, and $80 of annual income. In 1829, seeking an increase in his pension of eight dollars a month, he assessed his "reduced circumstances" in these dire terms: While a widower still supporting a son and three daughters, he could no longer work at all. His estate, when his debt was deducted from his property, amounted to only $111.50; his property afforded him an income of a mere $30 a year in rent and crops.

Receiving no support from his desolate father-in-law, Joseph took up the ultimate job of the poor countryman. He entered military service at the time of the War of 1812.[23] On his return, the couple settled ten miles or so up the Sandy Valley in the small village of Phillips, Oxford County, where their first child, Joseph, was born in December 1812. They then promptly produced at least seven more children who were recorded living with them in the 1830 Avon census.[24] Their ascent up the valley, which led from Phillips, to Avon, was concluded in Rangeley. Incorporated in 1855 on the banks of Rangeley Lake as a town of one thousand inhabitants, Rangeley is ringed by five Appalachian mountain peaks with elevations from 3,500 to 4,200 feet, the approxi-

mate height of nearby Saddleback and Sugarloaf Mountains, now covered
with ski resorts and summer homes.

Their ascent out of the valley in which there was no room for them
brought them within the shadows of the peaks of the Blue Mountains, a sub-
chain of the Appalachians. Surrounded by mountains to the north, south,
and east, the aged couple never returned to the valley below. There, where
Squire James Rangeley had purchased vast tracks of property, Joseph and
Catherine lived among their own kind: tenants, squatters, small landholders, neighbors, and in-laws like Luther Hoar, who had paid off his land by
working for Squire James Rangeley. Like the rest, the Boodrys came poor and
stayed poor. On thin and rocky soils and enduring long and snowy winters,
with the ice not clearing on the lake until late April or early May, they had literally reached the end of settlement. In Rangeley, the only significant industry was making nails, cutting wood, and making shingles. With a river too
shallow for navigation and only narrow steep trails for transport, all markets
were distant. These hilltop believers had to find their religious consolation
from occasional visits from Methodist or Baptist circuit riders.

Joseph had not delivered his family to a promised land. Instead, he had
brought them into a parsimonious backcountry, one so common to Maine,
Michigan, Wisconsin, and elsewhere in rural New England and the old
Northwest. At a glance we still recognize those places today. They are where
farming has always been poor, and the locals reside in small, dilapidated
dwellings among a scramble and a shamble of broken and discarded things—
the leftovers of generations living in poverty. The inhabitants who still bother
to work, cut and sell firewood, serve as hunting and fishing guides, and offer
their parents' and grandparents' worn goods for sale. Signs along the road
advertise lake cabins and rustic log lodges, hoping that passersby will be
lured into closer contact with successfully exploited nature.

Until his death in 1859 and hers in 1872, Joseph and Catherine battled a
landscape that began its decline almost instantaneous with its birth and their
arrival. Belonging to those so called "Makers of Maine," they were poor and
solitary creatures who consistently overran and outpopulated the lands they
inhabited. Necessity was never far from their minds. Indeed, in 1856, they

quit-claimed their land to son-in-law A. J. Thompson for the sum of $500
(with the exception of one cow, to remain Catherine's), on the condition that
he "provide them with suitable clothes, food, drink, medicine, nursing, and
all other things necessary for their comfort and support during their natural
life," otherwise, "this deed would be void and null."[25]

However, I must caution myself that I did not know the minds of these
people, Frances's great-grandparents, so I cast their narrative essentially, and
as best I can, out of biological and economic laws. Without memoirs, I lack
direct access to their inner landscapes, which always exist in forms of individual personality and character, thoughts and feelings, vices and virtues,
manners and gestures. History, I must remember, sentences the illiterate
poor to silence, and even more so, poor women whose very last names are
quicker to perish, and whose personalities, when unknown in living flesh,
are securely veiled behind the iron curtains of illiteracy and the tedium of
domestic life. I also must remember that the spread of money and consumer
society, which went hand-in-glove with the spread of the market and money,
was already omnipresent in modern history, and it shaped emerging inner
worlds of want, desire, and envy, the dimensions of which dramatically out-
grew the actual acquisition and accumulation of goods. Of the pre-industrial
consumer in England and America, Carole Shammas insightfully wrote,

> In the final analysis, the single most surprising aspect of the spread of new con-
> sumer commodities during the early modern period is that it occurred among
> a broad spectrum of people, at least some of whom were malnourished and/or
> poorly housed. The kinds of compromises made by lower-income households in
> the realm of consumption, as well as the various limits and restrictions imposed
> on their choices by masters, employers, markets, and the government, are more
> complicated than previously imagined. Paradoxically, the individual [which could
> have been any individual Boodry] who drank tea in a tea cup, wore a printed cot-
> ton gown, and put linen on the bed could be the same person who ingested too
> few calories to work all day and lived in a one room house.[26]

Hearts, passions, emotions, despairs, and hopes are hidden especially
deep in those whom we didn't know in flesh. We only know in rough their

outward appearances. We cannot animate their spirits or even offer explanations to curious facts we meet in the course of our research. But we can, without great imagination, reconstruct their material conditions: how Joseph struggled to uproot a stubborn pine, unearth large rocks, supply a winter's fuel, and scavenge the woods around; or how Catherine bore her children in pain, watered her garden, and probably helped lamb, an act so important to mountain agriculture.[27] We also know that even if they escaped the fate of being squatters, they had not come to the land of sweetness and honey. Even in Rangeley, the landlord's shadow fell far, and, as the local history of Rangeley makes clear, the successor of Lord Rangeley was unusually cruel. Surrounded in west and north by wilderness, with impoverished valleys to the east and ocean to the south, they found themselves encircled by the same necessitous circumstances the Boodrys had known since banishment from Arcadia and their exodus from old Plymouth Colony.

Their migration to the mountains of Maine delivered them to a place that could be labeled *Ruin Corner, Deadendville,* or *Hard Scrabble.*[28] Their story, however, is not only what they endured but that they persisted, and in so doing displayed that heroic steadfastness for which the poor who are to survive have no substitute. After all, they had actually fared as well or better than their kind. They had raised a family, lived long lives, and won graves at the very front of the local cemetery, which were marked by two tall soft white headstones, one of which had broken in half between my first and second visit to Rangeley in the course of researching this long family history.

Down Into the Valleys of Wisconsin

Set on duplicating his father's goal of having a place on the land, Sylvester was as destined to leave Rangeley as his father was to get there. By the time Sylvester, born in 1819, left Rangeley in the 1830s, it had already begun to show more potential as a tourist attraction for Maine and New England fishermen than as an agricultural or timbering community. In fact, Rangeley singularly flourished after the Civil War as a lakeside resort in the mountains, and so it remains, though in sharply diminished state, to this day.[29]

Sylvester left Rangeley for what appeared to be the thriving village of Clinton, Maine, located on the Sebasticook River, in the Kennebec Valley. There he joined his brother, Leonard, who, rejected for military service in 1853, mysteriously died on board the ship *Antarctica* bound for Liverpool in 1855, and his sister, Lucy, whose husband, Andrew J. Thompson, later appeared connected to Sylvester in Rangeley and Town of Main, Wisconsin, censuses. Organized as a plantation in the 1770s and incorporated as a town in the 1790s, Clinton first served as a ferry crossing, a mill town, and an east-west and north-south post stop. It showed economic vitality in the 1830s and 1840s, when it got two sawmills, a tavern, a carding mill, and a metal shingle machine, which was operated, along with a general store, by E. G. Hodgdon; his brother or relative, farmer James Hodgdon, was to be Sylvester's father-in-law.[30]

In 1842, twenty-one year old Sylvester married sixteen- or seventeen-year old Sarah Hodgdon. Working a small garden-size piece of land of eight acres sold to his wife in 1854, Sylvester had already declared himself in the 1850 census to be a farmer, even though the family's need for money made him dependent on finding seasonal work in town and at the mills. Showing not the least hint of infertility, the couple already had by 1850 six-year old Elizabeth, named for Sylvester's mother-in-law, and two-year old James (Frances's father), and one-year old Alice. Marcella, Mary, and Edgar quickly followed in succession in 1854, 1855, and 1856.

As is so often the case in micro-history, it is impossible to know what motivated Sylvester's departure for Wisconsin. Failures of farm income and wages afflicted the majority of small landholders and farmers in central Maine. But in all likelihood, he was another victim of "Ohio Fever," which swept rural Maine, New York, and the rest of backcountry New England at the start of the nineteenth century. Waves of tens of thousands of prospective settlers moved west toward the fresh lands of the old Northwest—the territories and states of the Great Lakes. Again in Maine, as in Massachusetts, family size and economic need outstripped available land and cash. In the tradition of their parents and grandparents, the grown children and young couples of rural Maine who could assemble the means to travel began their exodus toward new lands and opportunities. Filled with needs and dreams, they followed traditional inner tracks to new points west.

Proving himself a true son of Joseph, in 1856 Sylvester, with Sarah and five or six children in tow, set out for Wisconsin. They had sold their eight-acre parcel of land back to her father for a twenty-five dollar profit, which served as part of a grubstake. Though ambitious and hard working, Sylvester was a poor Johnny-come-lately. Arriving too late and with too little, he found opportunities as a farmer and landholder inevitably diminished and restricted to cheap, remote, and non-productive lands resembling those of the Maine left behind. On the outskirts of Plover, located along the Wisconsin and Little Plover rivers and a few miles from the growing hub of Stevens Point, Sylvester purchased for one hundred dollars an acre of wooded river bottomland. Here, on this small lot that furnished only enough land for a home, a garden, and a place from which he could depart for day labor and to practice his craft as a carpenter, Sylvester carried on a six-year economic experiment. He again failed to be more than another poor man desperately clinging to family and land. His wealth had not appreciated an iota; in fact, an 1862 county assessment valued his acre parcel at only seventy-five dollars. Immeasurably worse, his wife Sarah died, after having given birth to two more children—Georgianna in 1857 and possibly Clara, who may have been the cause of her mother's death, in 1860.

Without his helpmate, with seven or eight surviving children and land of value only as a place for a home, forty-year-old Sylvester did what great numbers of poor rural males did. Like his kin in Maine, Michigan, Connecticut, and elsewhere, and his father a half century before, he joined the army. He may well have had patriotic motives—he took up the great and mighty cause of saving the union and ending slavery—but he went to war to earn money that would pay the bills and might just possibly purchase a decent forty acres.

Leaving his younger children in care of his older children, which for the poor is a common means and necessity, Sylvester returned to Rangeley, Maine, where, counting on one's best support, he dropped off his youngest child, Clara, with his sister Trifena and her husband Daniel Hoar. He returned to Wisconsin, whence he was mustered into service in Oshkosh in

September 1862. Described as five feet, ten inches, with gray eyes, Sylvester joined Company E of the Wisconsin 32nd Infantry as a private. He received, I calculate, a combined bounty of approximately $200 (from local, state, and federal governments), pay of $12 a month, and an additional $5 a month for his dependents.[31] Sylvester earned his pay, and what bonuses came his way, with thousands of miles of marching and camping under General Sherman's command in southwestern Tennessee and northern Mississippi and the campaign against Vicksburg. After patrolling in the territory of Grand Junction, in February 1864, the 32nd participated in the Meredian Expedition into northern Mississippi. It then subsequently moved to Tennessee and Alabama, before joining General Sherman at Atlanta in August 1864.[32] As the war dragged on, though, Sylvester had been increasingly absent from his regiment and the battlefield. He took a five-month furlough in 1863, from which time his reactivation might have merited an additional bonus of a few hundred dollars. He was subsequently sick in the South and in Illinois in 1863 and 1864, until he was returned to Wisconsin for treatment. His illness culminated in his final release from a hospital in Madison and from military service on August 22, 1864.[33]

As fatigued and battle-worn as he may have been, Sylvester returned from the war undiminished in energy and ambition to put a family on the land. He was bred and disciplined to this—and this drive, more than any trait of national character or cultural ethics, formed the fabric of his being and the horizons of his imagination. In 1866 or 1867 Sylvester took as a new wife a young Prussian immigrant, who cared for his children and garden and produced yet more children. The young bride, Gertrude Anna Hanuf (Hermeth), known as Annie, was born about 1849 and was approximately twenty-five years his junior.

Showing also that the war had not stifled the colonizing network, Sylvester joined fellow Mainites and in-law E. G. Hodgdon, owner of the businesses in Clinton, in forming a new settlement in northern Outagamie County.[34] Called appropriately the Town of Maine, the new township stood between the Wolf River and present-day Highway 187. In 1869, along the river a mile south from Leeman Corners, Sylvester purchased, for the modest sum of thirty dollars, forty acres of farmland.[35] This was the very piece of land his son James, Frances's father, worked and aspired for his whole life, and Frances forever dreamed of having.

Among a network of poor hungering for land, and as part of a chain that reached from east to west far more than half way across the settled nation, Sylvester took his place. By 1870 the community had grown to 23 households containing 101 residents. Of this total, 46 were born in Maine; 28 in Wisconsin; 10, including a young woman named Ella Sayers, her two sisters, and a brother, in New York; 9 in Canada; and the remainder from a variety of places in the United States and Europe. Among the total 23 households, 13 husbands were born in states and nations different from their wives.

Annie and Sylvester produced eleven children, making him the father of twenty-two children in all, by the common family count (which may err by adding a child or two to the first marriage, because of a beguiling love of symmetry). In any case, Sylvester created a life's work for a genealogist and suggests the futility of tracking brothers and sisters, aunts and uncles, and cousins in large families of old. Only twenty-one in 1870, just one year older than Sylvester's oldest son James, Annie had taken on responsibility for a household that still held four teenage children from Sylvester's first marriage—Marcella, Edgar, Georgianna (the first of his children born in Wisconsin), and Agnes, 12—in addition to already two children of her own, one-year old Kathyrn and a few-months-old Cora. The last of the new brood was born two years before Sylvester's death in 1890, when my grandmother Frances, one of James's daughters, was already three years old.

Sylvester lived among family and old friends. Never mind that the land, like that of Clinton, was poor—so poor that one local legend says that even the rabbits pack lunches when they plan to cross the Town of Maine. After all, it also supported gardens, vegetables and potatoes, and pastureland for a team of horses and a cow or two. Abundant berries, fish, and deer supplemented diets, and there were those all-important seasonal jobs in the woods and at the nearby mills, which paid money to buy tools, clothes, animals, and a rare nice thing once in a while, and to pay nagging doctor bills and taxes. On his poor shrubby and marshy river bottomland, Sylvester drained and opened acreage for farming and pasturing. With hand tools including planes, bores, and a broad axe (still in his youngest grandson's possession), Sylvester, also a carpenter, built a first and then a large second home, which still stands on his land. He built a number of barns and few buildings, which were still standing in the 1990s. In this tiny township, numbering only one hundred residents in 1870, he witnessed the growth of small subsistence farms on the township's poor lands and saw a parade of activity on the north-south military road, which ran parallel to the Wolf River, connecting the productive northern woods to the active southern sawmills of Shioctin, ten road miles to the south. Local and transit business, in fact, gave rise to a few general stores and residences taking in travelers.

Sylvester lived long enough to see the fruition of his labors. He secured his land and witnessed his children, my great-grandfather James first among them, grow up, marry, rent, and start to buy small farms, and reproduce—and, in truth, continue to be rural and poor. Sylvester had remained faithful to the covenant. In all likelihood, never considering an alternative, he had done what his ancestors had in the swamps of Arcadia and on the poor lands of Massachusetts and Maine. On his deathbed he could rest content. He got land and was a true farmer.

The town cemetery still testifies to Sylvester's inheritance. Less than a mile south from Sylvester's farm, it has a rising knoll along the fence on the east end, on which stands a run of Boodry tombstones. Besides Sylvester and his second wife Annie, nine of their eleven children are buried in the Town of Maine and at least seven of his children from his first marriage, including Great-grandfather James and his wife Ella. The Boodrys share their knoll and the cemetery with other first settlers from rural Wisconsin, New York, Canada, and even Ireland, England, Scandinavia, and Prussia.

An Inheritance

Surely Joseph and his son Sylvester formed a moral inheritance of steadfastness. Nothing could deflect them from having a family and forty acres of their own. Unfaltering dedication to that end, and a matching discipline, organized their minds, directed their energies, and gave a moral core. While almost mechanistic in their search for family and land, their lives exemplified the heroism of unrelenting tenacity. At the same time, their stories merit talk of fate, fortune, and God's Providence. The narrative of their lives, though profoundly personal and familial, fuses with the history of the American rural poor, their movement west, and a European quest for land whose origins reach back to the Middle Ages.

Their migrations and settlements invite grandiose narratives and excite a range of theories and explanations.[36] To mind first comes the French *Annales* historian Emmanuel Le Roy Ladurie, who depicts the movement of the peasantry of southern France from the thirteenth to the eighteenth century in Malthusian fashion. He treats the expansion and contraction of human populations in terms of long cycles of abundance and scarcity of food supply.[37] In good times, humans multiply and spread out on the landscape: overtopping the brims of overpopulated fertile valleys, they spread up into the foothills and even the low mountains. In bad times, accordion-like, human population contracts, retreating first from the highest and most marginal lands and eventually consolidating in the valleys. On this count, the movements and settlements of Joseph and Sylvester Boodry resembled those of the traditional rural peoples of France, Acadia, and Europe. In the service of primary biological impulses they ate, reproduced, and—when unchecked by hunger, famine, disease, and death, as was the case in most of colonial America and during the early Republic—migrated to new lands. And when they overpopulated New England and even the old Northwest, they spread out to the poor soils of marginal lands. However, this form of a Malthusian society does not explain all. At every point, social, political, economic, and cultural forces— diverse, interpenetrating, and all subject to historical change—trumped biology, shaping the reproductive family and its movement on the landscape. The household, a pinwheel evicting its progeny near and far, simultaneously functioned as the principal organizer of the individual family members' roles and activities. It also determined specific economic strategies, by rewarding certain behaviors and commanding social relations and familial assets. The head of the household usually determined who went and who stayed. The

nuclear family, which ruled sovereign, was the vehicle of American migration and settlement.[38]

Other factors shaped the exodus of the Boodrys and the poor. Money,
which turned land into real estate, became a primary instrument for satisfying need and measuring want. Economic calculation, consequently,
became ever more indispensable with society's mounting dependence on
distant markets, the increased consumption of goods and services, and the
risky, even perilous, act of mortgaging one's land. Military service, a perennial
first and last employer of the rural poor, also attracted the landless. It offered
Joseph and Sylvester, their cousins, neighbors, and poor contemporaries, the
cash to buy land of their own. At the same time, the very opening of new
lands by governments and commercial agencies singularly dilated imaginations and ignited energies.

My family contained no celebrated explorers or settlers. It opened no
fresh path for the nation's westward advance. Instead, it was composed of
impoverished Johnnies-come-lately. Its exodus depended on humble means,
shared sojourns, and cheap mass transportation. It tested family members
against trees, rocks, poor soils, and harsh climates. It challenged them to
build new homes, establish villages, and make true and loyal neighbors. But
even after the driving quest to put the family on the land lost much of its
material and biological underpinning with the coming of birth control, the
formation of the industrial city, and the closing of the frontier, it still kept
hold on the inner dreams of subsequent generations. In fact, the more it lost
hold on society at large, the more it seemed to take individual minds like my
grandmother Frances Boodry's captive, to fill them with a deep inner urging
for a simpler and more basic time.

5

Migrants West

Some families define themselves by where they settled and stayed. Other families, like mine, are distinguished by journeys and crossings. Their stories, involving individual courage, risk, tenacity, and persistence, fuse with sweeping national narratives of the opening of new lands, innovations of transportation systems, and epochal manias. Historians of families like mine must weave together stories of individual families and narratives of national transformations. Lending their hearts to stories of a singular migration, they have to test their heads on such matters as changing economies and demography, the rise and decline of industries, and mutations of whole environments and societies. Each of my composing families tests me on themes of migrants and immigrants. The Amato and Notaro families of Sicily and the Acadian Boodrys demonstrate the most recent and the most ancient of my migration stories.

Grandmother Frances's maternal family, the Sayerses, who intermarried with the Boodrys, are the subject of this chapter. Of obscure English origins, they left their impoverished life in St. Lawrence County, New York, on a steamboat for the developing region of Wisconsin's Lake Winnebago. After a decade, without establishing themselves on the land or finding steady work, they trusted their fate to the railroad's promises of new settlements in Kansas, where they homesteaded two more places before retiring to a small town in south-central Kansas, not far from where east-west and north-south continental trails cross. They traveled farthest west of any of my families, and more than the others, they belong to those poor and restless Americans of whom poet Stephen Vincent Benét wrote:

> Americans are always moving on.
> It's an old Spanish custom gone astray
> A sort of English fever, I believe,
> Or just a mere desire to take French leave,
> I couldn't say. I couldn't really say.

An ethnic accounting of the marriage in 1867 of Sylvester Boodry's son
James to Ellen Frances Sayers, the fourth daughter of Leonard Sayers, could
be depicted as a synthesis of the two great and opposing families of Europe,
the French and English. However, this betrays, as ethnic explanations often
do, a simpler and more humble fact: James and Ella married for the sake of
their personal wishes and practical needs. James and Ella shared a contemporary rural inheritance based on enduring marriage, unregulated production, endless toil, and aspirations to establish a secure condition for old age.
By strength of will and necessity-cropped imagination, they were simply and
totally their parents' children. This humble condition set them apart from
the refinements of wealth and luxury of choice, as well as the quarrels of
kings, the distinctions of theologians, the arguments of philosophers, and
the well-turned words of poets and writers. Their family creed was the givens
of everyday life: the need to earn one's daily bread and secure one's place as
best one could against hunger and debt. Formed around the trinity of family,
work, and land, it stood on the legs of a faithful and hardworking husband
and wife, a mutually helpful family, and cooperative neighbors, who equaled
their weight in gold in migration as in settlement.

However, bred on the same begrudging poor and stony New England
soils, the inheritance Sylvester and Leonard fashioned was more than a creed.
It was also a calculation. The spread of markets, the infusion of capital, the
circulation of money, and the availability of cheap land led all nineteenth
century North Americans to a complex and finally inconclusive arithmetic
that sought to judge available capital, risky migrations, possible rewards, and
varying risks. Land, in particular, gave rise to the most important and complex formulas. It could be bought, sold, rented, borrowed against, willed,
and, of course, speculated on. Land, the most and least tangible of things,
anchored wealth, afforded subsistence, provided income, and furnished
security for old age, while awakening dreams and occasioning speculation.
People as humble and common as the Sayerses and the Boodrys saw the connection between land and money. Cheap travel and the chance for cheap
land tilted the equations of many in favor of going west.

Sylvester and Leonard also became market and migratory creatures. By choosing to join the widening and lengthening trail west, however, they did not abandon traditional concepts of the family and forsake the help of relatives and neighbors. Going outwardly west, their inner compasses continued to point back east. Like that of so many contemporary New Englanders and Europeans, the settlements of both the Sayerses and the Boodrys in Wisconsin constituted a kind of New England micro "colonization."[1]

Leonard Sayers

While many factors undoubtedly accounted for Leonard Sayers's emigration from St. Lawrence County, New York, to Wisconsin, he made his choice after years of deliberation. Leonard learned upon the death of his father to look to himself for his fortune. In about 1837, when he was fourteen, he took up an apprenticeship in carpentry, which remained his principal livelihood. In 1847, in Oswegatchie Township, twenty-five-year-old Leonard met and, after a short courtship, married twenty-year-old Charlotte Augusta Hynes. Sworn to be life-long companions, helpmates, and fellow economic calculators, they lived in Oswegatchie for almost a decade before going west.

Charlotte was born in Waddington, New York, on December 2, 1826. She added a religious intensity to their marriage. At seventeen she became an avowed Methodist Episcopal, a type of fervent Christian, who were so common as a consequence of the religious revival that swept upstate New York in the 1820s and 1830s. She was the fourth daughter of the sixteen children born to a literate Irish immigrant, William M. Hynes. Hynes was born in Dublin in 1792.[2] After being educated in England, he returned to Ireland, whence he migrated to St. Lawrence County, New York. There he taught school for several years until about 1827, when he crossed the river to teach in Brockville, Ontario. After a long career as an educator, during which he taught mathematics at a university in Montreal and served as a school superintendent, he published a newspaper. A staunch Presbyterian throughout his life, he married the daughter of a Loyalist Presbyterian family, Margaret Burrell, with whom he had six children. When she died around 1832, he married Mar-

garet's sister, Mary. They had ten children, whose occupations suggest that
mobility ran more downward and sideways than upward: one became a physician, while others joined the ranks of painters and housekeepers. Retiring
in the 1860s, Hynes went west himself to Cleveland, Ohio, in order to live, as
was a common tradition, with his youngest daughter.

The origins of Leonard's own family appear to be in eighteenth-century
Norfolk, England, where biological and economic laws, not those of race
or ethnicity, principally governed the emigration of the majority. Some
were drawn into the fateful embrace of London, where work, money, but
also death abounded; for those who wanted to continue their agrarian family economy, including 125,000 rural English, Scots, and Irish, the American
frontier promised fertile lands for the taking in the fifteen years between the
end of the Seven Years War and the Revolution.[3] However, in the old country
as well as the new, the Sayerses seemed as much attached to crafts and day
labor as to farming.

Whatever the exact reasons for their immigration, it is certain that the
Sayerses arrived too late and too poor to get decent lands even in remote St.
Lawrence County, New York. The Sayerses fell afoul of the harsh law that
governs immigrants everywhere: the best lands in the valley go to the speculators who originally bought them from afar. Second pick of lands goes to
those who arrived first with the most money. Those who come after occupy
the meager interstices of the valley or move up into the surrounding hills.
Like the Boodrys from Massachusetts and Maine, the Sayerses from New
York tilled and gleaned weak lands and worked humble jobs.

The New York they came to in the 1830s had been settled for only a generation and was in the process of being redefined by the American and Canadian
canal system and the emergence of steamboat travel on the Great Lakes. In
1800, New York had barely surpassed Massachusetts in population. Its 589,000
people belonged to a republic of five million, whose population center from
north to south lay within fifty miles of tidewater; New York's interior was little more settled and was not much easier to penetrate than when La Salle and
Hennepin found their way to the Mississippi.[4] St. Lawrence County belonged
to the frontier. With no developed water route into the heartland of the

continent in 1800, "nowhere," noted Henry Adams, "did eastern settlements touch western. At least one hundred miles of mountainous country held the two regions apart." The shore of Lake Erie, where alone contact seemed easy, remained unsettled. "In 1800, as in 1700, this intermediate region was only a portage where emigrants and merchandise were transferred from Lake Erie to . . . Ohio valleys." Western New York, Adams elaborates, "remained a wilderness: Buffalo was not laid out; Indian titles were not extinguished; Rochester did not exist. . . . Utica contained only fifty houses. . . . Albany was still a Dutch city, with some five thousand inhabitants."

Leonard's father, James Sayers, immigrated into St. Lawrence County after his cousin (or possibly brother) William Sayers (1781–1864), arrived around 1815.[5] Like his many ancestors from Norfolk, James practiced the common rural craft of carpentry, rather than farming, while no doubt renting a small acreage for gardening. The 1830 census for Oswegatchie Township, St. Lawrence County, indicates that James was living with an unnamed wife; son Leonard, born in 1823, was seven years old; and a daughter whom we take to be Leonard's sister, Hannah, about three years younger than James.[6] His poor and transitory neighborhood was a kind of zone for sorting out immigrants: eighteen of James's nineteen neighbors in 1830 had moved by the time of the 1840 census.[7] With no records for James and his wife after 1830, it is assumed that they died, orphaning Leonard and Hannah some time between 1830 and 1840. In any case, by 1840, eighteen-year-old Leonard was already out and working on his own as a carpenter; Hannah was married to widower Eliphalet Pope, a one-time Macomb County supervisor; by 1847, when she gave birth to their daughter Jane.[8] In 1846, the year the Mexican War began (and the year before his marriage), Leonard surfaced again. A court martial to try delinquents from military service was convened in his house, suggesting he was being charged.

The 1850 census reveals Leonard, still grappling to secure an economic footing in St. Lawrence County. With a little property and boarding a renter, he was living among neighbors from England, New York, and Ireland, whose average real estate value of $2,500 was far above Leonard and Charlotte's. Still identifying himself as a carpenter, twenty-seven-year-old Leonard was the

head of household, which included his twenty-three-year old wife Charlotte (Hynes) Sayers, their daughters Margaret, three, and Mary, one, and
seventy-two-year-old Patience Rosegrant (alternately spelled Rosecran), the
mother-in-law of Charlotte's older sister, Frances Hynes Rosegrant.[9] Leonard
and Charlotte may have supplemented their income by caring for Patience.
Certainly Frances's husband, Franklin, showed impoverished Leonard and
Charlotte that money can be made by the purchase and sale of land. He first
succeeded in St. Lawrence County and then duplicated the feat to the west in
Russia Township, Lorain County, Ohio.[10]

Leonard's own blood cousins did not match Rosegrant's in acumen or
luck in real estate. Going inland and upland to the southeast end of Lawrence County, William Sayers and his sons purchased small and poor parcels of eighty, forty, and fewer acres. They were the scraps and leftovers from
the partitioning and repartitioning of immense original tracts, such as the
3,670,715 acres of St. Lawrence County and western New York, purchased for
eight pence an acre, or "at a price of a loaf of bread per acre," by real estate
mogul Alexander Macomb and his "silent partners," in 1792.[11] Lagging behind
Massachusetts, Pennsylvania, Virginia, and North Carolina in population,
New York, it was argued, needed to put its land to use for the sake of economic development.[12] If the Sayers cousins were to succeed in agriculture, it
would be on rocky and uneven ground. For the sake of minimal cash income,
they had to join their crafts (which was blacksmithing, in the case of William's son James) to their farming.

Many of the Sayerses, who filled the ranks of barkeepers, craftsmen, and
laborers in England, started out as modest rural workers and gardeners in
the Town of Oswegatchie, where Leonard and his family resided in the 1830s.
In fact, the census still recorded thirty Sayerses living there in the 1850s. In
1839 Thomas Sayers, a son of William, bought two pieces of property, one for
$29.15 in 1839 and another for $500 in 1844; his son Samuel bought two equally
small pieces in nearby DeKalb County in 1849 and 1850 for unrecorded sums.
Not far from Oswegatchie, where I assume Leonard and Charlotte lived in
the proximity of her in-laws the Rosegrants, a road leads across Depeyster
into the Town of Macomb. There one finds another epicenter of the family

in Macomb Township's Pope's Mill and Oldsville Cemetery, where more than fifty Sayerses are buried.

Pope's Mill, Town of Macomb

In Macomb Township, first settled in 1805, the Sayerses, in the 1850s, joined earlier immigrants, who came from Vermont and New York's Mohawk and Cherry valleys, and from England, Ireland, and Scotland.[13] They settled some of the worst land in St. Lawrence County. Set in a glacially raked landscape, the Town of Macomb is pockmarked by woodlands, rocky knolls, wetlands, small lakes, and Black Lake. Streams and creeks crisscross it. While there are narrow and oblique productive valleys around Pope's Mill, the land, comprised of light soil and extensive sand plains, its surface broken frequently by gneiss and white limestone, disappoints any tiller of the soil.[14] With only one arable acre out of three or four, this land is more fit for grazing than tilling.[15] Long winters, characterized by sharp cold and deep snows, add to the difficulty of travel on a landscape of changing elevation and winding roads, intersecting streams and ponds.

Pope's Mill was settled early, and the Sayerses arrived just in time to witness its decline. Built around a mill on Fish Creek installed in 1816 by Timothy Pope, the town got its first general store and public school in 1835. A post office came in 1838 and Methodist and Episcopal churches welcomed believers starting in the early 1840s.[16] With, I surmise, the exodus of the young already coming a decade or even two earlier, Pope's Mill and Macomb Township's actual demographic decline in raw numbers dates from the Civil War. Drafts, bonuses, and patriotism scoured the northern countryside for the poor willing to serve the cause. Like the rural Boodry men, three of Leonard's younger Sayers first cousins (Edward, son of William Jr., James, son of Fortunatus, and Benjamin, son of James) answered the call to arms. Benjamin's service papers and his mother's request for a pension—an act that generates rich government documents for the family historian—reveal far more than an individual fate. They expose the economic conditions of a poor northern family prior to and after the war.[17]

Benjamin Sayers, the second child of nine recorded children of James and Jane (Thurling) Sayers, was born in 1837. The farm on which he was raised proved no ark on the sea of need and hard times.[18] Benjamin left his parents' farm to supplement the less than one hundred dollars a year that his father earned by farming and blacksmithing. At twenty-one years of age, in 1858 or 1859, Benjamin followed two cousins and other Macomb County contemporaries in going west to "booming Illinois" for work. At Little Rock, Illinois, 140 miles west of Chicago, apparently not finding work or money, Benjamin enlisted in the Union Army. In a first letter to his illiterate parents, he promises to send the significant sum of fifty dollars with the next available post. He explains that he has lent out money among his comrades for safe keeping, which he will collect as soon as the paymaster appears. He queries whether his brother received the five dollars he sent him for the Fourth of July, and he relates, with justification to his parents as a farm boy would, how he and his fellow soldiers had taken some green corn from enemy fields: "[They] made this terrible [war] and now they must abide with the loss of a little green corn." In a letter dated October 16, 1862, from a camp near Crab Orchard, he reports long marches and spending the last two or three days in the rain without shelter. He asks about a trunk mailed to him, wonders how the apples and butter sales at home have been, and cautions he may not be heard from for a while, since they are on another long march.

A third letter, dated January 12, 1863, described Benjamin's death. "Dear Friends," W. D. Wagner began, "Benjamin with 211 and others in company was killed" in what is known as the Battle of Stones River, near Murfreesboro, Tennessee. Between December 31, 1862, and January 2, 1863, Union and Confederate forces lost approximately 13,000 men apiece, roughly one-third of the total men engaged in what proved an important yet depleting Union victory. "After falling back" and leaving the dead and wounded in the hands of the enemy, Wagner wrote, Benjamin's unit retook its position, where Benjamin's body was found. "He had been stripped of his clothes, knapsack, and the twelve dollars Benjamin claimed he had a few days before."

Twenty-four years later, when Jane Sayers, Benjamin's widowed mother, applied for a pension, Wagner's affidavit gave a different account. He swore that Benjamin, two days prior to his death, had given Wagner eighty-five dollars to mail home but, unable to post it, Wagner returned it to Benjamin, who had it at the time of his death. Wagner also vouched, perhaps only giving truth to the old soldier's lie, that having buried Benjamin, he knew that Benjamin was shot in the forehead and died instantly. (Another soldier offered conflicting testimony, claiming that Benjamin died as a consequence of being hit in the neck by a musket ball.)

Other affidavits described Jane Sayers's economic condition. She resided alone; her buildings were but a small frame house and very poor barn; half of her land was "bare rock." Her husband James, who died in 1868, had not supported her since 1854. In June of that year, Benjamin's brother Matthew swore that James was injured falling from a house; then, in July, of the same year, he was kicked in the chest by a colt. He could no longer farm or do blacksmithing. A neighbor, who had known them since 1837, estimated that their small farm of sixty acres was worth only fifty dollars a year rent. Another neighbor appraised its sale value to be worth not more than fifteen dollars an acre, while yet another validated a debt against the farm of four hundred dollars at the time of James's death.

Additional affidavits made Jane's case for indigence by attesting to her inability to work and her complete dependence on others for survival. She was more than eighty years old in 1890 and judged to be feeble; one party wrote that she was "in danger of immediate dissolution and, if relief is to be afforded her, it must be done within a short time." In August 1891, after four years of petitioning, a pension of twelve dollars a month was approved. Jane died in September 1892, having received about $150 in pension payments. There was no doubt a nation filled with Janes.

The West Beckoned

The experiences of the Sayers family, like those of the majority of Macomb Township settlers, forcefully counseled emigration. They told Leonard and Charlotte that their search for well-being was futile. They could not accumulate property or goods that would protect them against indigence and provide comfort in old age. Perhaps, and there was the rub, no land could. It had to be bought, kept, and mortgaged, but its value, measured by a changing real estate market, was not predictable. Leonard and Charlotte needed no education to see how its value rose and dived like a kite in the shifting winds, fluctuating as much as 50 percent or more in the course of a decade, depending on a mixture of local, regional, and national economies. During this insecure time, when money was increasingly necessary for survival and before pensions, Social Security, and life insurance bricked the walls of one's house, all but the richest heard the wolf constantly howling at the door.

Leonard and Charlotte witnessed the declining plight of the Sayerses in the decade they chose to emigrate. In 1850, when cousin Benjamin's grandfather, William Sayers, was seventy years old, his real estate was assessed at $1,000. In 1860, its value, without calculating debt, had depreciated to $600. It appears that his sons fared no better.[19] The land around Pope's Mill did not afford security; it only chained a family to a life of work, worry, and debt.

Leonard and Charlotte, in fact, were born to a staging ground for westward migration. St. Lawrence County, whose demographic turbulence (comings and goings) makes it a black hole for genealogical research, was barely settled before it began to lose population to the cheaper and available lands of the old Northwest. This emigration began as early as the 1830s and by the 1850s became nearly uniform throughout the six traditional states of old New England—Rhode Island, New Hampshire, Vermont, Connecticut, Massachusetts and Maine. As the latter two states had lost population to the fresh lands of Ohio and Michigan, so St. Lawrence County's decline coincided with the opening of Illinois and Wisconsin in the 1850s. The population of St. Lawrence county grew from 500 in 1800 to 55,000 in 1840; growth then dramatically slowed, as shown in the 1850 and 1860 censuses, with populations respectively 68,617 and then 83,689. By the end of the Civil War in 1865, St. Lawrence County actually had declined to 80,994. Macomb Township mirrored the county's population in its descent from its apex of 1,800 in 1860 to 1,400 in 1890. It then lost an additional fifty percent of its population in the first half of the twentieth century.[20]

Pope's Mill, which I visited a few years ago, seems today less a living place than a site of a brief and fleeting battleground in the great war of American demographics that pitted local and indigenous forces on one side against the markets of the Atlantic seaboard and the great fertile fields of the Midwest on the other. It reminds us of the speed at which the New England frontier was settled and abandoned. Along a bend of blacktop highway, at the intersection of Route 58, County Road 184, and miniscule Dam Road, where the township's first mill thrived, the remnants of the village stood in a state of virtual collapse. On the front porch of the general store, on which a cooler still hums, a sign hung in the window: "Closed for inventory." No date for reopening was indicated. A few hundred yards up and down the road from the store, there remained a handful of well-kept houses and clear yards that seemed to stand in defiance of the surrounding decay and disorder. One long two-story dwelling, prominently perched on high ground just off the road, appeared to be in the act of breaking apart like a grounded ship. It looked down on a sloping farmyard, with collapsing sheds and rusting machines, where two cows grazed. All this reminded me why Frances's maternal grandparents, somewhere near the start of this decline, left New York for Wisconsin around a hundred and fifty years before my visit.

Off to Wisconsin, Then on to Kansas

The West's tug on Leonard and Charlotte began a mere seven miles from Pope's Mill at nearby Morristown, a small port on the St. Lawrence River. From its a dock, a cheap ticket took one west on one of many scheduled steamboats, churning downriver and through the Great Lakes to a litany of the era's promised places—Rochester! Toronto! Cleveland! Detroit! Milwaukee! and Chicago! How could anyone hearing that departing whistle, not share, if only vicariously, the rush and thrill of starting afresh, at time when land was cheap and plentiful?

The idea of going west awoke a speculative fever in both farmer and artisan. In just three years after 1816, indebtedness to the government for public lands increased nearly 600 percent, and in 1820 the government reduced the minimum purchase from 160 to 80 acres at $1.25 per acre. Between 1810 and 1820, Ohio sparked the jump west; its population shot up from 230,000 to almost 600,000.[21] Illinois, which had achieved statehood in 1818, Michigan in 1837, and Wisconsin in 1848, and then Minnesota in 1857, were principal magnets of the emerging waterway system, which reached from western New York and Ontario to what would become the new national heartland.

With the completion of the Erie Canal and corresponding Canadian canals in the 1820s, regular and cheap steamboat travel delivered migrants to their dreams. They dropped them off along the shores of Lake Ontario at Rochester or Buffalo or continued along Lake Erie to Cleveland, where the Hyneses and other families associated with the Sayerses got off. Venturesome immigrants, like Sylvester Boodry's cousin Nathan, stayed aboard until the port of Detroit, which afforded access to the potential farmlands of southern Michigan. Immigrants of the 1850s and 1860s like the Sayerses—or yet my forbears, the Linsdaus and O'Briens, extended their trip twice as far. They went north up Lake Huron, around the tip of the Lower Peninsula of Michigan, down and across Lake Michigan to Chicago, a port for the blossoming lands of Illinois, Indiana, and Iowa, which was served in part by a nascent railroad system. From Chicago, land-hungry newcomers like the Sayerses backtracked north, both by water and land, from Chicago to Wisconsin, where rich southern valleys offered prospects for good farming, and northern waters and woods beckoned with bountiful timber and bustling mill towns.

Leonard and Charlotte began their trek west in 1855. They traveled with five of the six daughters born to them in New York—Maris Margaret, Mary Adaline, Hannah Augusta, Ellen Frances (my Great-grandmother Ella), and Charlotte Eliza. Harriet Eliza, their sixth daughter, had died in infancy in 1854. With Illinois and southern Wisconsin already settled by earlier waves of immigrants, it is not surprising that Leonard and Charlotte moved inland and north. They followed the Fox River from Green Bay to Lake Winnebago into east-central Wisconsin. Chicago and Milwaukee were all-important staging grounds for Wisconsin immigration. Hopefully, in these burgeoning towns, money and resources could be accumulated for the move inland. Located at the southern end of Lake Winnebago and reachable by water from Lake Michigan, Fond du Lac served as an important local entry point into central Wisconsin.[22]

By 1860, Leonard and Charlotte and their five daughters, along with their recently born son, Charles, had established themselves on the western shore of Lake Winnebago, between Oshkosh to the south and the recently settled town of Neenah to the north. As revealed by the 1860 census, they were living in the company of six other New York families. This implied, if not a colony, at least participation in a common regional migration pattern. Leonard's sister Hannah, her sixty-one-year-old husband, Eliphalet Pope, and their five children were their immediate neighbors, as was another Pope family, also descendants of the founder of Pope's Mill.[23] Beyond seniority of age, Eliphalet's wealth made him the leader of the group. In the 1850 census for the Town of Macomb, Eliphalet and Hannah had property valued at $1,800. The 1860 Wisconsin census valued their property at $3,000, which was many times the $600 of real estate owned by his thirty-year-old son, Martin Pope, and the $500 listed for Leonard and Charlotte.

Leonard built a log cabin on his twenty acres and began clearing the land for farming by cutting and burning the woods. Later, he constructed a house and a small barn, which elevated the estimated worth of his real estate. On this small farm Leonard and Charlotte duplicated the economic behavior they had learned as children in St. Lawrence County and continued to reproduce as nature dictated. They added seven more children to the family in Wisconsin. Their five new daughters were Henrietta Ida, Susan Ann, Alice Lillian, Carrie Lura, and Mary Augusta; their two young boys were Charles and Leonard William Jr.

Their children proved vulnerable to disease and accident. Two of the daughters born in New York died, Hannah by natural causes, while Mary Adaline was burned to death when the coal oil stove she was starting exploded. In 1877 their nineteen-year-old son Charles slipped on the bark of a rotten log and fell, causing his gun to discharge and mortally wound him in the head. Leonard and Charlotte's sole surviving son was Leonard Jr.

During these years, their older daughters left home at an early age, following a typical strategy born of necessity. The oldest, Maria Margaret, led the

way. When only fifteen, in 1863, she married impoverished Thomas Wright
Allen from a founding family of the Town of Maine. In 1870 census they are
recorded as having a meager $600 of real estate. Ellen Frances (known as Ella),
mother of my grandmother Frances, outdid Maria Margaret by a year, marrying James Boodry in 1867 when she was only fourteen years old. In the 1870
census, James and Ella were living with an Allen family, evidently Thomas
and Maria Margaret, in the Town of Maine, where their land was assessed at
a mere $100. Not to be left behind in the race to maturity, independence, and
shared poverty, younger sister Charlotte Eliza followed suit: In 1870, when fifteen years old, she married recently widowed Reuben Sweet, a name that I
recall lilting its way through my grandmother Frances's recollections. Having
returned to the Town of Maine after fighting in the Civil War, Reuben had
married one of Great-great-grandfather Sylvester Boodry's daughters, Alice,
who died in childbirth in 1868. Reuben was a restless man, in the mold of his
own and her father, and they moved six times between their marriage in 1870
and 1897.[24]

Poor country girls all three, Charlotte, Ellen, and Maria took what life
offered. They married poor countrymen and did with them what their parents had done. They rushed to marriage. Without contraception, they sped
to perform their Biblical duty to multiply. As part of a chain reaction and
chain migration, they all married men from the Town of Maine. They offered
proof that circumstances channel wills and circumscribe imagination,
and that tradition and imitation in the older rural order formed a ring that
equally fit generations—at least during the settling of West.

The 1870 census, however, records an advance on part of Leonard and
Charlotte. Their property value had doubled from five hundred to a thousand dollars in the preceding decade, although they had not added any land
or increased the value of their personal property. Living now among the
influx of foreign-born Austrians and Prussians, including the family of John
and Elizabeth Linsdau, my mother's great-grandparents in nearby Menasha,
Leonard's closest neighbors included a younger Pope family whose property was valued at a miniscule two hundred dollars. Leonard still identified himself as a carpenter, in contrast to the majority of his neighbors who

declared themselves to be farmers. Undoubtedly, Leonard's economic strategy remained the same as it was in St. Lawrence County. He would rely on his wife and younger children to cultivate the small garden farm, and on his older children to pick up day work and farm work, while he practiced his craft to earn the cash essential for their basic needs and for saving to buy better land—and to pay taxes. I suspect he found sufficient work in the 1860s building schools, businesses, and homes, as well as barns and farmhouses, in the growing communities of Neenah, Menasha, Appleton, Oshkosh, and Fond du Lac.

Life, however, never got easy for Leonard and Charlotte's family, and it took a decided downturn with the 1870s depression, which proved deep and protracted in the Fox River Valley. Their daughter Charlotte (Lottie), born in 1855, once wrote that her parents were so famished they prayed for meat. And, to their amazement, no sooner had they finished praying than a deer appeared at their door. Leonard lamented, "If only the hammer on my old flintlock were not broken, I could kill the deer." Showing her ingenuity, Charlotte picked up a carpenter's hammer, had Leonard steady the gun, she hit the bullet with the hammer, and so firing the gun, dispatched the deer. Young Charlotte recounted another tale of her mother's pioneer virtues. Hearing a pig squealing in the pen, Charlotte rushed into the yard to see a black bear dragging one of her "porkers" away. Up to Daniel Boone in courage, she pushed her candle in the bear's face, causing him to retreat into the chicken coop. Charlotte slammed the door shut on him and called neighbors, who came and killed the bear—and, though this is not reported in the family story, no doubt helped skin and eat it.[25]

Leonard and Charlotte had made a profound effort to create a home in the Badger State. They had raised their first batch of children and had decently buried two of them in the Neenah town cemetery, where they had bought eight burial plots, as if to stay. But at the end of two decades, they celebrated no victory over scarcity; their own lot remained common, full of travail.

Wisconsin had not satisfied their New York dreams. Despite their labors and ordeals, they had stood still in time. They had not driven the wolf from the front door. Their work and land had not brought them security, and they remained unimaginably far from luxury and choice that glimmered for upper-class townspeople on the main streets of Neenah and Menasha.

In fact, their prospects for a secure old age dimmed as the 1870 depression wore on—as commerce was stalled; agricultural prices remained depressed; mills didn't produce; real estate values were in decline; and foreclosures— sheriff deeds on property—multiplied. Work was scarce and carpenters like Leonard, always plentiful, were now a dime a dozen. In 1877, Leonard, who was fifty-five and Charlotte, who had given birth to thirteen children and was fifty-one years old, were again pushed to emigrate.

They looked again to land ownership as a solution to their condition and the path to a secure old age. It was hard to resist the plethora of railroad ads promising extraordinary opportunities in the fresh lands of Kansas and Nebraska. As was the case almost two decades earlier when they left New York, they envisioned fresh and cheap land and the building of new towns as a chance for a decent retirement. How could they, who followed the steam-boats into the heartland, not heed the promise of millions acres of land in Nebraska and Kansas! Opportunity and risk had become their culture.

Kansas called, "Yeoman strong, hither throng!/Nature's honest men,/ Will make the wilderness/Bud and bloom again."[26] Distant Kansas, rekin-dling youthful dreams in their old bodies, was, as Wisconsin once was, but a mere cheap trip away. Pioneer-settlers Leonard and Charlotte left behind twenty years of work, family, friendships, and community and boarded a train at the nearby station, as once they climbed aboard a steamboat, and set out for another new garden, a fresh Arcadia, a Kansas of abundant, bountiful, and promising lands.

Last Stop, Kansas

Leonard and Charlotte traveled as economically as they could. In fact, the young children were afraid their parents were abandoning them when they were forced to stay behind to travel with another Kansas-bound family who could take advantage of free railroad fares for a limited number of children.[27] Their first stop in Kansas was Wea Township in Miami County. There they established themselves on an eighty-acre farm, which placed them less than twenty miles south of Kansas City, less than a half-mile from the north-south Osage Division of the Missouri, Kansas, Texas railroad line, and only a mile and a half from the village of Louisburg.

To the satisfaction of Leonard the carpenter, they were joining a prairie place in the making. As could be seen in a useful 1878 historical atlas and plat book, bridges, roads, buildings, and schools, which provided work, were still under construction.[28] The newly settled town of Louisburg made Wea Township, with a population of 2,200, the most populous of the county's fourteen townships, which collectively had 14,500 recently settled inhabitants. The Sayerses, having traveled beyond their own past, settled without New York or Wisconsin relatives or neighbors. They were the only couple in its fifties, and theirs was the only family that had children born in Wisconsin. Leonard Jr., 19, worked on a farm, while Susan, 15, Alice, 12, Carrie, 10, and Mary, 8, were all described as attending school. Only one family, with seven children, was as large as theirs. Leonard made himself an excellent exception by describing himself as a carpenter amid rows of farmers.

The changing and turbulent community of Wea Township manifested a "transciency" typical of nineteenth century North American frontier settlements.[29] Kansas was at the epicenter of the veritable explosion that transformed the Great Plains into a wheat belt and a cattle industry and a rural revolution that tripled the number of farms in the nation between 1870 and 1900.[30] Kansas also stood at the center of a great continental transformation, attracting both foreign-born immigrants, who themselves were establishing a second or third home, and native-born Americans, like Charlotte and Leonard, who made Kansas their last gamble. The railroads delivered a whirlwind of peoples to vicissitudes of shifting opportunities, changing prices, and climatic disasters common to an arid land. Severe fluctuations characterized the whole period of settlement and made more losers than winners out of settlers who came without sufficient money to survive a year or two of bad times.

Leonard and Charlotte experienced the precipitous growth and decline. With its population concentrated in the east, Kansas had only about a hundred thousand people in 1861 at the time of its statehood. It had a stunning 360,000 three hundred and sixty thousand residents in 1870, more than a million and half in 1888. Thereafter decline took over during the next two decades. During the depression years of 1888 and 1894, immigrants were in full retreat, especially from the state's arid western lands. Counties barely born in the west lost as much as two-thirds of their population in the 1890s.[31] Leonard and Charlotte knew the turbulence of a new state whose population of 1,300,000 in 1885 counted only 350,000 born in Kansas.[32]

In 1883, at the apex of the Kansas boom, Leonard and Charlotte uprooted themselves once again. They followed the lead of their son-in-law Albert Peachey, a widower with two small children who had married their daughter Henrietta. Starting a new teaching position at Sunny Slope in Sumner County, Albert encouraged Charlotte and Leonard to follow him to the booming area of south-central Kansas. This time the dream-inducing train tracks, which in the 1880s had expanded from three thousand to nine thousand miles in Kansas alone, led Leonard and Charlotte to Sumner County, located south of Wichita near the Kansas-Oklahoma border. The nearby Flint Hills defined their eastern horizon. Their western borders were delineated thirty miles to the west by the Wichita-Salina line, which coincides with a rise of elevation from eight hundred to sixteen hundred feet and the division between eastern tall-grass and the arid western short-grass ecological zones.[33]

Having made money in Wea, Leonard purchased a 320-acre farm in Creek Township, with $2,500 and the help of a $1,100 mortgage.[34] A road that bordered one of their two 160-acre parcels of sandy-soiled land was called Eden Road. The following year, in 1884, Leonard sold his land for $4,700. Here in western Kansas, approaching the limit of good farmland and near the end of the period of settlement, Leonard and Charlotte had finally caught a break, or succeeded in the art that brother-in-law Franklin Rosegrant had modeled in St. Lawrence County decades before. The profits on this one single sale surpassed decades of his income as a carpenter.

They had managed to sell their property just as county land, now 40 percent under cultivation, reached its maximum price. After 1885, an absence of rainfall and declining grain markets resulted in a precipitous drop in land prices over the next five years. In freshly settled western Kansas where "the chance of surviving economically for five years on 160 acres [of homestead] land dwindled with each passing meridian," depopulation began.[35]

However, this time speculation had paid off. Leonard and Charlotte could buy a place and retire in modest security in town. Leonard bought two lots for $680 in Argonia, where he practiced his life-long trade of carpentry. There he built Charlotte and himself a modest home, which is still standing. That year the *Argonia Clipper* boosted the town's prospects for future rail service and touted the "Paradise" of the surrounding country: "the rich alluvial sandy loam soil is peculiarly favorable to withstand almost any drought or excessive rainfall 'failure,' being unknown in this part of the world." The *Clipper* crowed, as if at the beginning of the American covenant, that here is a "city set upon a hill whose light cannot be hid." Of course, it also printed complaints about muck and mud, running and rabid dogs, too much drinking, and unethical peddlers of lightning rods.[36]

I would guess that neither high civic praise nor low civic complaints would stir sixty-three-year-old Leonard. He had the comforts of village life and the self-satisfaction of a home of his own. Charlotte, as if she had finally arrived in the valley of choice, was welcomed into the new Church of Christ (rather than the town's recently organized Methodist Episcopal church). In 1885, to put last things in order, Leonard drew up his will. Anticipating his own death, he deeded the home to Charlotte. However, in 1896, one year short of their fiftieth wedding anniversary, Charlotte died. In the same spirit of reciprocity, she willed the property for the maintenance of Leonard. True to what they both had believed and wanted from the outset of their migration, property had proven the life raft of old age. Proceeds from the sale of the home maintained Leonard at his daughter Carrie and son-in law Charles Shapper's farm until his death at eighty-two in 1904.

At the End of the Trail

Fittingly, Leonard and Charlotte, grandparents of my restless grandmother Frances, found their final home in a land of trails. Here buffalo, Native Americans, and Spanish explorers had once passed, and the nearby Oregon Trail and California Trail led 350,000 settlers to the west between 1841 and 1867.[37] West of the Flint Hills and east of the Arkansas River, Leonard and Charlotte found themselves almost dead center between two northern branches of the Chisholm Trail, along which Texas cowboys moved their animals to railheads at Ellsworth and Abilene. Here in the Wellington Lowland, where prairie agricultural land begins its ascent to the arid High Plains, they ended a lifetime journey midway on the continent.[38]

In youth they had fled the rocky edges of the Adirondacks, and now in old age they settled on the threshold of the ascent to the Rockies. Doing what necessity required and transportation permitted, Leonard and Charlotte had distinguished themselves as members of the distinguishing breed of migrating American poor. They had not drunk to the dregs the intoxicating glug of Yankee restlessness, that singular potion of want and envy, desperation, and speculation that sent its New England consumers zigzagging across the opening lands of the west, desperate not to miss an opportunity on the land. Perhaps the best-known example of that type is Charles Ingalls, father of Laura Ingalls Wilder, who told her family's story in *Little House on the Prairie* and subsequent books.[39]

At the end of their own trail, Leonard and Charlotte drew their Kansas family emotionally around them. Their affection won them the reputation among the neighbors of being the "kissingest family around."[40] But, from the point of community, they had come to rest on thin soil. Now light-years distant from New York and decades gone from Wisconsin, they fully belonged to south-central Kansas, where populations flowed in and poured out, especially to Oklahoma, where the last free national homesteading and the last great American land rush occurred.

Leonard and Charlotte's children illustrated Kansas's role as a national turnstile. Four daughters married and settled in Oklahoma, with one moving on to Oregon and one to the Southwest. At nineteen years old, born in 1870, daughter Carrie, alone, stayed put and avoided the dispersal. She married a thirty-nine-year-old local farmer of German stock in Milan, had twelve children, and cared for father Leonard until he died.[41] Leonard Jr., the only

surviving son, became a regional traveling salesman. After marrying Lilly
Burtram in a hotel in the nearby railroad town of Wellington, Kansas, he
returned home to Argonia only to find, according to Cousin Irene Kolmen,
that his new bride could not live comfortably in a household with "so many
women . . . each wanting to be chief." One of Leonard's Wisconsin sisters,
whom I take to be my great-grandmother Ella, wrote, suggesting that he and
his wife return to farm in Wisconsin, which they did. Living one farm away
from Ella and James Boodry in Town of Maine, on a raft of their own, Leonard
and Lilly had seven children. One of their daughters, showing that old habits
don't die easily, married and had fifteen children. By 1904, Leonard and Lilly
had died, and another of their children, Jenny, proved that exception (which
might simply be historical change) is potentially inherent in any genetic
chain. Orphaned, and adopted into a husband-and-wife acrobatic team, she
ended up in Baraboo, Wisconsin, where in 1910 she became a trapeze artist
for the traveling Ringling Brothers Circus. I see her on the high wire, balanc-
ing her and the Sayeres' way toward home.

6

A Memorable Death, a Common Lot

Anecdotes, tales, myths, and lies—they are all stories, and stories are often the best and most repeatable part we have of our family's past. They can join the individual and the universal and save them, as the humanistic studies should, from smothering concepts, timorous hypotheses, and impersonal abstractions. They hook our interest, drive wonder and query. They form the knot of the past we cannot forget. Long and short, complex and simple, told only once, repeated ad infinitum, in the form of dramas, satires, ironies, and tragedies, stories form the nexus between past and present. Hiding and revealing, confirming and conflicting, in their testimony, stories stand guard as the inner significance and outer meaning of a family. Often our only source, they are also our best source. Success in our research depends on their deciphering; good writing depends on their just telling. Stories bring us to their teller—be it a laconic uncle or a compulsive aunt raconteur—and we suffer where and how their words and reality meet.

As much as any, the single story of James Boodry's rabid death shaped my understanding of the family's past and life and death. It also made me aware that my understanding of things grew out the stories my grandmother, grandfather, and mother once told impressionable me. As I search the past, I discover I am the stories I am impelled to tell.

In the Old Testament, a man's "lot" in life was literally the land assigned to him, and so in times following, the land a man owned determined his fate.[1] I was especially drawn to the lot of my grandmother's father, James Leonard Boodry, second child of Sylvester, because of two telling photographs and the story of his horrid death. I think of him frequently, and when I do, I cannot easily put him or his death out of my mind.

He looks out at me from his wedding photograph, taken in August 1867. He had just turned nineteen. I shiver at our similarity of looks. It is as if he

James Boodry and Ellen Frances (Ella) Sayers at their wedding, 1867

and I were the same person, as if his genes jumped three generations and then, dominating all others, made me his spit and image. Take him out of his high leather work boots and his baggy, ill-fitting coat, and put him in my high school prom tuxedo, stand him in front of my father's 1956 Chevrolet, and we are one and the same person. Our faces, hands, body, and posture match, although I imagine below his baggy clothing he was far more muscular than I and felt more confident about getting married and taking up a life with a woman, children, horses, sawmills, and the poor fields of central Wisconsin than I did at the same age, preparing to set off for the University of Michigan.

In a second photograph, he, with his wife and two children, is aged and worn, though probably only in his mid-forties. He looks crazed and pursued. He gazes straight ahead, but somehow inner forces blind him to what stands in front him. Almost as if he is bewitched, he seems to be draped in a cowl of fear. His eyes beacon torment. For me they express a life overrun by work and necessity.

As photographs rivet me to him, the story of his death captivates me. More binding than any genealogical connection and more compelling than a social science or abstract historical accounting of his life, his death fastens me to his fate and convinces me, my hope to the contrary, that God does not spare anyone a miserable death.

A Death Among Deaths

A family, like any group, passes through time and change collecting, modifying, discarding, and forgetting stories. In the process of doing this it knits itself into one, recasts itself, comes unraveled, and unless written, is finally entirely forgotten. One of the most powerful sources of stories, the counter pole of origins and births, is that of death and dying.[2] One way we know ourselves and this life is by recitation of stories of how our parents and grandparents died. Back in time and across into the lives of uncles and aunts and cousins and their children, we gather ourselves around our collection of stories of death. For any one family, there are deaths of every sort—single and collective, long and short, close and far away, known and mysterious, at home and at work, in the course of childbirth and military service—by explosion, lightening, fire, drowning, scalding (like Rosalia's oldest son Joe), suicide, and all imaginable diseases. With great historical variation, due to changes in environment, society, and other factors, they take uneven numbers of young and old. The effects of a death on a family, and what society makes of it, constitute the primary memories of any given death.

Forming a pathway of recollection, we know ourselves by inventorying our family's deaths. However deeply we bury the dead below monuments of stones and words, they rise back up. Bloated with strong emotion and unsatisfied obligations, they float to the surface of consciousness and can haunt us, like the body my uncle Bill literally kept afloat for a full day and then couldn't let sink over a lifetime. After his ship went down in the Mediterranean, off the coast of North Africa in 1943, Bill, a medical corpsman, kept his dead friend's body with him for eighteen hours until they were pulled from the sea. Bill never could bury his friend's body; it floated in his mind with all the buoyancy of the irrepressible great war and young manhood. And after the war he didn't return to Detroit, but went to Boston with his new bride, Margaret from North Carolina, to live in an apartment in the house of his friend's mother. There with Margaret and his newborn child, Mary Ellen, he worked nights at a bakery for a few years until my father, mother, and I drove out to Boston and brought them back to Detroit.

So different from Bill, my father, of an earlier generation and contrasting experiences, offered a different view of male heroism. Caring for his mother and fatherless sisters, and then my mother and me, was his battlefront. He never dwelled on the past or spoke of his memories of that time. Practical to the bone, with no storytelling urge within, he kept the past at bay throughout his life. He found no pleasure in recollection and no responsibility for its perpetuation. He had no time for keeping the past alive in the present. My father judged war stories, in which my Uncle Bill enfolded himself, to be an act of self-indulgence and even political interest. Everybody, in his view, had survived something. In the here and now, it is better to get on with life. Like a traditional peasant, my father was a servant of lean necessity.

Fittingly, when his time came, he died instantly, severing his relations with life quickly, cleanly, and economically. He suffered a massive heart attack at home, while watching the University of Michigan basketball team playing its final game for the 1989 national championship. While my mother developed several, slightly variant, versions of his last acts and words, his death itself was undisputedly swift, and she never digested it. I had received one notice from him of its coming three months earlier, during my last visit to Detroit. Uncharacteristically, he told me of an ominous incident he had experienced. After washing his car, he suddenly found himself on the ground, unable to get up. There he remained for a quarter of an hour or so. He forced me to review his well-kept business papers and gave me instructions what to do at the bank if he should die.

My mother died otherwise. After my father's death, she spent thirteen years with us in Minnesota living independently, until she decided that she had gone as far as she could on her own. She entered a nursing home, where she lived her last two and half years. Having suffered a few bouts of depression and many bodily humiliations that come with aging—perhaps none as profound as tremors and the loss of the use of her hands—she turned her indomitable mind to the act of dying. She had taken one fall too many, and after what was to be her last fall, she chose, with our implicit permission, not to eat or drink anymore. I continued to talk to her as if her coma had not made her impervious to my words. I assured her it was all right to die. I took the fact that she stopped breathing just as I entered the room as her final gift to me—and as a sacrament of loving memory, I continue to die her death.

The death of my maternal grandfather, William Linsdau, was not dissimilar to that of my mother. The closing years of his life had heaped indignities on this good-natured and prayerful man. Over a span of several years, he watched his wife physically and mentally deteriorate as a result of a succession of strokes. In his last years, loneliness tormented him most. He ate more and more television dinners and grew fonder and fonder of his dog, Skippy, and even more insistent that visitors exchange greetings with the animal before entering his house. When he awoke in the hospital from a second and more severe stroke and found himself unable to talk coherently and make us smile with his jokes, Grandpa Linsdau turned his back to us and died.

My paternal grandfather, Antonino Amato, died a quick and unexpected death at the inopportune age of thirty-three. In contrast, his wife Rosalia died, at seventy-seven, a long, long death from emphysema. Over a decade, she coughed, more and more. At St. John's Hospital, where my Grandfather Linsdau had died, we stood vigil during her last days. My father decided to have her glucose withdrawn, but death was hesitant in coming. Her faltering breath, that long, faltering, and raspy pulling in and that thin, eerily irregular emission of air, persisted through the afternoon, the evening, and into the early morning hours until, at last, it mercifully stopped.

These deaths of my parents and grandparents were but a few of the path-ways my family took to death. But no death in my family's past captured my mature imagination as much as that of my great-grandfather, James Boodry—my grandmother Frances's father. James's death merited him ban-ner headlines in the June 25, 1909, *Appleton Evening Crescent*. In capital letters it declared, "BOODRY HAS HYDROPHOBIA." "Well Known Hostler," the subti-tle declared of James, the stable caretaker, "Who Was Bitten by Sick Dog a Month Ago, Developed Hydrophobia Yesterday Afternoon, and is Now Said to be Fatally Ill—Terrible Suffering." Mr. Boodry was "in a violent state and his sufferings are terrible. He is being constantly guarded by several men, all of whose strength is required to restrain him. He froths at the mouth, snaps at everyone coming near him and seems to be filled with burning thirst, which can not be allayed because the mere sight of water would make him more violent." The paper declared his case hopeless, "Not even the famous Pas-teur treatment at Chicago," the article reports, "can save Mr. Boodry from his agony which death alone can end."

"A bull terrier," so the paper account read, "had bitten Mr. Boodry a month earlier. Working at Dr. O. N. Johnson's veterinary hospital, Mr. Boodry found it necessary to stop a fight between the terrier and Dr. Johnson's own Italian bull. He bent over to pet the terrier, only to have the animal sink its teeth in his nose making an ugly gash on either side of the bridge." The article went on to explain that a post-mortem examination of the terrier (which in fact would have been superficial, as they had no means to examine the tissue) showed no sign of hydrophobia, and so, the paper explained, Mr. Boodry was not sent to the Pasteur clinic in Chicago, which alone had the rabies vaccine, developed by Pasteur in 1885.

The following day the *Crescent* reported James's death on its front page. His violence had increased as death drew closer. During the afternoon, two strong men were unable to restrain him; they secured him with a straightjacket procured from St. Elizabeth's Hospital until he died. His funeral was officiated by the minister of Appleton's Presbyterian church, into which his family had been received the preceding year. He joined Boodry hill at the head of the Town of Maine Cemetery.

His death had an immediate effect on Appleton. Doctors sent a boy bitten by the same dog to Chicago for treatment. City officials decided to kill or license and muzzle Appleton's estimated 750 dogs, of which 300 were unlicensed and more than 500 ran free. James's death ran like a deep underground stream in the family mind. It coursed thereafter in his wife, Ella; his two surviving sons, Chester (Chet) of Hortonville and youngest child, Tom, whom I knew as my deaf-mute great-uncle; in their five daughters, Maggie Wing of New London, Sadie Terrill and Lulu Preston of Shiocton, Mrs. Agnes Johnson of Crandin, and my grandmother, Frances Boodry of Appleton, who told me of his death when I was a boy. When I was forty, I taught at a Unitarian Minnesota summer camp that was infested with bats, and when I buried a bucket full, James's rabid death flew up powerfully within me. Family deaths make metaphors by which we measure life.

Dark Fall: Instructions on Killing a Bat

I. A Night's Vision
Before your face
It sliced the room in two,
Cut it into a hundred parts.
And worse was that unholy vision
That rode on those dark wings.

My great grandfather Boodry's rabid death
Lived on in my grandmother's memory

For sixty years:

Veterinarian in a remote Wisconsin township

He knew the bite he received had no cure.

Young, with a family yet to be raised.

He had himself strapped down on a table.

When his convulsions became strong,

He had his friends shoot him.

II. A Day's Plans and Reason for Revenge

Now it is morning.

Plan your revenge.

Hang a bucket, half-filled with water,

At the opening,

Where you heard them dressing their wings

All night long.

Remember,

The bat is not a bird.

Its flight, like human history,

Begins with a fall.

It must fall to rise.

And do not forget

The bat is a creature of sin,

The smallest of the fallen angels.

It flies the downward flight of all matter.

Death entered the world on its wing.

It flies at night,

Celebrating the first fall,

Anticipating the descent of all things.

III. Tomorrow's Certainties

Tonight,

When darkness swells,

There will be an end to them.

No falling, swooping start,

No night flight of screeching expectations,
Only a watery grave
In a brown plastic scrub bucket.

Throughout the night,
They will struggle against the water
And one another.

They will swim and float.
They will climb, scratch, gnaw.
And each truce with death made
Will be broken by the fury
Awakened by a new fallen bat.

In the coming light,
They will become a slowing circle of life,
A raft of darkness and wing.
And you will peer down
At that swirl of creatures.[3]

James's death never quit me. It wound itself around my memory like a vine of wild honeysuckle wraps itself around a young tree—and can make a fine walking stick. I remember how my grandmother told me that James snarled and snapped at those around him like a mad dog, and that when his convulsions became worse, his friends tied him down. Then they blindfolded themselves and shot him to death. On my visit to Wisconsin over three decades ago, his grand-nephew Alex Johnson, son of daughter Agnes, disputed this story. He claimed James died before his friends, who were planning to shoot him, had to.

Apples That Fell Close to the Tree

James knew the Town of Maine intimately. He, the oldest son of founder Sylvester, was there at its beginning. Born August 22, 1847, in Clinton, Maine (the township's mother colony), James arrived with Sylvester just after the Civil

War. In 1870, the township population reached 100 residents, while the county itself doubled from 9,600 in 1860 to 18,500 inhabitants in 1869. The 25 percent of the land developed in the 1870s involved small farms of only eighty, forty, and twenty acres.[4] They saw the erection of farmhouses and barns, some of which Sylvester built, and which principally sprang up along the township's main north-south river road, the Shawano Highway. Parallel to the log-filled Wolf River and passing along the vestiges of the seventeenth-century Indian garden and village, Questatinong, the highway took loggers, teamsters, and suppliers on their way to and from northern lumbering districts. A primary employer, lumbering accounted for the building of two small commercial centers in the township, Leeman on the north end and Stinton a mile south. Increasing foot and horse traffic along the highway affirmed the growing connection between logging on the upper Wolf River and the southern mills of the Fox River Valley. Lumbering accounted for the growth of Shiocton, a mill town five miles south of Leeman, standing on the Shawano Highway and at the confluence of the Wolf and Shiocton Rivers, and the growth to the south of the important mill towns of Oshkosh, Neenah, Menasha, and Outagamie County's principal town, Appleton.

Leaving the full households of their parents at their marriage in 1867, James and Ella entered the adult world of reproduction and work. Joined in Ella's Methodist Episcopal church of Neenah, the young couple brought to the marriage dowries of loyalty and a determination to work hard. Their vows would not spare them the travail under which humans had labored since Adam and Eve were evicted from the Garden. With neither land nor animals, and only the energy and hope youth can muster, they yoked themselves to the perennial condition of the rural poor: never having adequate land or sufficient money until death did them part.

The Town of Maine, on the one hand, was truly their home. There was the progeny of prodigious father Sylvester and his young Prussian wife, Annie, with whom he replicated the eleven children of his first marriage. Almost all of Sylvester and Annie's children remained in the township or migrated no farther than the nearby countryside. Nine of their eleven children were buried in the Town of Maine, as were at least seven of his children from his

first marriage. In turn, eight of James's surviving children filled out a large
extended family network in the town and the nearby countryside. Further
weaving the nest of family, Ella's sisters and brother and many of their children also married and lived in there. On their little raft of forty acres of land,
with siblings as immediate neighbors, James and Ella lived tucked in among
such friends and original fellow settlers as the Spauldings, Thompsons,
Allens, Sweets, and others whose names, along with that of the Boodrys,
gather in clusters on the flats and hillocks of the Town of Maine Cemetery.

Beyond the social landscape, James and Ella—like country folk in centuries past—knew the physical landscape of their corner of Maine like the
backs of their hands. They knew the river, where to fish it, how to hunt its
lowlands, and which berries and mushrooms to pick along its banks. On a
landscape filled with wetlands and thickets, James and Ella knew the value of
the lands on which they could grow crops, tend gardens, pasture animals, and
plant apple trees, which flourished in Outagamie County. James timbered his
father's land and drained what wetlands he could into the Wolf River. Beyond
that, his need for cash led him to work on roads and do the work of an axe
man and a teamster. Like the other men of this poor and puny valley, he went
north in the winter to work in the lumber industry and probably south for
occasional employment at the mills of nearby Shiocton.

The Wolf at the Door

As much as James and Ella were at home in the Town of Maine, they
never really established themselves on its land. With no capital to begin
with, they started married life in 1867 as hired hands. In the 1870 census
they are listed as living with Ella's sister Margaret and her husband
Thomas Allen on a small farm valued at only $600. James and Ella owned
only $100 dollars worth of land and had an equal amount of personal
property. Then, in 1883, after more than a decade of working as a hired
hand and a teamster, doing what his impoverished but hard-working
kind were doing across rural America, James bought his own forty acres.
He and Ella promised to pay $400 for the acreage, which was ten times

what Sylvester had paid for his land along the river a decade before.

Finally, after sixteen years of marriage, ownership of forty acres initiated them as full members of the community. Though we do not know the level of debt of this family of six, surely, like so many small landowners of the century, the wolves of debt (the tax collector, banker, doctor, undertaker, horse jockey, and others) frequently knocked at their door and reminded them that they only had a precarious hold on the land. They could tend their gardens, hunt, fish, and canvas the countryside for food, and James might work as much as he could as lumberman and teamster, but this guaranteed them no permanence in the Town of Maine. The fact that their families had been in the nation more than two generations didn't count. They were no more certain of tomorrow in the Town of Maine than grandfather Joseph Boodry had been on the slopes of the state of Maine. Not unlike their ancestors and the poor of the countryside since time immemorial, they might conclude that their sole accomplishment was the replication of themselves and production of surplus children to be plowed back into the rural under-classes, who would be a reservoir for the society's expanding need for labor.[5]

As the rural poor, they constantly stared into the changing face of debt. Everything they needed cost money. Driving horses made James, if he owned his own team (a measure of status in the countryside since the Middle Ages), worth approximately $300, the price of a good pair of draft animals. Yet his pay as a teamster, if he earned the contemporary industry standard, was only $26 dollars a month.[6] A year of steady work at this wage would have netted James $300, surely a puny amount when measured against need, much less the pettiest indulgences. It left his family, even with a paltry additional annual farm income of $100, short of the capital to secure his land or undertake emigration to diminishing arable western lands.

Perhaps there were many individual reasons, aside from their growing family, why they never migrated to Milwaukee, Chicago, the Dakotas, or central Kansas where Charlotte and Leonard Sayers landed in their last days. Surely, James and Ella were hit by the bad economic times of the 1870s. By the 1890s, when they both were in their fifties, agricultural depression had shut the doors on western migration. Low prices for wheat and high shipping costs made farming in even the best of valleys difficult, and immigrants and settlers were retreating back East from the dry, boom-or-bust lands of the great western prairie. The greater movement, in which my families enrolled, increasingly led from farms and villages to mill towns and finally to the industrial city. Those streams, which had sources in the rural depopulation of New England, drew even from the recently settled Midwest and West and became torrential at the end of the century.

A Mill Town

In 1901, when James and Ella were both more than fifty years old, they left—or, more than likely, were forced from—their forty-acre farm. They moved, with no apparent assets, thirty-five miles south to the emerging industrial mill town of Appleton, the queen of the Fox River Valley, whose waterpower rivaled the best sites of New England.[7] In Appleton, as the rural poor do who leave the countryside for town, he became a day laborer. There he remained in menial work, living in rental properties for the rest of his life. Their south and slightly southeast descent to Appleton, was a mere two-day journey. It was nothing in comparison to those westward voyages of father Sylvester and father-in-law Leonard. Nevertheless, for James and Ella, it was immense journey from which there was no turning back. Life in town would never be that of life in the township, but as for the rural poor, east, west or even south, the yields of land did not equal the wages of town. The market increased its grip, and money took a tighter hold on both need and want. Money bought land and houses, goods and services. It intermingled and commingled country and city lives and imaginations.

James and Ella were part of a movement that left fields untilled—let them return to brush and trees—while farm folk moved to the nearby mill town to make an ever-needed dollar. They brought their horses, now detached from plow, carts, and skids, and set them to pulling the distinguishing carriages, and the omnibuses, and streetcars, which (along with Appleton's "Dinky," reputedly the nation's first electric trolley), formed the skeleton of an emerging transportation system, for those who could afford the fare.[8]

Appleton, located in southern Outagamie County, was both county seat and an emerging mill town already in the 1850s. It was financed by eastern capital, which espied the potential waterpower of the steeply descending Fox River. The town soon saw the building of two flour mills, one paper mill, four sawmills, two lath mills, one planing mill, two sash and blind factories, one chair factory, and three cabinetware plants. A leader in the regional lumbering industry, Appleton boasted that it out-produced Madison, Oshkosh, and Fond du Lac. Appleton not only built its own plants and houses but projected its commercial power into the region by constructing plank roads across wetlands and bridging the Fox River and other rivers and streams. By the middle 1860s, Appleton, which supplied distant Chicago with lumber, drew to its emerging plants—one of which, the first in the United States, was a sawmill operated by electricity—displaced farmers and loggers throughout the region.[9]

James and Ella came to Appleton at a time when across the nation the traditional rural way of life was ending. They left behind five decades, or yet one might suggest a thousand years, of horses, woods, and small farms, for electricity, lights, machines, and the crucible of changing town life. They were entering the industrial city, a place where mass, national, popular, and commercial cultures converged, the equation of land and survival was melted, and family was alloyed as a new unit around work and wages.

Of course, James and Ella were not ignorant of or indifferent to town life. Actually, the city came to them before they went to the city. It entered their hearts and lives in the form of new needs, fresh wants, and novel and unimagined innovations. It came by the medium of the Sears catalogue and with the visits of relatives who told of the powers and wonders of Chicago, Milwaukee, and the growing towns of the Fox River Valley. The city came with the canals, the tracks, and actually directly impinged on them with the nearby flourishing small town of Shiocton. Only a few miles from their home place, in its 1870 heyday, Shiocton, a significant lumbering center, had five stores and three hotels, a hub and spoke factory, a planing mill, a handle factory, and one of the largest sawmills in northern Wisconsin, which cut millions of feet of white pine and hard woods until the surrounding area was depleted of timber and it became a backwater. In 1900 economic renewal came with its transformation into a major vegetable and flower garden center.[10]

The new century did not begin for James and Ella with the election of Theodore Roosevelt, the building of the Panama Canal, the Boxer Rebellion, the Anthracite Coal Miners' Strike, or the flight of the Kitty Hawk. It simply started on that day in 1901 when they crossed Appleton's city limits. After almost four decades of searching for a place on the land, they washed up on the shores of Appleton, the flotsam and jetsam of an older economic order that had been breaking up on the shoals of a money-driven economy for more than a century. They entered a society where population was concentrated, machines were truly powerful, and body, mind, and taste were linked to the nation.

Living in rental housing a few blocks from downtown, James and Ella encountered a world and a class that did not exist in the Town of Maine. Appleton mirrored a nation whose wealth in the last decade, despite the depression of its first four years, had increased from $65 billion to $88.5 billion and whose income went from $12 billion to $18 billion. This prosperity was, according to American historian Harold Faulkner, distributed "shockingly unequally," "with 200,000 people controlling 70 per cent of the wealth"; as a survey of estates probated in five Wisconsin counties reported, the poorest two-thirds, in which James and Ella fit, owned only 5 percent, and the poorest three-fourths only 10 percent.[11]

On the paved streets of Appleton, James and Ella witnessed these inequalities. They passed mansion row and saw their well-heeled and clothed superiors, whose bodies were not bent and distorted by years of hard manual labor and whose days were not determined by work.[12] In palatial homes the elite had running water and toilets; the most ostentatious touted eight fireplaces and a library and was completely wired for electricity. Conspicuous in dress and social appointments, the wealthy informed the town newspaper of travels to New York, Washington, D.C., Philadelphia, London, Paris, and the world. They sneered at the raggedly clothed and smelly people, like James, who did the town's necessary work. The youth of the elite, conscious of taste and with disposable incomes, sailed, rowed, frolicked, and attended well-advertised concerts, plays and musicals. Prospering Appleton high society set a price of admission to a new and luxuriant world, which the older generation of country and day workers could not afford or even imagine entering.

James looked through the glasses of old country life at the spectacles of these new urbanites. He and Ella saw the students of Appleton's Lawrence College, who, so unlike their own Frances and Tom, had four years of leisure to study and to select the life they would live. Daily, these self-adorned aliens, who by providence or fortune had escaped toil and dirt, bore witness to a free and sparkling world. They paraded and promenaded on foot and in carriage. A few of the most adventurous, gaining the attention of every passerby, showed up on the streets to demonstrate their horseless carriages. Here was a revolution of speed, steel, and small gasoline engines, which would soon displace the medieval worlds of stone, wood, and horse. James and Ella could only look on this contemporary invention as the era's audiences did on the magic escapes of Appleton's very own native Harry Houdini.[13]

Ella and James arrived in Appleton a year after seventeen-year old Edna Ferber, who, like Houdini, was another Hungarian Jew associated with Appleton. Ferber offered some of our very best portraits of contemporary Appleton. She was a cub reporter for the *Appleton Crescent*. Born in Kalamazoo, Michigan, to a Hungarian Jewish family, and raised, in her own words, on Chautauquas, political rallies, parades, circuses, and books, Ferber's job in Appleton constituted her first step in a career that led to national prominence. She described Appleton, a town of fifteen thousand, as "a lively town, decent, literate." The rich equipped their homes with the best, sent their children to the University of Wisconsin at Madison or eastern schools, made their daily ritual the reading of the *Milwaukee Sentinel*, and took frequent trips to Milwaukee and Chicago for theatre and opera. "The women," Ferber noted of the town trend-setters, "wore quite well-made clothes and smart—but not too smart—hats. They knew what was fashionable and bought it." Belonging to the emerging age of travel, they invested "their earnings in new-model automobiles and lavishly laid them at the feet and the threshold of European statues, cathedrals, museums, ruins, and hotelkeepers."[14]

Living in Appleton did not mean that James and Ella lost contact with the Town of Maine. The 1901 Outagamie Directory for Maine lists stepmother Annie, who still clung to her 40 acres; stepbrothers, Raymond who, born in 1878, owned 80 acres, and name-sake Sylvester who, born in 1874, also owned 80 acres. (Sylvester later committed suicide by hanging in 1929, when he discovered he had purchased a team of horses with the heaves, a pulmonary disease.) Of course, in addition to Ella's brother, Leonard Sayers, who owned 40 acres, there were sons Chester, listed in 1903 as owning 40 acres, and Edgar, recorded in 1904 as owning 60 acres. The land the brothers bought and speculated on—some of the least tillable and the worst in the township—was sold within a few years.

Ella and James took family stories of the Town of Maine with them to Appleton or had their supply regularly replenished with each visit from one of their children, cousins, or friends still living there; my grandmother carried that mix of Gothic and nostalgic stories with her to Michigan, where she passed them on to me. She told of her crazy older sister Sadie, a seasonal recluse who hid in her house for long periods to avoid contact with the world, but was always betrayed in the winter by fresh tracks in the snow from the house to the outhouse. Grandmother Frances sprinkled her talk with darker stories; she contended that "one of relatives" was the source of a famous national pickle recipe.

When James and Ella arrived in Appleton in 1901, they had more to do than celebrate the new century and bathe themselves in Rexford's fashionable melancholy. Such matters as these belonged to a class with spare time and left over feelings. During their first years in the new town, James and Ella had to attend the marriages of Lulu, Chet, and Margaret. They still had to care for eleven-year-old Frances and seven-year-old Thomas. (Their youngest child, Irena Cusilla, who was born 1897, died before the family arrived in town.) Thomas was of particular concern. He was deaf and mute, and the year before coming to town—perhaps influencing when they came—a goat wrapped its rope around his neck and choked him. Without the resources to pay for a special school for the deaf, though he would attend one later when a teen, they sent Tom, like his sister Frances and other siblings, to work as soon as possible. In 1910, young Tom is noted in the *Appleton Directory* as working at the "wireworks" and living at a new address with his recently widowed mother, Ella.

When I was a young boy, Uncle Tom's kindness attracted me, and his muteness fascinated me. Once my parents, grandparents, and I went to Tom and his wife Wilda's small apartment on the near east side in Detroit. We gathered around a small kitchen table covered by an oilcloth. The men had a beer, and they prompted Tom and his deaf and mute wife, Wilda—who was better than Tom at signing and, in a screeching and agitated voice, articulating words—to talk. When conversation faltered for lack of subjects, Tom took out a broom and, holding it in both hands a foot or so from and parallel to the ground, he jumped over it forwards and then backwards.

During their first years in Appleton, defeat pressed all around Ella and James. Their eldest son, Edgar, and his young family apparently failed on the land. The 1900 census for the Town of Maine indicates that he was a farmer, living with wife, Florence, and three children, ages six, three, and one, on an eighty-acre farm. In 1904, he and his family were living in Appleton, and he was working as a carpenter. (Also, either reflecting an error or a serious split in the family, or just possibly his death, he is not listed in James's obituary among James and Ella's living children.)

Chet's prospects offered no hope that the family would climb out of their condition, either. Initially, he had promise. In 1902, at twenty-six, he married Effie Castellion. In 1903, he purchased a miserable piece of thicket and wetland. Chet went downhill from that point on. In the 1910 census, married with four children (two sons and two daughters), living in Hortonville, Outagamie County, he described himself as a day laborer who did odd jobs, which included being a chimney sweep. A chronic alcoholic, he obsessively moved from place to place, and, according to cousin Delores Johnson, eventually left the essential care of his wife and six children to his oldest son, James.[15]

In Appleton, James, Ella, and their family were transformed from rural poor into urban poor. With their move to Appleton they became renters. They rented two different homes before James's death in 1909, when Ella moved to another apartment before ultimately living with her children

until her death. Identified as a farmer on the 1897 birth certificate of daughter Irena, James held a succession of poor jobs in Appleton. In the 1904 *Appleton Directory* he was described as working at a canning factory. In 1906, he was a teamster, and at the time of his death in 1909, he served as a hostler—a stableman—for a local veterinarian. He was probably lucky if any of these jobs yielded a wage of a dollar a day, the going wage for unskilled mill workers. However, I find it fitting that James ended his life caring for horses, the creatures that symbolize a rural order begun in the Middle Ages, with which he had worked over a whole lifetime.

A traditional rural man, James passed his life with horses in field and in forest, on road and in stable. He delivered his family to the center of a world that was displacing his kind and his children to a world in which the Boodrys, these distant children of Arcadia, would again have to remake themselves. In taking the family to Appleton, he put my young grandmother Frances in front of a distorting mirror of wealth, talent, pleasure, and outward self-satisfaction in which she would struggle across a lifetime to recognize herself.

Appleton told Frances who she wasn't the moment she arrived in town. It gripped her even tighter in 1906, when, as a girl of only seventeen, she began her work as a dressmaker at stylish "Mrs. Adams." This job accompanied her during a brief stint at business school in Clintonville, and it undoubtedly swept her up heart and soul when she took up the contemporary music, theater, and arts of the valley in the company of the stylish Catholic Linsdau brothers from the nearby mill town of Menasha, Emmett and my grandfather William. They ushered her into the footlights of urban life in the Fox River Valley.

I don't know what impact her father's death had on Frances, although to have one's father die a miserable and highly public death from hydrophobia must have humbled and angered her. I know it angers me. I find myself shouting out, "God, why do you let us, our kind, die the worst of deaths! Dogs' deaths!" In any case, within a year of her father's death in 1909, Frances married William Linsdau in a Catholic church. They moved to nearby Neenah where Frances gave birth to my mother in 1912. Then Frances and William set

Chet Boodry, my mother's uncle, 1930s

out for the great industrial city, Detroit, where she never found her quadrant or freed herself from that star pulling her back in time and deep in imagined place to the Town of Maine. She spent her decades in Detroit, that immense valley city, looking for a deeper and calmer bay—which she never truly had in her childhood Town of Maine or in her adolescent Appleton. No new house could locate a missing home, could furnish the precious, healing, magical forty acres for which she yearned.

7

Jacob,
the Rise and Fall of a Plebian Patriarch

Unless we would deny the humanity of our family and the humanistic goal of history, we must not sacrifice families and the individual lives of their members to impersonal laws and generalizations. At the same time, we must not make a family a captive of a facile metaphor or worn literary motif. Nevertheless, family history over the long course or for a single generation requires themes, explanations, and narratives. While at times, we struggle to find organizing themes, at other times, especially in more recent times, when we have greater knowledge of our family and its social differentiation appears under way, we find ourselves with multiple and even conflicting themes. I found this to be the case in writing of my maternal great-grandfather, Jacob Linsdau. Jacob came from Prussia as a boy, and he was more successful than his brothers, while remaining identified with German culture. He got a good job at the mills. He married an Irish woman, who had a little money. They had a brood of promising children. He ran a neighborhood saloon on the first floor of their dwelling, the platform for his eight years as alderman on the city council. Then his experiences gave truth to the words of the Athenian statesman Solon, who told the incredibly rich and powerful Lydian King Croesus that no one should be judged happy until he has lived out all his days. Croesus later lost his son and was defeated and captured; things turned against Jacob. In this way I am forced to tell the story of this distinct family, composed of unique individuals and different ethnicities, which experienced the formation of modern industrial society and the birth of mass popular culture, principally as a simple story: the rise and fall of an immigrant.

My mother's stories carved a special corner in my heart for Jacob, the grandfather she called Jake. Her anecdotes about him animated his memory. I still cannot return to Menasha, on the southwest end of Lake Winnebago, with its canals and bridges, mills, bars, and churches, in many of which, one way or another, he had a part, without keenly feeling that I am in his territory. I feel a special kinship with him as a self-made and fallen saloon-keeping patriarch. Indeed, when I discovered that the well in the New Testament at which Christ encountered the Samaritan woman was traditionally thought to be Jacob's Well, I renamed the poem I wrote in 2002 to commemorate my mother's death.

> At Jacob's Well
>
> *When she was young,*
> *Ethel jumped barrels,*
> *Skated circles around life,*
> *And ringed the world with words.*
> *When she was married, and a mother*
> *She was the beacon star of a man and a boy's universe.*
> *As a grandmother, she saved her best play for children.*
> *Until the end, Ethel retained her quick tongue.*
> *German poet Goethe's last words were*
> *"More Light!"*
> *Samaritan Ethel,*
> *Who drank abundantly from her own past,*
> *And memories of her saloon keeping grandfather Jacob,*
> *Last said,*
> *"Give me a drink!"*

My mother knew Jacob for only the first six years of her life. She constantly repeated two stories about him as if they were the marrow of her memory of him. He was the jokester who sent her and her younger sister Mabel to catch farts with paper bags, promising a nickel for each one. And then there was the one about Jake and the church parrot. The local priest had decided to get rid of the foul-tongued bird. Corrupted on the play yard by school children, the parrot couldn't complete an Our Father or a Hail Mary without unleashing a stream of expletives. Once settled into the apartment over the bar, and with no gratitude to the master of the house, the "feathery biped" became a tattletale of high order. He consistently and automatically reported Jake's frequent descents to the bar below. No sooner would

Jake begin to sneak out than the parrot squawked out, "Pa's leaving!" When Jake retaliated by covering the parrot's cage before his exit, the thankless informer, nevertheless, screeched out, "Pa's leaving!" as soon as it heard the first step squeak.

Ethel, however, depicted Jacob as more than a jokester, and she did it with more than anecdotes. He was a man locked in conflict with his wife, Mary Jane O'Brien Linsdau, who had a sharp tongue of her own, especially when the defense of home or children were involved. Their household, by Ethel's account, was an abiding contest between two strong and opposing personalities, magnified by Jacob's firm adherence to German culture of beer, music, and sociability, and Mary Jane's commitment to an Irish culture of story, word, and song. Ethel described the fundamental axis of family life tilting between the two floors of their building. It moved between the family's large living quarters upstairs, where Mary Jane assembled quality goods (silverware and green glass, some of which I have), taught manners, and sought to raise proper and literate children, and Jake's bar and workspace below, from whence wafted up the smell of stale beer and smoke and sounds of men drinking and conversing.

My mother relished telling me that Jake got the last word. A loud German band escorted Jacob to his grave, where he lies today on a prominent hill in a well-appointed row of family tombstones, on a slight knoll near the center of Saint Patrick's Cemetery, which gathers Catholic Irish, German, and Polish alike. He is interred there next to his beloved Mary Jane, their six-year old son, Francis, Mary Jane's mother, Mary (Allen) O'Brien, and Jacob's mother, Elizabeth (Bavelski) Linsdau.

This tension between a husband's bar and a wife's gentility belong at the center of this chapter. But it is a second to the tragic theme of the rise and fall of a plebian patriarch, which emerged from my research and grew out of my increasing identification with him. At the end of his life Jacob saw the world he had so successfully assembled unravel. He had achieved in a single generation what the other men in my family and the majority of immigrants had not accomplished in several generations. Arriving as a young German immigrant in the emerging mill town, Menasha, he adapted his inheritance and

Wedding photos of Jacob Linsdau and Mary Jane O'Brien Linsdau, 1871

invented a German-American identity to take advantage of the new country's freedom and opportunity. He married advantageously. His wife, Mary Jane O'Brien, daughter of a successful Irish Catholic canal digger, bore and raised seven children. He had found steady work for his whole life as a lathe

man at the city's dominant wooden works industry. In his part-time bar, he established a political platform that led him to serve on the city council for four two-year terms. But these successes in domestic and public spheres, no mean accomplishment for a first-generation worker, did not prove a secure foundation in either domestic or public worlds.

A Young Immigrant in a New Mill Town

Of all my ancestors in all my families only Jacob Linsdau, who came as an eighteen-year old directly from West Prussia, mastered the valley into which he first immigrated. He took root in Menasha, Wisconsin, on the northeast corner of Lake Winnebago, which shared a border with twin mill town Neenah, three miles south of Appleton and ten miles north of Oshkosh. His family had made its momentous voyage in 1866, the year Russian Dostoevsky opened the kingdom of the irrational with *Crime and Punishment*, Swede Nobel invented dynamite, and Protestant Prussia, the home of the Linsdau, defeated Catholic Austria in a war for Germany and its soul. Leaving the popular northern port of departure, Hamburg, the Linsdau family sailed on the *Washington*, to Québec, where they arrived on June 22, 1866. Traveling directly from Québec, they came up the St. Lawrence River and across the Great Lakes to Menasha. The immigrant Linsdau family included Jacob's fifty-two-year-old father, John, listed on the ship's manifest as a farmer, his forty-eight-year-old mother, Elizabeth (Bavelski), and three siblings: August, twenty-three, Mary, sixteen, and Anna, twelve. They came from a village of the common name of Neudorf in West Prussia.[1]

I can only guess about the cause or combination of causes that accounted for their emigration. A general economic-demographic explanation suggests that the Linsdaus, like other Prussian farm families and European rural peoples, found themselves without sufficient land or money to live in an increasingly commercial era. In turn, industrialization set the already mobile Prussian population in motion, which amounted to a true revolution in the ratio of urban and rural dwellers.[2] As early as the late 1840s, North America became a magnet for the peoples of Germany, Poland, and Scandinavia in search of home. Two additional direct political causes could have motivated the family's timing of departure. The Linsdaus, Catholic, had three sons eligible for the draft by bellicose Prussia, which attacked Catholic Austria the very month they arrived in the United States. A less dramatic but more likely reason, especially in light of their immigration directly to Menasha, may have been the existence of an immigration chain. Just perhaps they were encouraged and even informally sponsored by Prussian friends.[3] In any case, John and August signed naturalization papers soon after arrival, indicating that the family had come to the United States to stay.

Menasha, though barely a decade old, was already a thriving town with a growing immigrant population.[4] With two water routes soon connecting it to Lake Michigan and the outside world, Menasha had been incorporated as a village in 1853, and by the time Jacob and his family arrived it was composed of thirteen small factories, three small flour mills, and 125 workers.[5] The year of their arrival, local German Catholics organized the parish of St. Mary, the Linsdaus' home church, and a year later they started a parish elementary school.[6]

The waterpower of the steeply descending Fox River, and waterways dug in the early 1850 by Irish immigrants, including Mary Jane's family, gave rise to a cluster of sawmills and grain mills in the twin towns of Neenah and Menasha. Their optimistic leaders praised the potential of the two towns—Neenah for flour milling and Menasha for woodenware. Touting their combined population of six thousand inhabitants, the editor of the *Island Times* argued in 1866 that all that was needed was a shared railroad, which would run thirteen miles to Winnecone, where it would join the Milwaukee and St. Paul Railway, and thus open the twin towns to the entire Midwest. "We will become the Pittsburgh of the West," concluded the editor's economic paean.[7]

Of course, in combination with the direction and capital of an eastern elite, this was dependent equally on the backs of the immigrant labor force. Jacob was a member of those Catholic ethnic working classes that drank beer, danced polkas, practiced marksmanship, and went squirrel hunting in the nearby woods. Showing that they had come to stay, they built impressive churches—St. Patrick's for the Irish, then St. Mary's for the Germans, and finally St. John's for the Polish. The mass schedules of all three were omitted from the town paper.[8] Belonging to the Menasha plebes, Jacob and his kind went on foot, not in carriage, and thus knew the town's muddy and even perilous streets. Poor roads, blanketed with dust, manure, and muck, could be impassible in the winter and swallow nightwalkers with great holes caused by new construction and incomplete sidewalks.

Menasha's streets also hosted crimes, scams, and shams of all sorts. Standing rivalries, bizarre incidents, and irrational occurrences, reported in the paper, played on inhabitants' gullibility, multiplied their fears, and intensified their grudges and resentments.[9] As if to stress the dark and dangerous side of the under classes of Menasha, the paper, which one week announced the coming of the opera to Milwaukee, reported a brawl at Menasha's German Concordia Hall, to which the Linsdaus belonged. In all likelihood, the editorial conjectured, Irish from Oshkosh came over to fight rather than dance. After all, a good fight was the best of entertainment for the young at heart. Fire, however, was a far more deadly threat than fisticuffs. Death, also, burned brightly and brusquely in the town, coming frequently, quickly, and indiscriminately in the form of epidemics of spinal meningitis, influenza, and black smallpox. Sunstroke, scalding, asphyxiation, and drowning punctuated everyday news. But all things considered, life in muddy, violent, and mortal Menasha was, one can guess, superior to the northern European countryside left behind, for here Irish, Scandinavian, German, and Polish immigrants stood a chance of finding work, making money, and assembling a life and space of their own.

Menasha was no Garden of Eden. In this earthly valley immigrants would have to work, save, cooperate, compete, and plot to have a home of their own. Death, sickness, and madness still roamed freely in the valley. Only three years after their arrival in Menasha, father John died. This left, as indicated by the 1870 census, widowed Elizabeth living with two sons, August and Jacob (who was still in school), and two daughters, Mary and Anna. Her property was valued at five hundred dollars and her personal property at one hundred dollars.

By the early 1880s the family had dispersed and rearranged itself. Elizabeth, doing what the old and widowed commonly did, was found living with her younger daughter Anna on a small farm in adjacent Calumet County. John's death also accelerated the children's dispersal into the world to marry and form their own households. However much marriage was moved by passion, the formation of an economic household dictated its schedule.

Marriage followed class lines, for it was imperative that one should marry one's kind—someone who understood and could share a hard and life-long ordeal. Catholicism, also, functioned as moral connective tissue for the working classes, as Jacob and his brothers and sisters showed. In Menasha it bridged unions between the northeastern Germans and Poles (who were intermarried in Prussia) and the Irish.[10] Catholicism would help, in particular, I conjecture, when there existed a disproportionate number of marriageable candidates from one gender or the other.[11]

Jacob's elder brother August also married a neighborhood Irish girl, Catherine Hughes, whose family had arrived in Milwaukee as early as the 1840s. Both the Hughes family and Jacob's in-laws, the O'Briens, spoke English, had been in town a decade before the Linsdaus arrived, and, most significantly, had amassed more land and wealth than recently arrived but far more numerous Germans.[12]

Marrying the Irish Girl Next Door

In marrying the girl next door, Jacob did what the poor had always done: He made a convenient marriage when he was ready to go into the world. No expensive, distant, and laborious courtship was required. He married a family and a person with whom he was familiar and must have found compatible. They took binding vows before their communities. They pledged to advance their household through inescapable hard work, unregulated reproduction, dedicated childrearing, and participation in mutual aid systems with parents, siblings, and even certain neighbors. They left their wedding joined in a lifetime partnership.

Mary Jane knew that in marrying Jacob she got a healthy, energetic, and ambitious man. He labored to learn English, and he was intent on securing a good job at the mills, which he did. Surely, he stood tall in contrast to what might have been her first measure of a husband, Mary Jane's own older brother, Richard. Richard returned home from the Civil War having suffered, as veterans so frequently do, an irreversible defeat in life. He was deaf from cannonades of the artillery and plagued by the terrible and unrelenting bane of hemorrhoids. A subsequent lifetime of menial jobs and small regional migrations strengthened his family's tether to poverty.[13]

Mary Jane, in turn, did all Jacob could expect. She bore him seven children—Richard Austin (1873), John Timothy (1875), Francis Xavier (1879, who died in infancy), Leo Emmett (1882), Mary Elizabeth (1887), my grandfather Joseph William, (1889), and Mabel (1895, who died when six years old). Mary Jane built a comfortable household for her husband, children, and her own mother, who lived with them. Observant and pious, Mary Jane took her Catholicism seriously. To the pleasure of any young man who understood that a good marriage might equal in wealth years of work in field or mill, Mary Jane's trousseau came packed with ample cultural and material goods that would help them establish a place in the world.

Her Irish family was at least a generation in advance of the Germans in settling the Fox River Valley.[14] In the 1855 census for Menasha, Timothy O'Brien and his wife Mary Allen O'Brien, both born in Ireland, are reported belonging to a household of five males and three females. Mary Allen's father Richard and his wife Elizabeth Fox Allen, both of whom were born in Ireland, were living in a household of five males and four females. (Their friends William and Bridget Hughes, also born in Ireland, had three daughters, including Catherine, who married August.) The Allens, Foxes, and O'Briens, who intermarried with the Hugheses and the O'Rourkes, formed Menasha's first Catholic Church, St. Malachi, which as a structure was a mere log cabin located along an Indian trail.

Typical of the pre-famine Great Lakes Irish immigrants, the O'Briens, the Allens, the Foxes, and the Hugheses had worked their way west helping build the expanding American canal system. The Erie Canal, completed in 1825, delivered them to Rochester, New York; from there they went to the Welland Ship Canal, which opened in 1829 and, linking Lake Ontario and Lake Erie, led them, I conjecture, to become residents of St. Catharines, Ontario. From there the O'Briens stopped off for a year or two in Indiana—possibly to work on the great Wabash and Erie Canal—before joining the Allens, who had migrated to Wisconsin's Lake Winnebago and the Fox River Valley.[15] River masters in that community had conjured a winning water route from the

Great Lakes down the Fox west and south to the Mississippi, challenging Chicago as a connection.

The O'Briens, the Allens, and the Foxes utilized the strategy of plow and spade on their migration west, as the Boodrys and the Sayerses used the New England strategy of plow and ax. The plow for land and spade for cash served the Irish poor—both Catholic and Protestant by faith—in their migration and settlement in North America, which began at least two or three generations before the Great Famine of the 1840s. In contradiction to American views of Irish immigrants as the famine-driven people who were Catholic and uniformly lived in large cities, the pre-famine Irish settlers of Ontario and New York, who numbered into the hundreds of thousands, were a rural people divided roughly evenly between Protestants and Catholics. Not dissimilar to the Scots who emigrated because of the Highland Clearances and excess English country folk who left central England, the Irish emigrated to avoid death by overpopulation, grimly foretold by Thomas Malthus. They hopped borders and seas in search of work. Canals and cheap land were their guiding stars west. The strategy of plow and spade yielded savings that permitted them to follow expanding river transportation and canal work in the Upper Midwest. Not that different from that immense stream of ambitious New England poor, each generation of my Irish ancestors hopped and jumped west, human locusts of a sort, ever seeking, ever finding, an equilibrium between necessity and dream, between cash and land.[16]

In the 1850s, with money made, land hoped for, and twenty to twenty-five years elapsed, the Allens and the O'Briens and their kind moved northward from Indiana, Chicago, and Milwaukee to central Wisconsin. The Fox River Valley, freshly opened by the forced removal of the last Ho Chunk (Winnebago) people after 1846, was caught up in a pitch of feverish development.[17] With Fond du Lac established in the south, Oshkosh in the center, and Appleton staked out at the northern end of Lake Winnebago, eastern speculators quickly bought up the principal lands of Neenah and Menasha, both to build new towns and to profit from the sale of real estate. With economic development hinging on building a system of canals and dams, the chance to work on Neenah's and Menasha's waterways brought Timothy and Mary O'Brien and their daughter Mary Jane to the area. They could have wished for no more: here was finally a chance to buy land, start a small farm on which they housed and fed their family, and have paid work building a region's waterways and then working in its mills.

As early as 1854, Timothy O'Brien purchased a small two-and-one-half-acre piece of land on Plank Road that led to Appleton. He bought it for two hundred dollars from Mr. Doughty, one of Menasha's founders. In the 1860 census, Timothy described himself as a farmer, not a laborer, who headed a family consisting of his wife, Mary Allen O'Brien, and five children: Richard, Elizabeth, Timothy, Mary Jane, and Dennis. Mary O'Brien's brother, Richard, and his wife, Elizabeth (Fox) Allen, appear to have come to the region with more resources than their daughter and son-in-law. In the 1850 census, Richard, only thirty-two years old, and Elizabeth, twenty-four, had been south in Lamartine, Fond du Lac County, where they held real estate valued at one thousand dollars. Ten years later, they were living in a house on Menasha's Broad Street, set on a large lot on which Jacob and Mary Jane also built their primary residence. Richard worked on the Menasha dam and canal. The Green Bay and Mississippi Canal Company ledger for 1856 recorded him as heading up a team of thirteen workers (in all likelihood fellow Irishmen) who used an undetermined number of horses, for which he was to be paid $45.50. He was given an additional nine dollars for acting as a foreman for six days.

So in marrying Mary Jane O'Brien, Jacob Linsdau married into hardworking, responsible, and ambitious stock. At the same time he inherited the successes of Timothy O'Brien, whose widow Mary lived with her daughter Mary Jane, to whom she ultimately deeded her property and willed her money in 1893, several years before her death. No amount of labor on Jacob's part would have secured what he gained by the simple act of marrying the Irish girl next door.

A Job in the Mill and a Saloon in the House

A good marriage, a combination of craft skills, and a head for management allowed Jacob to succeed in the valley as his brothers August and John did not.[18] He outlasted the contraction of production and employment that swept the entire valley from 1873 to 1879, which, as we earlier observed, sent carpenter James Sayers and his wife Charlotte to try their fortunes in the well-advertised fresh lands of Kansas.[19] And no doubt Jacob and his family benefited from the subsequent growth of population and economic activity in the town and region, which saw Winnebago County population increase from approximately 20,000 to 60,000, while that of Menasha more than quadrupled from 1,500 to approximately 7,000, from 1860 to 1900. A second railroad that connected the town directly to the northern white pine lumber country transformed Menasha into a principal wood milling center, which by the 1880s housed three large sawmills and two large woodworking factories, using six million feet of timber annually, and the beginnings of a local paper industry.[20]

Jacob's particular skills as a leader and a carpenter, which according to my mother even took him on occasion to Milwaukee to carve those altarlike bars that grace the town pubs, differentiated him from the common mill workers and redundant rough carpenters. They probably won him a position as lathe foreman at the Menasha Wooden Ware Company, where Jacob worked the rest of his career.[21] With a workforce totaling approximately 225 men, making it Menasha's largest employer, Menasha Wooden Ware evolved, all to Jacob's benefit, from a low-paying company relying on seasonal workers into the town's best employer.[22] Its workers in the 1870s already received a dependable $40 a month for a six- or even a seven-day week, in comparison to flour mill workers, who received only $30 a month. By the 1880s, skilled workers like Jacob earned $50 to $60 a month.[23] With wages such as these, amounting to $600 or so dollars per annum, a fully employed worker could meet annual costs for food, fuel, rent, and other living expenses. If working-class families like the Linsdaus and O'Briens could pool the additional incomes of wives and children, they could put aside resources for a rainy day, buy a home, seek out farmland, or yet begin to buy, for the sake of display and respectability, non-essential clothing and non-utilitarian household goods.[24]

Doing what many entrepreneurial individuals did throughout emerging

industrial and ethnic America (as is still the case in Menasha and my wife's
region of coal-mining Pennsylvania), Jacob further supplemented the family
income by running a bar at night on the first floor of his house. Taking up only
half the first floor, the bar left the other half for his woodworking, a horse and
cart, and later, a bicycle shop. Additionally, the bar strengthened the family
position by supplying daily news and gossip about the local community, while
fueling Jacob's local political ambitions. Joining economic and communal
functions of the household on one floor under Jacob, and the familial and
emotional household on a second under the control of Mary Jane, their house
was a substantial building. With dimensions of fifty by fifty feet, it was built
of cream-colored brick, which characterized the bigger and better homes
of the period. Still standing, and now providing lower-cost apartments on a
block with a bar and auto-repair shop, the Linsdau house dwarfed the average
wood-frame homes set on small lots of forty by eighty feet.[25]

The prominence of the Linsdau residence placed them in the center of
Menasha's activity and commerce. The home was located on Broad Street,
which, as indicated by its name, serviced Menasha's docks and served as the
town's principal commercial avenue until the railroad and highways superseded water travel. Their home looked south across the Fox River toward
Doty Island. Only two blocks from St. Mary's church, Jacob's residence and
bar was located among the Catholic working classes.

A Prominent Alderman

Jacob's rise to prominence in his community did not stem from his work
at the Wooden Ware Company but from his role as a town alderman and a
saloon owner. *Jacob's well*, so to speak, like ten to twenty bars in town, opened
after work and closed sometime before midnight. More than "a watering
trough," and perhaps the most influential German bar in town, it played an
important social, cultural, and political role in ethnic Menasha. Gathering
news and gossip from street, mill, fraternal organizations, and church, and
registering resentments and complaints, Jacob's saloon proved a place politi-
cally to caucus. It appeared to have mobilized Jacob even more than his cli-

ents; in 1883 he first threw his hat in the arena, running for a two-year term as alderman.

Jacob eventually served four two-year terms, in 1885–86, 1887–88, 1893–94, and 1895–96, as one of two aldermen in the fourth ward. Jacob won his first election in 1884 by a slim margin: ninety-nine to ninety-four. He boldly ran against and beat out rival New Englander Elisha Smith, the founder of Menasha's pail factory, which failed in the economic downturn of 1872. His son Charles reorganized the company as the Menasha Wooden Ware. Voicing the interest of wet Catholic immigrants, Jacob opposed Smith, a known and ardent prohibitionist, who donated to Smith Park on the condition that "any spirituous, malt, ardent or intoxicating liquors or drinks in any quantity whatever," were prohibited, along with such low-brow entertainment as circuses, adult games, and camping. On Sundays more restrictive laws permitted the park's use for only religious and temperance meetings.[26]

Though adamant in his position that town minutes be published in the area's German newspapers, Jacob, nevertheless, fully mastered both everyday English and the governing language of Robert's Rules of Order, so rich in "whereas," "be it resolved," and other arcane terms. Alderman Linsdau was never shy about speaking out. On the contrary, he strongly expressed opinions and deftly seconded proposals, which, with few exceptions, passed on such regular but vital issues as zoning, assessments, taxes, and welfare cases like the "man who was unwilling to keep his mother or pay for her keep." He also sat on such important boards as those for health, the poor, and bridges. Although his votes were generally free of direct self-interest, except for voting to renew his own saloon license and a few other small affairs, they were not free of class and ethnic interests.[27]

Alderman Linsdau consistently supported progressive causes, believing that Menasha must keep up with sister-city Neenah, in particular, and progress, in general. He voted to raise levies for roads, bridges, sidewalks, graveling, sewers, electrification, lighting, and telephones; he was unwavering in his support for a fund of forty thousand dollars for building a high school and favored the establishment of a public library. He supported keeping streets clean, prohibitions against running dogs, the hiring a second policeman for night patrol, and, representing the committee for the poor, he made a motion for allotments of wood for the needy, who suffered winter worse than any other season. Voting for the purchase of fire engines, bells, and hoses, he moved to increase punishment of firebugs. Fire was a constant threat to homes and mills. In a single memorable incident, in May 1877, fire destroyed six mills and a lumberyard before it was brought under control.[28] A disaster of equal proportion occurred in 1886, when a paper mill explosion killed eight workers from Jacob's home parish and ten workers from other parishes in Menasha.

Concerned that the city keep its credit rating, Alderman Linsdau urged the government to be prompt in paying its debts.[29] At the same time, Jacob, consistent with his notion of the benefits of an active government, supported equalizing and raising taxes, which had the effect of driving industrialists, with few exceptions, to build their mansions in Neenah, which had lower taxes. (To this day, rich and mansion-filled Neenah is upper-class, distinguishing it from working-class Menasha.) Revealing his class bias and apparently not afraid of reprisal at work, Jacob argued that the wealthy should pay more in taxes. In one instance, he affirmed tripling the taxes of the Menasha Paper and Pulp Company, from one thousand to three thousand dollars.

Defending his and his own kind's interests, Jacob adamantly defended the interests of saloonkeepers, especially against the imposition of a discriminating tax burden on the saloon business.[30] During his terms in office, Jacob repeatedly took the side of saloonkeepers and their patrons during the "drinking wars," which pitted populous Catholic Germans and Poles and less numerous Irish against an alliance of upper-class Protestant New Englanders in early prohibition campaigns, marked by the 1893 founding of the national Anti-Saloon League, a milestone in the emerging temperance movement.[31]

In January 1897, Jacob found himself at the center of a local cultural maelstrom that churned around bars and dancing and exposed his personality. He was the only alderman who refused to summon saloon owners Rohloff & Utley and Joseph Krautkramer before the council in order to consider the revocation of their liquor licenses, which cost fifteen hundred dollars to purchase, for willfully and unlawfully selling liquor to minor John Gronof-

ski, who appeared at his job at the Menasha Wooden Ware Company intoxicated. Not mincing his words, Linsdau claimed that he had looked into the
matter and decided that "both the father and son Gronofski were habitual
drunkards, the father as bad as the child." He threw fat on the fire by saying
that he allowed his children to drink beer, and he defied anyone to say—
although soon many would be able to say—they had seen any one of his children drunk. "The whole thing," Linsdau concluded, is the father's, not the
saloonkeeper's, responsibility.[32]

Alderman Miner replied. He did not see what Linsdau's children had to
do with the case and contended that this was a matter of law, to which Linsdau retorted that he believed that "the council was a body of men and ought
to act like men. At any rate I am a man and I don't care what the rest of you
are. This case is ridiculous. If it were brought to court, it would be dismissed
at once." Despite his passion, Alderman Linsdau's motion for dismissal was
called and failed.

The following day the editor the *Menasha Evening Breeze* took Linsdau to
task:

> *Alderman Linsdau knows how to bring up a family so that they will not drink too*
> *much at the beer barrel when they are turned loose at it; but he apparently has*
> *not learned the art of being a dignified gentleman in debate. His remarks last*
> *night in the presence of ladies who visited the council room were questionable.*
> *Indeed, they would not be considered suitable had none but men been present.*

Four days later, on January 18, the local Union Temperance League, whose
circuit speakers visited Menasha in the 1870s, took action. With Methodist
and Congregational church members singing hymns, the Congregational
Reverend S. T. Kidder made "a strong plea for the protection of boys and
urged people to stand by the aldermen who are striving to see that the law
is maintained."[33] On the issue of drink, Jacob stood as Kidder's foe and represented majority Catholic and ethnic Menasha, which, as late as 1895, still
had twice as many foreign-born residents as native born; the town's taverns
sponsored horse-drawn floats featuring men dressed in their Sunday best
with their mugs held high.[34] In any case, Jacob and his sort defeated Kidder

and his kind. At the January 22 council meeting, motions to dismiss charges against Rohloff & Utley and Joseph Krautkramer were passed four to three, with Linsdau casting his yea and Alderman Whipple, the other representative of the strongly Polish and German Fourth Ward, absenting himself from the meeting.

The End of a Plebian Patriarch

In June 1898, a year and a half after Jacob left office, the Semi-centennial Souvenir Edition of *The Menasha Press* featured Jacob as one of the town's most prominent men.

> *J. A. Linsdau, a prominent citizen of the fourth ward, was born in Germany in 1847, and immigrated to Quebec in 1866, coming to Menasha in the same year. During his thirty-two years of residence here Mr. Linsdau had figured prominently in business and political circles and for eight years served as an alderman from his ward in the city council. In that capacity he took a firm stand on questions ... and was known for his fearless advocacy of whatever he believed to be right. At present he conducts a well-stocked liquor store and hall in his brick block on Broad Street, and his affairs are prospering. For many years after his arrival here he followed the trade of carpentering, and also acted as lathe foreman for the Menasha Wooden Ware Company, but during the past twelve has been engaged in business. Mr. Linsdau is a member of the Germania Society in whose affairs he has always taken a commendable interest.*[35]

Twenty years later the family used these exact words for Jacob's obituary. At fifty years of age, two decades before his death, Jacob had reached the apex of his public arc. In this two-class mill-town society, he had not climbed the imposing wall that divided worker from owner. In fact, the division was exacerbated in the last decades of the century by walkouts and strikes across the whole valley.[36] The principal grievance of labor against ownership focused on the primary complaint that there was "no chance to graduate to foreman, superintendent, or businessman." What Jacob had done earlier was increasingly impossible after the prosperity of the 1880s receded. Most students, including the Linsdau children, went to work in the mills before finishing high school; education did not yet offer compensatory careers. "As the century came to a close," a newspaper article remarked, "a subtle but major change had occurred. A new generation of workmen would become a caste of laborers unable to pull themselves up by the bootstraps, as the mill owners had themselves done a generation before."[37] The frontier of opportunity, almost always so brief and ephemeral, had closed in Menasha. Hope for money and the things it could buy receded.

Immigrant Jacob had not climbed far enough to free his family or himself from subservience to the mills and their wages. Neither profits from his saloon, nor prestige from political office, nor Mary Jane's dowry, had spared the family from the closed fate of being mill workers. His children remained captives. Their lives would be seen as tedious, humdrum, and testing when they, the children of Menasha, looked in nearby mirrors of prosperity, so much on display in contemporary Neenah, where a dozen millionaires and their imitators had built impressive mansions. There the rich put their wealth on full display with yachts and sailing races, outings and parties. The Babcocks of Kimberly Clark Paper Company put on one such party for a friend's daughter in their most spacious and lovely mansion, which had a half dozen fireplaces and a book-lined study (which my wife and I recently saw, thanks to a generous descendant). To the party they invited six hundred guests and brought black servers all the way from Milwaukee to cater the social event.[38] From the shadows of Menasha's mills, Jacob's children watched a world engaging in diversifying and intensifying leisure promenaded on the streets of Neenah and on Menasha's own Brighton Beach.

The 1900 edition of *Bunn's Menasha Directory* left no doubt on what side of the street the Linsdaus, as a family and clan, sat. It listed Jacob working as a millwright (a person who designs, builds, or repairs mills or mill machinery) at Wooden Ware. His son Emmett was described simply as a laborer (a worker without a place of steady employment), and son John, married and no longer living at home, as working at Cook Paper Company. Brother August, who lived on Plank Road, was also listed as laborer. One of his two daughters, Nellie, was working at the Gilbert Paper Company. The 1905 directory indicated that the family still remained part of the Menasha's laboring classes. Both Emmett, and now Jacob's youngest son, my grandfather, sixteen-year-old William, had joined their father in working at Wooden Ware. Daughter "May" now worked at Gilberts Mills.

The 1910 town directory only confirmed that the family's destiny was still tied to the mills. Jacob, sixty-seven years old—my very age as I first sat and wrote this passage—still labored at Wooden Ware, which hired approximately 50 percent of Menasha's workforce. In 1910 my grandfather William, who once worked at Wooden Ware, now a young man of twenty-one and married, also worked in Neenah at the Bergstrom Paper Mills, while May, still living at home on Broad Street, worked at the Jersild K. Company. The family exception to mill work, Emmett, identified by his more formal name, Leo, in the directory, was described as a photographer.[39]

A Man's Home Is Only Partly His Castle

Though the principal breadwinner, owner of a bar, and city alderman, Jacob was not the undisputed king of his own household—for he lived with Mary Jane O'Brien. In addition to all the powers she held as a determined woman, wife, mother of his children, keeper of the hearth, and guardian of the second floor, Mary Jane had yet one greater power: She had owned the property on Broad Street since 1886. In 1899, her mother Mary deeded her interest in her adjacent property—Lot 22, Block 18—to Mary Jane for one dollar "on the condition that she be provided for the rest of her natural life good and wholesome food, medicine and medical aid, . . . suitable clothes, with a bed, bedding, and the payment of her funeral expenses."[40] Business mortgages on the family property by Mary Jane, its owner, of $550 in 1890 and $900 in 1895, suggested that she had significant control over the household money, while the debt, absent additional investments in property, implies significant borrowing against limited assets.

An inverse ratio might apply: as tall as Jacob may have stood in public, he may have been short at home, where clear commands do not cut through the tangle of emotional underbrush. A father can labor years to dig a deep well, from which he believes that his children can draw good and lasting waters, only to see his children refuse to drink the water or spit it out. I suspect, which is often all a family historian can do, that as his children aged, he had good reasons to prefer the foamy suds of the bar below to the brew of heady, strong, and independent personalities above. Aside from his mother-in-law Mary, who lived with Mary Jane and Jacob until she died in January 1900, there were under Jacob and Mary Jane's roof in 1905 children John, Emmett, Mary, William, infant Mabel, and Austin's Danish wife from Neenah, Dorothy (Theda) Jorgensen, and their three children, Dorothea (Dorothy), Donald, and Robert—but not Austin himself.

All of Jacob's children defied or disappointed Jacob. With each of his seven children inflicting a unique pain on him, Jacob suffered deaths, mistakes, ingratitude, and wrongs. Austin perhaps caused the worst pain. In 1903 he ran away from home, abandoning his wife and their three children. Was he too sick to work? Could he not live in Menasha without supporting his own family? Knowing only that he publicly sang and organized bicycle races, we are left, as genealogists and family historians so often are, with a fact that, standing alone without story, becomes a solitary unexplained megalith on an empty landscape. My mom said he didn't really run far away at all— nowhere distant like California, the mysterious place where popular myth romantically assigned contemporary familial runaways. Perhaps he only fled to a farm in a nearby township, where he took up a life as a hired hand. Perhaps he committed himself to the poor house—or yet the sanatorium? My mother said that Jacob was left in the dark about Austin, so as not to reopen the wound his oldest son had caused. They let Jacob, like a blind Leer, believe that Austin never contacted home again. Theda hid the fact that he had written during these years and even sent socks for his children from the sanatorium, where he was dying.[41] In 1908, Theda herself, only thirty-four years old, died of tuberculosis, perhaps caught from Austin. Jacob and Mary Jane took their grandchildren into their care.[42]

If Austin's abandonment struck Jacob with a single blow, Leo Emmett repeatedly disappointed Jacob over his whole youth with his ingrained preference for the arts, writing, and music over work. As part of a first generation that tasted the abundance and leisure of wage-earning industrial society, Emmett, for industrious Jacob, who was nevertheless a bit of showman himself, must have been the cricket who sang away the fall, ignoring the coming of winter. A mutant from, and at odds with, the family work ethic, Emmett loved the stage. As early as 1900 the Oshkosh newspaper summarized a minstrel performance in which he participated at the Germania Opera House. Angry working-class patriarch Jacob would have had Emmett find work, but Emmett—clever, charming, and handsome—sought an audience. My mother, who like Homer and the Greeks of old didn't offer a name without attaching a description to follow identification, depicted her beloved godfather Emmett as the nemesis of Jacob. He was "a mama's boy," who hid behind the skirts of Mary Jane. On one occasion, Mary Jane literally hid Emmett in the apartment above from irate Jacob, the wrathful father below. She indulged Emmett's love of words and preoccupation with the arts—which included music, playwriting, stage performances, and photography. For a few years, seeking to join art with making a living, Emmett set up his own photographic studio. My collection of his photos for a small "illustrated history of Menasha" and postcards, with "Linsdau Studio" printed in bold on the back, features images of the town's streets, buildings, plants, bridges, and an active town of stylish people, automobiles, parades, and his own peers and relatives, including my dapper-looking grandfather and his first cousin Bernard, obviously dressed in their Sunday best.[43]

Proving himself a versatile entertainer, as old-timers often were and had to be, Emmett, when on stage, sang popular tunes, told jokes, carried on pantomimes, and imitated Irish brogue, which he no doubt modeled on his mother, grandmother Mary Allen, and her relatives. He did his imitations and jokes, which were often one and the same, in return for drinks at bars well into his fifties, when he lived on the east side of Detroit. When my grandparents were dating, around 1910, he toured his vaudeville acts to nearby Green Bay, Oshkosh, and Appleton. In fact, my grandmother bragged that Emmett once recruited her and my grandfather for one of his shows. As a beloved, story-filled, and well-entertained grandchild, I remember my comic grandfather as one who could play the part: he was always stomping his foot to music, clowning by putting on women's hats, and punctuating his

William Linsdau and his cousin Bernard Linsdau,
in a photo taken by William's brother, Emmett

long and complex humorous stories with short Pat and Mike jokes. On his Horner Harmonica, key of C, he could belt out a handful of popular tunes of his day. His repertoire, which often set his dog a howling, included his favorites, "Sidewalks of New York" and "Bicycle Built for Two."

One of my most precious heirlooms is a typed copy of one of many of Emmett's works, "Uncle Dick's Will." Described as a skit in one act, it is written by Emmett Linsdau and to be played by Miss Malenofsky & Emmett Linsdau. Its subject and theme was a world entirely alien to earthy and practical Jacob's. Protagonist Jack's opening lines confess his bad luck. His measly old Uncle Dick, who must have been "Looney, crazy, drunk, intoxicated or plastered, made a will requiring Jack to marry his pug nosed, freckled face, ignorant country cousin, Alice." His answer to this dilemma comes when he remembers Alice's absolute determination not to marry a farmer, in the disguise of which he will meet her at the train station the next day. Equally condemned by Uncle Dick's will to an unwanted marriage to Jack, whom she takes to be a rube, Alice finds an answer in her memory as well. She remembers how he had an aversion to actresses, especially the snobbish ones from New York. So at the Menasha train station, playing-acting Alice encounters cousin Jack disguised as a farmer. The remainder of the short play is one of discovery, based on an initial mutual agreement that New York is bigger than Menasha, though Jack resists believing that it could be larger than Milwaukee. Finally, in the course of a warming conversation, mutual confessions are made: Alice admits that she is only a telephone girl on the stock exchange and never was on the stage at all. Taking off his disguises, Jack says, "I ain't no darn old hayseed." They concede that they have fooled each other—"one horse apiece," they conclude, using an old phrase for "being even." The curtain comes down, with the two in love and willing to become rich by satisfying their uncle's will. Jack admits, "I have taken quite a fancy to you. I'd like to paddle your canoe." And Alice reciprocates by admitting she knows "no one in the wide world, whose tootsie wootsie I would [rather] be." So Emmett ingratiates himself to a Menasha audience, willing to satirize a New York high society that assumes farmers, the very stock of his ancestry, are a bunch of rubes, hayseeds, and clodhoppers.

Aunt May, probably at graduation from nursing school, about 1914

However, Emmett's drinking caused Jacob more pain than his superficial plays and play-acting. He was the public drunk whom alderman Jacob had publicly declared he would never raise in his family. According to my mother, Emmett once, suffering hallucinations and delirium tremens, paraded downtown nude and sporting an umbrella. Emmett added to Jacob's disappointment when he married an unwed mother, Marie Nys from Green Bay. Shortly after the wedding, Emmett and Marie left her first child with her parents and followed restless older brother John to Detroit. They also had hopes of better times afar.

Sister Mary Elizabeth, my mother's favorite "Aunt May" and my favorite great-aunt, also defied Jacob in a singular way. May worked in the mills as late as 1910, when she was twenty-three. In all likelihood influenced by the opening of the Theda Clark Nursing School in Neenah, May decided that she would become a nurse. Jacob saw this vocation in which women handled men's naked bodies as equivalent to becoming a prostitute. But despite Jacob's vehement objections and a deep rift between them, May, always of strong opinion and singular determination, went into nursing and then went on to serve as an army nurse in World War I and a Detroit public health nurse. May, who never married, was the only of the Linsdau children to establish herself in a career, in what was at the time a new and emerging profession. The youngest of Jacob's living children, my grandfather William, surely disappointed when he married a Protestant from Appleton. But the young couple may have placated Jacob when she converted, married in the Catholic church, and bore two children, while William worked at a paper mill in Neenah and stayed in town until Jake and Mary Jane died.

A Stranger at Home

As family troubles pilloried Jacob at home, so a dark cloud of suspicion and accusation formed a nimbus around his head in public. With the U.S. declaration of war against Germany, Jacob saw his new fatherland turn against Germany and the German culture in which he took pride. Even though Jacob had married an Irishwoman, the daughter of an early settler and a member of St. Patrick's Church, and even though he conducted himself as a good and loyal American and even a local official, he did not escape the taint of being German. Once war was declared against Germany in 1917, it did not matter that his family left West Prussia fifty years before. Nothing would spare him and German descendants throughout Wisconsin, from suspicion. His local Germania Benevolent Society's *Victory Handbook*, which included recipes from its members, was a dry leaf in the strong winds of enlistment, loyalty oaths, the selling and buying war bonds, and the call to fight the Huns. Jacob, like other German immigrants across the country, had invested an adult life in embracing the United States, while trying to keep a tradition intact. But intentions no longer counted. Dual identities were forbidden; dual associations in any form were suspect.[44] Jacob was made an alien in Menasha.

Living in one of the zones that the Wisconsin Loyalty League counted in its Sedition Map as "most infected by Pro-Germanism," suspicion fell on Jacob and the Winnebago Germans.[45] My grandmother Frances told me of an evening when she and a groups of friends were hauled to the local police station because a passerby heard them speaking German. My mother, who near the end of her own days enjoyed saying, to get a laugh, "It's hell to get old!" described the last year of her Grandpa Jacob's life, suggesting that the bar was still open and he still led the band: "He couldn't lead the German band anymore. People stopped drinking at his bar. Some even paraded down the street and threw rocks at his bicycle shop, which he had set up on the bottom floor next to the bar." With a candor never shown until her waning years, my mother recounted the family's repudiation of its German inheritance by changing its name from Linsdau to Linsdeau, thus changing the distinct German "au" sound to the softer French and English "oo" and making an orthographic attempt to be taken as French or Irish. More than once my mother told me that to celebrate the surrender of Germany and the end of the war, May bought her a new dress, gave her an American flag to wave, and marched her in Menasha's victory parade. And then, as if it this were connected to France, my mother would break out singing the first line of the French national anthem, the Marsellaise, "*Allons enfants de la Patrie / Le jour de gloire est arrivé.*"

The Last Cup

The last cup to be drunk in life, as if to make our farewell easier, is often the bitterest. With neither energy nor chance to start anew, last defeats wound irretrievably. There are no fresh dreams to dispel disillusionment. Hope no longer sparks an earthly heart; desire no longer arouses old bones; wish has run out of one. No longer prominent in the town below and never lord of the apartment above, everything Jacob had made and won had been taken back. Never a prince, disarmed by age, Jacob was left a defeated plebian patriarch. The very well he had dug in this new land had gone dry.

The historical curtain came down on the drama of Jacob and his generation of immigrants. His migration was forgotten and his settlement depreciated by his children, who lived in an increasingly industrialized and rapidly modernizing world. Cars and trucks began to travel where horses once plodded. First the train and then the automobile sped toward a new order of connectivity, wired by electricity and telephone. In cities, education and leisure defined an emerging middle class, while the markets and fashions of Chicago and New York took up in their prying hands the rest of the nation. As instantaneity approached simultaneity, Jacob himself moved from the temporal to the eternal. On April 10, 1918, coincident with the last great German spring offensive, Jacob died. His death was celebrated with a mass at St. Mary's, his home church.

The Queen Must Die, Too!

In February of the following year, as the Allied Powers gathered to put the world together with ideas and newly created democracies, Mary Jane died. She spent the last days of her widowhood in her second-floor home alone. May was serving as a Red Cross nurse in Fort Sheridan, Illinois. Emmett and his wife had joined his brother John in Detroit, where he worked on the lowest rung as a day laborer at what was called "gang work." Only William and Frances, with my mother Ethel and Aunt Mabel, living in next door Neenah, stopped in to comfort Mary Jane.

Mary Jane's remarkable long black hair had turned completely white. A cherished family letter to son John Linsdau from his wife Barbara offers a last description of Mary Jane: "Poor Ma, I didn't think when I left her that it would be the last time I'd ever see her. I will never forget how she looked when she stood at the top of the stairs in her white nightdress and her white hair down: She look so sad, poor old dear." Barbara continued, seeking to console John, who had gone to Wisconsin to be with his mother at her very end, "Her suffering is over now, and I hope that she is with Pa again, so don't grieve so hard dear and make yourself sick. You know she would rather be there than in this cold lonesome world, when the one you love has gone."[46]

Mary Jane was an invalid during her last years, according to my mother, as a result of a local priest's curse. Mary Jane and Jacob, so the story runs, had a six-year-old daughter, Mabel, who died in 1901 after a two-week bout of brain fever. She was buried at St. Patrick's, where Jacob and Mary Jane were married and their children were baptized, with a display of wealth. On the following Sunday, the priest, whom I construe to be long-time St. Patrick's parish priest and reputed English scholar, Father Dekelver, chose, as his unmistakable target, the Linsdau family sitting in their pew before the pulpit, and sermonized against those who wasted their money on the dead. (No doubt, he exhorted under the theme of Christ's words, "Let the dead bury the dead!") The family responded by getting up and filing out of the church. As Mary Jane, the last of the family to leave, crossed the threshold, the priest shouted at her, "If you leave this church, you will never walk again." She left despite his curse, and a while later, Mary Jane never walked again. After this incident, Mary Jane and Jacob no longer attended St. Patrick's but went to St. Mary's, the German parish, which buried them both.[47]

The priest, in any case, had not cost Mary Jane her faith. One of John's granddaughters said Mary Jane, without her Jacob, spent her lasts days sitting among her religious statues, praying. She wore wool robes next to her skin and prayed the rosary continuously, showing particular devotion to one of the most passionate and familial of Catholic images, the Sacred Heart of Christ.[48]

8

Cousins of the Tongue

Cousins are woven in and out of a lifetime's experience. They are few and many, near and far, old and young, pretty much the same, and oh-so-terribly different. Cousins, fellow grand-children, both make a family and constitute society. They establish pathways and vestibules, they are boundaries and walls. Mirrors in which we see and know others and ourselves, cous-ins reveal a group's capacity for both duplication and change. Usually of greater numbers, of diverse degrees of proximity, and spanning generations, cousins more than brothers and sisters illustrate a family's potential for variety—the dominant but incalculable combina-tions residing within a parent's genes, ways, and actions. A given collection of cousins can be labeled as a set of stray atoms, distinct mutants, unanticipated deviations—or simply odd balls. Surely cousins, who mix the family's genes with those of many others, form the cusp between family and society. In studying them, we grasp the formation and dissolution of the family; we trace the family's settlement and migration, upper and downward mobil-ity, practice of virtue and adherence to vice. Family historians must measure any project they undertake by the number and types of cousins they intend to include, for they define the reach of our research and the breadth of imagination. And I found in the case of first cousins Ethel, my mother, and Vern, son of William's brother Emmett, cousins use each other to determine a fixed point in the changing heavens of modern society.

Ethel bubbled over with energy and enthusiasm. Pert and perky, she verged on stuttering when she talked. Her wit and lip often outraced reason, her anger and generosity constantly outpaced her good sense. Keenly aware of her own physical energy and buoyancy, speed of gesturing and speech, Ethel cast herself to the subject of the popular song of her youth, "Five foot two, eyes of blue/ But oh, what those five foot could do/ Has anybody seen my girl?"

The spillover of Ethel's kinetic energy might just have landed me in the second grade in speech class as a stutterer, soon diagnosed as simply trying to talk too fast. I never disputed her strong arms, having received a few solid hits from her wooden whipping spoon. To ward off intruders, she kept a sawed-off pool stick handle in the front closet of our home on Evanston Street. She once advised her longtime friend, Violet, whose husband Ray was drinking too much and staying out too late, to shove him down the basement steps when he came home. Mom had strong and quick legs as well. On one occasion, to my embarrassment, she beat two of my ten-year old friends in a half block race. She once ran hurdles in grade school, and she wanted to jump barrels for one of the local Detroit skating clubs, but her father wouldn't permit it. Well into her thirties, she was quick to put on her ice skates when the pond in the field beyond the house froze.

Ethel had a strong streak of independence. I once saw her dress down a man who took his dog to a school yard "to do its business." She also informed a ticketing policeman, measuring the distance between the curb and the inside tire of a parked car, that if he had nothing better to do than this, she would never again give a penny to the city police fund. She undoubtedly modeled her sassiness on her father's standard command to the insubordinate world, "Kiss my ass!"—and on her favorite Aunt May's come-hell-or-high-water attitude. Like the working-class youth of her generation, by sixteen Ethel had quit school and was contributing to the family pot, something I was automatically expected to do a generation later when I lived at home while teaching high school in nearby Royal Oak. Ethel held a variety of jobs, including line work at Roseville pottery, but the job she most recalled was clerking in the mid-1930s at Benhur Sobin's Five and Ten Cent Store. She opened the store in the morning, sold all sorts of goods, and cleaned up at night, which required covering the food for the next day and sweeping the store with sawdust. She impressed on me, exactly why I was not sure, how important Sobin considered selling something to the first customer who entered the store. Apparently, the Sobins thought well of Ethel, who could read and count well, was quick to catch on, and had the gift of gab. They transferred her to their cousin's retail store in Toledo, where she lived alone. At one point, she claimed she considered marrying Sobin's son, who was studying medicine at the University of Michigan, but declined him when he was emphatic about not wanting to have children.

My mother had a mean streak, which, as she admitted with a degree of braggadocio, she displayed in taunting her younger sister Mabel and continued throughout her life when she got angry with someone. Her temper was formidable. But she also had a generous disposition, which was rich in sympathy, understanding, and forgiveness. She always found time and energy for family, friends, and neighbors. Regularly she plunged into things heart first, only to surface to disappointment when she experienced ingratitude. Ethel particularly liked to join and direct children in play. Like a big sister, which she was, she sponsored children's games, told them jokes, played cards, set up playhouses, and formed them into groups. She did this with the neighborhood children, my cousins, and my own grandchildren. She frequently issued the plaint that it was too bad she could have only one child—and how circumstances and events discouraged her and my reluctant father from adopting additional children.

What most distinguished Ethel was her loquaciousness. Cousin Vern Linsdau, a talker himself, said of my mom, "The tongue will be the last organ to go on that woman." The connection between her mind and tongue was nearly instantaneous. It was impossible at times to tell which fired first. She frequently talked herself into her thoughts and her feelings. Words provided the materials out of which she assigned meanings. Once she misnamed or mispronounced a name or thing, so it was dubbed and so it remained thereafter. Ethel, granddaughter of Jake the bartender, stood out at banter, which along with bestowing and utilizing nicknames played a large part in her and her generation's ribald humor. The speed of her wit outmatched all reasoning and made it hard for me to deny the power of intuition over rational explanation. In any case, the burst of words that often constituted her greetings and farewells threw slow-tracked people off balance, which she enjoyed doing and bragging about up to very last years of her life. Someone would say, "Hello, Ethel!" and Mom would shoot back, "What did you say?"—a pause— "Why did you call me 'Asshole?'" To people who asked her how she was doing, she frequently responded, "Half and Half," and then reminded them that was name of a brand of pipe tobacco. And she nearly predictably shot back the less than picturesque, "It's hell to get old!" When she was in her early eighties, she told a fellow resident at her senior housing residence, with whom she was waiting for a pizza delivery, "You get the pizza and I get the pizza man!"

Ethel was addicted to that widespread vice of overusing the telephone. With that big, black, heavy receiver in her hand, sitting on her sewing chair in the dining room, she, to use my father's phase, "hashed and rehashed things" for hours on end. Once, waiting for her to end one of her seemingly interminable conversations, I lay on my back, put two marbles in my mouths, and accidentally swallowed them. They were recovered a few days later—but still she talked on and on. As she grew older she seemed to have even less control over her talking. Occasionally, when engaged in what father called "a talking jag," she went too far in embroiling herself in the affairs of others, including those of her niece and godchild, brother Bill's daughter. Out in public, completely out of the blue, she would address a perfect stranger, saying something that was funny but at times made no sense at all.

A true grandchild of Jacob Linsdau, Ethel lit up the world with words. With pulsing energy and a remarkable memory, on her best days, she sparked and sustained conversation. With a wagging tongue, which may have been the magic wand that turned her son into a historian and the garrulous person he is, she enlivened the dull, sullen, reserved, and calculating world. On her bad days, her talk simply manifested the curse of the loquacious: talking too much and making too little sense.

Ethel continually canvassed her childhood memories to form a repertoire of favorite stories. She had a little neighborhood girlfriend whose buttocks had one white cheek and one black cheek. Ethel charged all the kids a nickel to sneak a peak at this two-toned rump, which was exposed by the simple dropping of her drawers in the alley. She reported herself chanting from her school yard toward the Protestant school across the road, "Catholic, Catholic, ring the bell/Protestant, Protestant, go to hell!"

Beyond these slightly off-color stories that won her attention at their first telling, Ethel had more serious and compelling family stories of Jacob, Mary Jane, Aunt May, and Menasha, of her mother and father, and husband Joe's family. These stories, a substitute for genealogy and family history, provided her with a well of tradition.

Stories Not on the Tip of Her Tongue

My mother's storytelling gave her a bridge to the past and a kind of identity spanning her disrupted childhood. Stories afford a kind of control and coherence to a youth in motion and change. When she was seven years old, with the deaths of her grandparents Jacob and then Mary Jane, Ethel and her family left Neenah and Menasha for Detroit, where they enrolled in the poor working masses and the bridges to their extended family did not hold. Far more damaging, Ethel annually or at least biannually was moved from home to home and school to school, making her always the new kid on the block. She had the love of her own parents and the benefit of being treated as Aunt May's favorite, a privilege that her good-natured sister Mabel and much younger brother Bill did not enjoy. Nevertheless, Ethel had to affirm her own independence and worth. She did this with a ready tongue and quick wit—and confidence that she was cute. Of course, on occasions, she rewrote the past to fit her wishes, in no case as much as when she told all her middle baptismal name was May, after her favorite aunt, when in fact it was Maria, as easily translated as Mary or Marie, the name of Emmett's wife, whom she disliked.

Who her people were, where they came from, and what they experienced were not precise matters for Ethel—and she certainly never had a thing to do with written genealogy or establishing anything like a precise family history. She could be aggressively indifferent to details. Although she knew she was part German, she professed herself at times to be fully Irish. If she acknowledged that she was mixed and an ethnic mongrel, she did it with a popular advertising phrase: "Yes, I'm Heinz—57 varieties." She would follow this with admission that she was French, either because "Linsdeau," the family's recently adopted name, might somehow be French or because the Boodry family was, way back, French.[1] But Ethel didn't care whence her Irish family came or how it got to Menasha any more than she cared what kind of German Jake was, or what Jake's mother's last name was, or that one of Jake's brothers left for the north woods of Wisconsin, or that his two sisters married Poles. Ethel had no interest in the refinement of details or the preservation of the whole.

Except for Grandmother Frances's deaf brother Tom and his wife Wilda, the Boodrys were consigned to oblivion. Except for Grandma's Sayers's niece, Alice Johnson in Neenah, with whom we traded visits just after World War II and Christmas cards for endless years, the Sayerses were ground by time into dust. There was only the story of the rabid death of Grandfather James Boodry, who died before he ever held her close or took her hand for a walk. She also had a single story of Grandmother Ella Sayers Boodry, who never won Ethel's liking. Unlike Jake and Mary Jane, Ella had no home of her own for the young Ethel to visit. Poor and without gifts to win a granddaughter over, she had no repertoire of jokes and pranks to spark a young child's glee and affection. Sometime in the early 1920s, Ella came for a long stay at my grandparents' place in Detroit, but when she heard young Mabel ask her mother when grandmother would leave, Ella took offense. She left immediately, in a huff, never to return.

In truth, Ethel's stories of the Linsdaus were also few and select. She seemed focused only on her grandparents, Aunt May, Uncle Emmett, and his son Vern. During our wartime trip, we drove by Jake and Mary Jane's old home and continued on to visit cousin Bernard and his wife Louisa, the last Linsdau family left in Menasha. We were on the porch, within a stone's throw of the family greenhouse. My mother and father chatted, and then they played cards—Wisconsin's popular *Schafskopf.* We left, barely ever to mention them again, unless the subject of flowers came up.[2]

Ethel never reflected clearly on the poverty of her Wisconsin ancestors and relatives. Rather, she raised them out of it. She promoted Grandfather James Boodry from hostler to veterinarian, elevated Grandfather Jacob Linsdau from alderman to mayor of Menasha, and made the greenhouse a sign of wealth. She surely did not grasp the range of economic reasons that accounted for the emigration of John, Emmett, and her father, William, to Detroit; she said her father left a promising job in a thriving Neenah paper mill because Frances was jealous of his fellow women workers. It never

The last Linsdaus in Menasha:
Louisa, Bernard, and their daughter Gertie, with three employees, 1930s

dawned on her that her grandparents died poor—that the great two-story brick home in which they spent their lives was heavily mortgaged.[3] In fact, she had no idea that her father, the youngest and only child to remain behind with widowed Mary Jane, was the administrator of the estate and how little there was in the end. Divided in fifths among the four living children and one part for the children of long-absent Austin, each share amounted to only eighty dollars, after legal and funeral expenses. The distribution of the money was accompanied by a division of a handful of personal goods, including the green glassware, which went to our family, and the family Bible, which went to Emmett's family.[4]

While Ethel vividly recalled participating in the local World War I victory parade, she never reflected on the social factors that caused the emigration of the second generation of the Linsdau family from Menasha. I never heard her consider why all the Linsdau children, including her beloved May, changed their name from the manifestly German Linsdau to the "Irish" or "French" Linsdeau. By leaving Menasha, were they quitting their German identity, while paradoxically turning their backs on the town where their father and mother had succeeded. Or, to state an even more complex question, more than trying to forsake an ethnic identity, were they trying to escape an increasingly rigid class condition, which preordained them to inferiority in a world in which abundance, leisure, careers, and choices were apparent?

Retrospectively, there seems little doubt that the Linsdaus were drawn to Detroit more than they were pushed out of Menasha. The essence of modernity and national progress, Detroit tendered the promise of cars, machines, steel, and the dynamic big city over and against a hometown of horses, mills, and fixed wages. To leave Neenah and Menasha for Detroit was equivalent for the Linsdau boys to leaving the bush leagues of mill towns for the big leagues of industry. To go to Detroit, a trip of approximately five hundred miles by land, was to arrive in the fastest-growing town in America. It was a chance to catch the biggest-breaking wave in the nation. Featuring by such inventions and innovations as apartment buildings, steam heat, the hydraulic elevator, the automatic sprinkler, improved roads, public transportation, parks, and electric street lights, Detroit proved a gigantic magnet pulling to itself hundreds of thousands of ambitious rural and town folks throughout Ontario and the Great Lakes region. Between 1900 and 1910, Detroit went from being the thirteenth largest city in the nation, with 285,704 residents, to ninth largest, with 465,766 inhabitants.

Detroit offered the Linsdaus what everyone wanted, a good wage. Already in the first decade of the century Ford Motor Company paid $2.50 a day, which equaled $650 a year for a single worker—and could mean an excellent income for a family of two, three, or four workers. Certainly, it was a lot more than the $1.00 to $1.50 made cutting trees in northern Michigan, on a small Ontario farm acreage, or in a Wisconsin mill. In 1914, Henry Ford, intent on producing not just cars for a nation but a nation that could afford them, raised wages to a revolutionary $5.00 a day. Terrifying businesses across the nation, Detroit became the pot of gold at the end of the rainbow for potential workers. The *Detroit News* reported in April 1922, "More people died rich in Detroit than in any other city in the United States during the past two years."

The Chance to Climb Down the Social Ladder

Ethel never considered that at least two Linsdaus, John and Emmett, went down, instead of up, the social ladder in Detroit. John Timothy, born in 1875, had been married and worked in Menasha's mills since he was twenty; he moved with his family to Detroit in late 1918, when he was in his early forties. Emmett, in his late thirties, arrived with wife Marie and their newborn son, Vernon, at the same time or a few months after John. First days were hard times for both families. When John and Emmett returned to Menasha in February 1919 to visit their dying mother, John's wife Barbara (Toenessons) wrote him, expressing their condition: She worried that John might catch the flu (the Great Influenza Pandemic of 1918 yet raged). She told him that she had put a ton of coal in the fruit cellar for $11.75. The brightest news she could muster was that their young son Bud (Gilbert) brought home $47 (a month's salary, equaling nothing like the famous $5 dollars a day!) for working Emmett's job as a gang worker, and the boss encouragingly said Emmett's job would be waiting for him on his return. However, Barb further wrote, "while the promise of work has given young Bud confidence that one day he will be able to start a family and household of his own, his older brother Jack [John Jr.] had fallen in the doldrums, for as much as he and his first cousin Bob [Austin and Theda's son, whom John apparently brought along from Menasha] scratch and peck, they cannot uncover work."

But she expressed happiness that Austin's daughter Dorothy had gone to see Grandma Mary Jane before she died, implying that some sort of misunderstanding had occurred between them; granddaughter Dorothy, with her mother and two brothers, had lived with Grandma Mary Jane and Jacob for many years after son Austin vanished.

In 1920 John suffered one of the principal causes of downward mobility and outright disaster for families: Barbara died, leaving him alone with four children. John's dimmed prospects turned black with a bad second marriage to a woman who proved the classic cruel stepmother to his beloved youngest daughter, Barbara Marie ("Toots"). Lending truth to Rosalia's proverb that "bad arrives on horseback and departs on foot," John suffered a severe groin injury at some point in his early years in Detroit, limiting thereafter his ability to do manual labor. For short stints he tried selling insurance and going door-to-door vending pots and pans. He found a more colorful occupation when working as a sheriff's assistant in rural St. Clair Shores: he conspired with Detroit's abundant "rum runners," helping them land where the authorities weren't. His last job, during World War II, was as a guard at an airplane plant in distant Willow Run, west of Detroit.

John, who experienced two house fires, never owned a home of his own. In fact, he lived rent-free for fifteen of his thirty years in Detroit with his oldest daughter, Viola Portzel, her husband, and their gang of ten children. One of these grandchildren, Patricia Walker, paid for his funeral expenses and tombstone. John, according to cousin Pat, was cut out of the same mold as Emmett and his brother William, my grandfather. John was handy with wood, talented in the arts, and had "a beguiling Irish charm," which won over even Emmett's hard-to-please Marie. John loved to shoot photographs and drive his car, which, on occasions, delivered him to a local bar. As workingmen once did, he bragged about famous barroom brawls in which he participated. At home, he entertained the family with jokes and stories, wrote songs, and played his guitar. Thanks to woodworking skills that all, including sister May, learned from their father, Jacob, John made chairs and furniture for the family. Like brother William, John supplied his grandchildren with bows and arrows, stilts, rubber guns, and whatever else he could make out of materials at hand. Out of vanity, he would never let his grandchildren call him Grandfather.

If John's assignment as eldest brother in the family was to keep the family together, he failed miserably, as oldest children often do, especially when siblings and their spouses fall to quarrelling. He was without his own home to host them, and he was without interests, money, or skills to a fashion community. All three families and May, the unmarried nurse, succumbed to a vortex of quarrels, in which small gets bigger and deeper. They swirled around Marie and Frances, May and Marie, May and Frances, and May and the Portzels. Considering John's daughter Viola to be fat, the rational and progressive May, who would have the family take hold of itself and pull itself up in the world, harshly judged the whole Portzel clan as dirty, poor, and irresponsible.

The Linsdau women were at war, and the men, as is so often the case, lacked the means to bring peace. Even their charm could not calm the swirling waters. After all, no drum beats as loudly and echoes as far as that which an angry family thumps. Family histories often amount to tales of anger, fury, and grudge, and stories of arguments, feuds, and splits. Marie and Frances were natural rivals. Having married men who looked so like each other, they were drawn into jealousy over their catches, which for women of their generation was often the sole, single, and all-important prize of a lifetime. Even though Marie had given birth to a Linsdau boy, Vernon, she carried the indelible mark of having had an illegitimate child before marrying Emmett. Frances, in turn, felt precarious and vulnerable about her own place in the family. Her large family, without a father, was poorer than that of Jacob and Mary Jane, and she was a Protestant who had converted to marry a Catholic. In search of self, I suspect, each looked into the mirror of the other. Vis à vis Frances, Marie experienced an inferiority, which was intensified by Frances's irritating air of superiority, which grew with Marie's disdain and cruel treatment of likeable Emmett.

Frances and Marie belonged to a class, time, and place of social differentiation. People's self-images were formed against a background of scarcity, on a table on which all was in movement and people took the measure of themselves and everyone else in relation to job, money, increased goods, home, and career. With those going upward and downward meeting themselves on every step, status, desperately suffered, was measured by all things, real and imagined.

Linsdau quarrels and grudges, spawned in the small towns of Lake Winnebago, were exacerbated in Detroit, as the three families and May sought to take root. Two or three decades passed when nary a word or visit transpired among many of them. Families, indeed, come apart and grow distant in many ways and for a variety reasons. In 1948, just a few days before my tenth birthday, I went with my mother, father, and grandparents to Great-uncle John's funeral in St. Clair Shores. I entered a room filled with strangers who, I was told, were relatives. They were gathered around a strange dead man. Even though he had lived nearby for my entire life, he might have been dead all along. We stayed for the rosary. My parents and Frances and Will talked to a number of people, but no one took me up in their arms as a beloved lost cousin, and I left with no idea how brothers and sisters grow apart. I remember a subsequent short visit to Emmett and Marie's small apartment on the south side of Jefferson Avenue on Detroit's near east side. Perhaps it occurred in the aftermath of the funeral. But I remember no details, except that the apartment was on the second floor, the living room was small, its one window faced out to the road, and I was stationed on a couch. Except for Aunt May, Ethel's episodic chronicle was all I knew of these Linsdeau great-uncles and -aunts and cousins until my research on this book began.

A Boy Cries, a Man Was Born

In the last decade of her life, my mom frequently mentioned Vern, Emmett's son, whom we last saw at my father's funeral in 1989. I hunted him down when

I started to write this work, sometime in the middle 1990s. Initial telephone interviews and then a visit to his home in St. Clair Shores assured me that he was a true Linsdau. Not only did Vern have a head of thick black hair, Mary Jane's genetic legacy, but he, like Ethel, was a person of tongue and wit. Fulfilling every family historian's dream, he had been keeping a journal since retirement. Its ten or so loose-leaf folders of pages written on computer were filled with his candid reflections on government, which he insisted is rarely to be trusted in anything; business, ever in need of honest workers and informed and principled bosses; morals, forever corrupted by individual and collective excuse-making; theology, which given the lot of man, must preach God's grace and human freedom; and marriage, the best thing that ever happened to him, in the form of a woman named Phyllis. It also gave intimate glimpses into his childhood, and his parents, and their relationship.

Just as Ethel had it, Vern's father Emmett was a mother's boy. Like the child of a spoiled generation, he preferred play and words to hard work. He clung to the apartment above his Gaelic-speaking grandmother, Mary, who took English for a *"haythin toong"* (a heathen tongue) and to the protection of his mother Mary Jane O'Brien. In the eyes of ambitious and determined Jacob, Emmett was a kind of city boy and an idler. Although Emmett was good with dogs, knew how to garden and make beer, and had woodworking and electrical skills that he showered free of cost on his Detroit neighbors' residences, Emmett's proclivity was for rest, and his calling, the profitless arts. He forever was singing Irish songs, except when his wife Marie was around. His skit writings stemmed from the songs and vaudeville repartee of one-liners he cultivated in the style of George Burns, Jack Benny, and Milton Berle. He touted his show around the Fox River Valley and took it as far away as Door County, Wisconsin. At the small St. Clair Shores Lakeview Theater, where people paid six cents to see a movie, he put on his version of tragedies.

Emmett turned work into play. While working as a janitor at the local Catholic church in St. Clair Shores, Emmett was plied with wine by Father O'Toole so he would speak "the true Irish brogue." He earned drinks by sitting on a bar stool at the Blue Goose and doing imitations of the east side's ethnic groups, including what he called "muskrat French." Like my grandfather, whose shenanigans were accommodated, Emmett "would occasionally dress up in Aunt's May's coat, with a lamp shade on his head, and in a falsetto voice get the girls"—which meant May and her life-long woman friend Herrick—"roaring with laughter." In the same entry in his journal, Vern wrote, "Whatever he did, he did well; he just never did anything for very long. The unemployed spaces were extremely long and he never had any hobbies that I was aware of until I discovered when I was middle aged, that drinking was his hobby."[5] Another entry read, "He was almost a lot of things but not quite."[6]

Reflecting on what his father's death meant to him, Vern confessed, "I can't say I was ever disappointed in my father, probably because I never expected anything of him." Vernon judged his father to be the archetypical sad clown. Smiling on the outside, crying on the inside, he was a good guy who never amounted to much. "Standing over my father's body," his tough and independent-minded son wrote, "I felt no overwhelming sense of being alone and frightened, of being forcibly torn from him." In their entire lives they had never been together. "We lived in the same house, but we lived totally separate existences; he in his misery, me in my detachment."[7]

Emmett's failure at work paled in comparison to his failure in marriage. Marie (Mary) Nys, a Belgian woman from Green Bay, was sharply disliked by my grandmother Frances and was despised by my great-aunt May. Perhaps hard-working Marie, who took in wash and even, for a period of time, worked at Hudson Motor, had reason to persecute her shiftless husband, but she won no sympathy from her son. Never, son Vernon contended, did Emmett deserve such an unforgiving and vengeful, splenic, and implacable hate as bestowed by hostile and spiteful Marie. "Everyone liked my father," Vern wrote and said, "but no one, my mother."

Once in the heat of a conversation, Marie tormented her son with her wish to hang herself. He responded by throwing her a rope. Well into his seventies, Vern was occupied with his upbringing, yet he simultaneously disputed the standard psychology. "If what psychologists say is true about the consequence of having a hateful mother," he once remarked offhandedly way, "I should have become a mass murder." He wrote in his journal,

Emmett and Marie in St. Clair Shores, early 1920s

All her life, she was so preoccupied with keeping records of each slight affront, each imagined insult, or as she liked to put it, each dirty dig, she had nei- ther time nor inclination for forgiveness. An impending verbal battle was evident when she went around the house for a day or two with slips of paper sticking out of her apron pocket. And from time to time she would pull them out and add a treasured remark that she didn't want to forget to use in the heat of battle [against] ... the target of her hatred-of-the-day.[8]

Once Vern encouraged Marie to read the Bible, which he was teaching at the Lutheran church. Puzzled by the Sermon on the Mount, she asked Ver- non if Christ *meant* to teach, "Love your enemies." Vern affirmed that indeed was the case. Looking "positively stunned," she asked, "Then how do you ever get even?" "Vindictiveness, implacable retaliation, for every real and imag- ined affront," Vernon wrote, "was the essential ingredient of my mother's character. To quote, 'vengeance is mine saith the Lord, I will repay,' only con- fused her more. The motivating force in her life was to exact revenge—get even—in spades!"[9]

The family lived in rural St. Clair Shores, midway between Detroit and Mount Clemens, along the south and east shore of Lake St. Clair. During Vern's youth, the area was largely uninhabited; dogs ran, small gardens abounded, and roads remained unpaved. They lived in a two-room shack on Raymond Avenue, which his father had built out of scraps, and perhaps stolen lumber, standing among empty fields and an irregular scattering of modest houses. The two rooms formed into an "L" shape, were "living room and bedroom (Mother and me), the smaller section to the east was the kitchen and eat- ing room, and everything else, I suppose."[10] The house itself had no indoor water or plumbing and only a worn rug draped between rooms. In addition to the house, there was the outdoor toilet and chicken coop, where Emmett was sometimes assigned to sleep for long periods of time. Rarely did their shed hold a car. Later, they added a small, unheated porch, where Emmett was sequestered season in and season out on the grounds that he had tuberculo- sis, which nurse Aunt May disputed. But the porch in the winter was not as cold as it was indoors, where icy, steely, unyielding silence held sway.

"I learned to live within myself, for myself," Vern confessed.[11]

Vern's boyhood memories of poverty never lost their sharpest edges. "A storehouse of ghosts," lacerating him with "humiliation," continued to pop up across his adult life. At reunions in later life, when old boyhood companions recollected Linsdeau poverty, cousin Vernon would turn "red with embarrassment" and struggle not to flee.[12] There was a nimbus of unwanted memories around his head. Many were particular and cutting: a mother who purposefully and spitefully displayed their poverty by the way she made a show of the laundry she had to take in, and a father whose "gold rushes" caused Vern's "pre-teen self-respect to ache." Once his dad, himself, and his stepbrother Joe, who was on vacation from Green Bay, built (with the help of a band saw paid for by Aunt May), a yard full of brightly decorated three-foot high wood models of the comic figures Mutt and Jeff to sell. Despite signs galore and lights strung up in the trees to advertise the business venture, they did not "sell a damn one."[13] Again, with the help of Aunt May, Emmett built a miniature golf course in their backyard using whatever he could scrounge up from a few local dumps. After plastering the yard with signs and stringing up lights for nighttime playing, the course drew a single customer: Vern's French friend Maurice paid his dime to play Emmett's backyard links.[14] The family car also injured the young Vern's sense of propriety—no time as much as when they plastered both front and the rear of their 1927 Ford with signs declaring "Green Bay or Bust!" and set off down their driveway and down the block blowing their "Ah-oog-ah" horn to call attention to their adventure on wheels.[15]

Vern most poignantly remembers the steps on the side of his childhood home:

> Most of the time I sat on those steps I was crying. That was my crying place before I was old enough to run away. My cryin' step—followed by my cryin' weed patch—followed by my cryin' private place in the woods. . . . But before I reached double figures, I was all cried out. The future, if I was to have a future was up to me, and crying hadn't done any good. When a fight started I quit getting out of the way. . . . I stayed put and forced them to fight in front of me, or

Vernon, on his "cryin' step," early 1930s

around me. That stopped most of the fighting, and dish throwing—then came the years of silence.[16]

The young Vern took refuge in surrounding fields and woods. There he had secret caches and inviolable places. Frank McGuire, an old, clever, and kind neighbor, married to a Huron Indian woman, made Vern a proficient woodsman. Frank took Vern up north to hone his young disciple's skills in felling trees, identifying plants, and tracking animals and humans across diverse terrains. When scarcely a teenager, Vern turned his rural skills into an income. He hunted and ran trap lines far out toward Mount Clemens, using what he called "an Indian walk"—something between a walk and a jog—to shuffle fifteen or twenty miles in a day. He sold the game he took and the pelts he harvested and used the cash to buy food and other necessities.

Young Vernon also had the support of his uncle John's family. Vern frequently made himself at home at Viola Portzel's. Large, musical, receptive, and constantly astir, Viola's household greeted Vern with open arms when he was a child. When older, he stopped off along his delivery route for a local dry cleaner. Young Vern also took unforgettable annual summer trips to Green Bay in order to visit his maternal grandparents and his half-brother, Joe, but he didn't receive a warm welcome there. His summer vacations almost predictably ended in a "disastrous boyhood incident," with Vern getting in a fight, trying out homemade explosives, or wrecking the Ny household's best cast-iron frying pan by cooking a greasy squirrel in it. Vacation invariably ended with Vern being shipped back home early at the express order of his incensed grandmother. Vern concluded that she hated everyone, even though he had true affection from his calm grandfather and his supportive Aunt Edna.[17]

Vern had another powerful ally in his corner: Aunt May. Having defied Jacob by going to nursing school, strong-willed Aunt May took up an Irish and modern American identity when she left the family home, staying in contact with the O'Brien side of the family. She rejected the good Catholic German name of Mary for May, and like William and Emmett, she changed her last name from Linsdau to Linsdeau. Aunt May even went so far as to celebrate her March 23 birthday on March 17, St. Patrick's Day. After a year of military service, during which she suffered a bout of influenza, she worked for a short stint in a mental asylum, then became a Detroit public health nurse. Even though city employees were sometimes paid with bankrupt Detroit's own scrip during the Depression, she had a better job than any of the three Detroit brothers. Unmarried—never to marry the one beau she had—she showered her attention on her favorite niece, Ethel, and nephew, Vernon. She visited them often, gave them small but significant sums of money, and had special gifts for them on their birthdays.

May taught Ethel and Vernon rules for building character in democratic society: They amounted to: Be independent! Believe in yourselves! Make something of yourselves! And, above all, don't take any guff! Vernon confessed to wishing May was his mother. He knew her to be outspoken and judgmental, someone who joined a temper to her prejudices. Golfing in the 1920s on Detroit's Belle Isle, May deposited her clubs in the canal into which her topped shot had just disappeared, never again to test her skill on the links. But in his journal, Vern recorded a time that hard-nosed May emotionally came apart. One day when she was on her rounds as a nurse in the black community, a child dashed out from between parked cars and ran in front of her, and she ran over him. Even though May was blameless, and the child's parents imputed no culpability and looked for no compensation, May felt otherwise. She paid for a fine funeral, stayed at the funeral home for the entire visitation period, attended the church services, and ordered and oversaw the installation of a tombstone. Aunt May could not forgive herself for the accident, and its lingering trauma almost cost her career. Long after the boy was buried, May continued to visit his parents, "not consoling them, but searching for assurance of their forgiveness."[18]

May incorporated Vern into her life. After she and her life-long friend Herrick (whose relationship Vern and Ethel never speculated upon) had rented housing together on the west side of Detroit for years, they decided to build a place of their own up north, on Lake Huron, above East Tawas. For a couple of summers Aunt May made Vern a worker in the building of a large two-story log cabin on a natural beach. Vernon helped imbed in the fireplace stones she and Herrick had gathered on their trips across the nation. Vernon also helped May, a fine wood worker herself, with the installation of a stairway made of logs cut in half, which led to the open loft above one side of the living room.

As a kid Vern was always hatching plans and always selling something—rubbing two nickels together. A Boy Scout, he led the other kids in the neighborhood with his dreamed-up ideas. He formed a local detective club whose first case was investigation of a dead dog. Good looking and with a shrewd tongue, Vern was not shy when it came to meeting young girls. He was also quick to win adults over to his cause. A straight-A student, young Vernon understood what he heard and grasped what he read. Graduating on schedule, he worked for a year before setting off to study engineering at the University of Michigan.

May encouraged him to go the university, but after a year, Vern, short of money, returned to Wayne University (later Wayne State) in Detroit, where a new period of his life began. Busy attending classes and working, Vernon and Aunt May stopped seeing each other and dropped contact. In 1941, earning twenty dollars a week, Vernon married Phyllis Beighey, a smart and energetic woman, around whom he put together his life and established a home of his own. They had four children: David in 1942, Robert in 1945, James in 1947, and Nancy, belatedly, in 1955.

With World War II under way, Vernon entered the important wartime plating and armaments industry, vital to Detroit's standing as "the Arsenal of Democracy." A combination of self-confidence, determination, willingness to learn, and knowledge, enhanced by turning a group of students into translators of an advanced German manual on plating, accounted for Vern's rise in the administrative ranks of the industry. After working for several firms, in the late 1950s Vernon started his own successful plating company. A devoted, clever, and hard-working wife underwrote Vernon's successful return to St. Clair Shores. Where he once cried on the steps of a shack, he now owned a lovely home on the lake, was president of the local school board, and joined the local Lutheran church, which he—grandson of Catholics Mary Jane O'Brien and Jacob Linsdau—deeply supported and whose underlying theology he sharply articulated and fervently embraced.

Yet during all this time of his ascent to prosperity, respectability, and, most importantly, his own internal solidity and confidence, Vern never visited May, and May never once met Vern's wife Phyllis and their four children. Indeed, they were only to meet again at Emmett's funeral in 1960. Upon seeing his favorite aunt after twenty years, Vern burst into tears. I cannot explain what separated nephew and aunt. Vern died before I could ask. Ethel never spoke of it. Phyllis seemed to have no idea that a separation existed. Their rift puts me before one of those unexplained gaps so common to families. I can look to Vern, and simply say that he numbered among the young who perennially forget the old when they chase the first opportunities of adulthood. I can look to May and hypothesize that a lack of respect or slip of common sense made her angry. Perhaps it was compounded when Vernon withdrew from the University of Michigan without asking for help or advice. It may have hardened when she was not invited to her favorite nephew's wedding or the baptism of his first child. Anger, an emotion that grows so well in so many soils, may have been in May's case fertilized by the sense that she, a spinster aunt, had no place in the life of Vern's young family. This very sense might also account for the minimal contact between May and Ethel during the first decade of my parents' marriage, even though she and Ethel kept in touch, and I recall at least two childhood visits to her lovely home on Lake Huron.

Alternatively, I might follow a less psychological tack, and adopt the kind of superficial explanation preferred by amateur historians of family and biographers. Maybe aunt and nephew parted simply because they were Linsdaus: they were by clan a spirit forged and honed out of Irish and German tempers, which disposed them, like good swords, to react swiftly to small slights and withstand long, hacking grudges. But I prefer to offer in their specific cases a general explanation based more on the society and their times than an underlying family characteristic. I would suggest that not just the Linsdaus, but the whole emerging working class, stood in a social state of disequilibrium. It filled their minds, families, and homes. Straddling countryside, town, and city, they were a mix of a differentiating rural poor and the emergent but inchoate working class. With community left behind in the countryside and only partially rebuilt in the new industrial cities, they lived in an age of increasing social mobility and differentiation. Of undefined money, work, property, education, and, in some places, career, the emerging working class felt unsure of itself in the world or their times. This left them unsure who they were and where they belonged. Consequently, they scrutinized their own family for the meaning, identity, respect, and community they lacked. In family they focused their strongest emotions and inevitably experienced the sharpest wrongs and deepest disappointments. The first and last buffer of human experience, family bore the revolution of popular culture and industrial society. Individuals, of changing inner dimensions, were born into households midway between traditional and modern society.[19] Amid such a profound metamorphosis, which we are yet to comprehend, I espy the long and deep silences of anger and misunderstanding that befell an aunt, a nephew, and whole Linsdau tribe.

A Last Look at Cousins

With the death of Herrick, May sold off the cabin. Now rather than spending her summers up north, she spent her winters in Bradenton, Florida. She would stop off at our houses for a few days on her return to her place on the west side. She encouraged me with words and occasional letters when I was at the university. Sometime in the middle 1960s, when she was in her middle seventies, she judged herself no longer up to the trip. She had Ethel find her a home near us, in which she could receive day care. There she remained until she died in 1970 at the age of eighty-three. Ethel administered her modest estate.

Vern, who never forgot who he had been and what he had become, increasingly turned to writing a journal and seeking his origins. There, well into his seventies, and thanks to information supplied to him by his son and other family members, and me, Vern found his real father, the one whose inheritance he could proudly claim, in Jacob. Grandfather Jacob, for Vernon, was a man who did what he had to and said what he chose to.

As my mom entered her sixties, more and more she referred to cousin Vernon and his success, as if cousins are the best way to know ourselves and our place in the world. This was also a way for her to elevate the status of her family. However, her mention of him never ignited in her a desire to see him. Even though he only lived a few miles away—"on the lake," she would point out—he could have lived a world away. It was their past that walled them off. As much as she admired him, she never cared to really know him, to reminisce with him, to examine the love of May they shared, or yet to chart their likenesses as grandchildren of Jacob and Mary Jane and children of the tongue. Cousin Vernon better served as a distant star in my mother's story-filled family galaxy. As she had her husband Joe and me, so her cousin had his wife Phyllis and three children. As much as she and her Joe secured a good life in Detroit, so Vernon and his wife secured a richer life in St. Clair Shores. She expected to see her cousin at certain funerals, and from time to time he (one of the very few bearing the name of "Linsdeau") would turn up in family conversation and even consideration. Once Ethel's sister Mabel, who seemed forever to be impulsively zooming around the east side from home to cottage, borrowed the luxurious but genealogically uninformative family Bible in Vern's possession. She gave it to my Uncle Bill, judging him its rightful owner. Vern, who never complained, never got the Bible back.

But there was no true reunion between first cousins Ethel and Vern. I could never quite understand why. My mother always spoke as if the final parting of their ways occurred on May 29, 1937, when Vern on his way up to the University of Michigan stopped and ate at her wedding. On her wedding day, which was also her birthday, Vernon would be the first in the family to try higher education.

To write this book I felt compelled to hunt down cousin Vernon in 1999. He was a smaller man than I imagined. Though already in this late seventies and ill, he expressed considerable energy. I was taken by his careful use of language. I, who was nursed by love and fostered by security, was awed by what he had emotionally overcome to be who he was. I was impressed by his humble confession that his life depended on his wife's love and his faith, which was recently so tested by the unexpected death of their youngest son. I couldn't deny a kinship with this newly found theological cousin. Equally intense about knowing who we were and searching a shared Linsdau past, we were fast approaching a conversation crossing generations when he became seriously ill and died in 2001. A grandson and great-grandson, first cousins once removed, were getting to know each other at Jacob's well.

9

Workers to the Bone,
East Siders to the End

We take ourselves and our families to be unique and of a singular history, and on no count does the responsibility of being true to this recognition press on us as much as when we treat our parents. Though we can rebel when young or across a lifetime, we know ourselves to be born and raised in the homes of their bodies and thoughts; to be embodiments of their genes, emotions, energies, and polarities, consequences of their steadfastness and sacrifice, folly and sin. We even believe ourselves, blessed or cursed with their luck, to be surrogates living out their fates, extending their covenant across generations. Piety and gratitude, anger and rebellion, commingle within us—heirs of Jacob—and dispose us to suffer again and again our parents' ordeals and humiliations, trumpet their victories, however ordinary and unnoticed, and re-voice their supplications for peace and justice. When we come around to write of their lives, we find ourselves in need of the skills of historian and novelist alike to grasp how we are theirs by accepted inheritance and conscious imitation and invention. Teaching us to untie part of the knot of our meaning, family history shows us how we made ourselves into the past and the past claimed us as its own. At least, this is part of what I discovered when I wrote of my Ethel and Joe.

My parents, Ethel and Joe, had an abiding loyalty to family. Their first obligations were to each other and to me. Their principal lifetime occupation was securing and maintaining a home in which Joe was the breadwinner and Ethel, the homemaker. Their second obligation centered on expressing respect for and seeing after the well-being of their parents, especially Grandmother Rosalia. As the oldest children in their families, they had enhanced obligations to their younger siblings, at least until they were out on their own. Family, as both nuclear and extended, required and justified work. The moral and emotional heart of the economic household, family constituted the end of their labor, discipline, savings, and self-sacrifice. It also ultimately defined well-being and security, which started with a need for subsistence and was transformed over four decades of work into a matter of having money in the bank, bodily comfort at home, and finally keeping up with the new inventions, goods, and pleasures of consumer society.

Home was the cockpit of their economic and private, emotional and intimate lives; it would also buffer their passage through a changing society and world. Though we were dependent on pubic institutions, home insulated us from surrounding communities and from the standardization enforced by changing mass, industrial, and national society, keeping our lives private, distinct, and valuable.[1]

Aside from a mixture of ethnic and American cultures, producing "a kind of biculturalism in spite of structural assimilation," to quote immigration historian Kathleen Conzen, a stripped down and uncluttered Catholicism, focused not on church and theology, but on faith and destiny, underpinned the primacy of family and home.[2] My parents' religion centered on God, not on biblically knowing Christ. It did not rely on the Holy Spirit or protector saints. Formed around hope for our well-being, their Catholicism was supported by a belief, as secular as religious, in fairness and kindness and in truthfulness and honesty. Ethel and Joe were what I might call reverent "peasant democrats." They did not speculate on theological matters or concern themselves with church affairs, did not order our lives around praying the rosary or making novenas; nor did they decorate the home with popular religious art, although my father, in conformity with Sicilian customs, wove palms into crosses after Mass on Palm Sunday and placed them behind the family crucifix. When I was young, as best I can remember, we did not attend church regularly or make frequent use of the sacraments.

My parents' everyday ethic rested on traditional senses of reciprocity and respect in combination with an unwavering belief in a democratic society. While Ethel and Joe enthusiastically embraced the fresh opportunities and the new goods that were offered after World War II, they never forgot prior hard times and deprivation. Home ownership, a goal of their marriage, measured security, displayed well-being, and constituted a reward for their hard

work, careful saving, and self-discipline. For them, first-generation Detroiters, owning a home carried all the real and symbolic power of unity and
security that a place on the land held for their rural ancestors, including
Grandmother Frances and her "forty acres." Ethel and Joe bought their home,
realized job security, witnessed the beginnings of the national Social Security retirement insurance, and enjoyed their own expanding wealth and consumption across the 1930s and especially the 1940s and 1950s. This veritable
revolution in societal well-being surprised them and their kind and delivered me to an unprecedented world of abundance, choice, and career.

I do not see my father and mother as merely members of the generation
that experienced and survived the Depression. Nor did they exclusively
belong to what recently is popularly called "the greatest generation of all,"
even though World War II profoundly affected their lives and the lives of
their families. Rather, in so far as I assign them to a generation, I treat them
as a cohort, which moved from youth to full adulthood across four distinct
decades, from the 1920s, to the 1950s. Living in the cauldron of a changing and
choice-filled city, they moved through time and society as a wave, encoun-
tering new events and possibilities. They danced to the same tunes, laughed
at the same jokes, tuned to the same radio stations, cheered for the same
athletes, and enjoyed first car rides, extended vacations, and a whole new
order of consumer goods. They also learned to depend on the same expanding public sector for education, public health, and Social Security benefits,
and to love and support the same nation and president (my dad loved Franklin Delano Roosevelt). They witnessed an identical set of local, national,
and world events, disputed the same affairs and issues, and joined in Detroit
what were common and epochal labor struggles associated with unionizing
America.

In the case of my family, the city provided more chances for economic
improvement and wider personal choices than ever known in rural Europe
or America. I join the very comprehensive assessment of the course of their
lives by economic historian Samuel P. Hayes in affirming that the city meant
positive change for the immigrants from countryside and Europe and their
children.[3] Though not fast nor uniform, their advance can be measured by

growing savings accounts, the purchase of houses and flats, a widening selection of consumer goods, a rising standard of jobs, and improved jobs and incomes. Mobility, though slow and occurring across two generations, was persistent and real; work, calculating, and planning bore material dividends; and over time they came to see their lives in the city, not as confined and inhibited, but as challenging, exhilarating, and improving.

On this count, I argue that the principal trajectory of my parent's generation went beyond the ordeal of the Depression and the test of World War II. A more comprehensive, though less dramatic, narrative line follows their success in securing family and home in emerging American industrial and urban society. This quest, anything but a seamless whole, fused traditional rural and modern industrial and urban values, making their achievements, true to their ancestors' primary goal and fruitful in choice, opportunity, and unprecedented advance by their children. In the end, I am prejudiced to write of them with, "a profound admiration for their steadfast determination to be heroes in their own lives."[4]

But to do more than make my parents silhouettes of a historical period, I must try to offer a living portrait of Joe and Ethel as two distinct personalities, members of traditional families who kept step with Detroit and American society from the 1920s to the 1950s.

The Meeting

Sharing lives, bodies, and times, my mother and my father were on many counts polar opposites. Quick-tongued, mercurial, and storytelling, Ethel was lithe and of superabundant body energy, while Joe, who worked and acted with alacrity, was practical, disciplined, and intelligent in his speech and gestures. Joe, like his cousins and his peasant ancestors, calculated what was economic in terms of what was necessary, and vice-versa. He did not waste time evoking the past or conjuring the distant future. He did not tell colorful Sicilian stories about things past or intense human encounters. With only occasional surges of emotion, he explained how things and people worked, described order and processes, and saved his positive prescriptions for such issues as why labor unions were good and Republicans couldn't be trusted. Ethel, quick of wit and filled with pride, replied energetically, fancifully, and exaggeratedly. With their whole persons they marked out differences of spirit on which philosophers produce tomes, while giving incarnate witness to the opposites of husband and wife. I cannot account for myself, as either existing at all or being what I became, except that Ethel and Joe met, and Ethel and Joe fell in love.

They met at a free outdoor summer street dance sponsored by Silver Cup Bread in 1932. At such dances, or in one of several dance halls that lined Detroit's east side, along Jefferson Avenue, young Italian, Polish, Irish, German, Belgian, and other working-class ethnic youth ventured out to meet the opposite sex and to see and be seen.[5] There they danced, struck up conversations, got to know one another, and if pleased, went on to date and ultimately became married east siders. Dancing, they forgot about the Depression—and an economy whose production, jobs, and wages dropped a quarter and a third from what they had been in 1929.[6] Dance by dance, partners shared accounts of their parents' old ways and divulged their own fresh hopes: besides the predictable need for a good mate and a steady job, there were the new possibilities of having only a limited number of children, buying a home, and getting a good jalopy.

Even though Joe may well have been twenty-year-old Ethel's first encounter with one of those Italians who helped fill up the east side of Detroit,[7] she didn't see their meeting as a cultural encounter or a matter of luck. Instead, she told a story of boldness and guile. Catching sight of Joe dancing with a blond, Ethel boasted to her girlfriend that she could take any guy she wanted off any blond. She wormed her way into a dance with him and then had several more before saying good evening. She had herself paged several times so he would be sure to remember her name, which Joe did. With his experience at Western Union, where joining names and addresses was the job, my father had no trouble locating where Ethel worked and lived, and he figured out what streetcar line she would take home. He was waiting for her the following evening when she bounded off the streetcar, taking a second step of many toward a marriage that lasted more than fifty years.

Joe Fits In

Polite, respectful, soft-spoken, diplomatic, and deferential, Joe broke down whatever stereotypes William and Frances might have held against Italians. Trim and handsome, with bluish-green eyes, regular features, a light complexion, and black hair, Joe would have passed the standards of just about any prospective working-class in-laws. Furthermore, Joe was self-supporting and independent. And most of all, he was a determined Ethel's choice. She had chosen him on the free dating market, in the very same way that the young Frances and William found each other a generation before in the Fox River Valley.

There were other reasons for welcoming Joe into the family. He treated Ethel well. He had found and kept a good job despite the difficult job market, and he did not voice a word of complaint about supporting his mother, sister, and three half-sisters. Working downtown, at the center of the telecommunication industry, Joe knew how the city ran, who was hiring and who was laying off. At home in the world of numbers and words he understood the rudiments of contracts, interests, and mortgages, and he eventually would do his own and their income taxes.[8] Joe was never shy when it came to picking up a shovel or joining in a home repair project, although he always acknowledged his father-in-law's superior skills in working with wood and metal.

Joe was well-equipped for life in the industrial order. Most importantly, he equated life and work. He trusted his own reason and didn't doubt the claim of his own labor; he was not swept away by his own words, or those of others. He did not nurse insults, harbor grudges, or seek to repay enemies, and he never expressed regrets about the burdens he shouldered so early in life. Marcus Aurelius, Stoic and emperor, could not have taught this Roman son anything about measure and duty, as Bill and Frances would witness: loyal and determined, a moderate and dutiful man, there was no crack in his character.

But anyone who played cards with my father or listened to him react to a contested sporting event knew he was not without feelings. Cards served not only to pass hours of obligatory Sunday visits to his mother-in-law's and long

My parents at their wedding, May 29, 1937.

Paul DeCarlo and Josephine Messina, their best man and bridesmaid, were also my godparents.

evening family get-togethers, but they gave my father a chance to bemoan his misfortune. He grumbled, lamented, and supplicated his cards as if he were a Psalmist and God would intervene to deliver him the good hand he deserved. He beamed when the right card came and he won. Over the years his plaints grew louder, and eventually my mother began threatening to stop playing with him unless his complaining subsided, which it might, for a hand or two.

He had other pleasures. A beautiful opera produced an expression of awe, while the changing plight of his beloved Detroit Tigers or any of a number of favorite Italian boxers made an accordion of his emotions. He didn't use irony, was not sarcastic, and although he was good-natured and laughed often, he rarely told a joke. He didn't use off-color expressions—in fact, he corrected me when I used my first curse word, "Nuts"—but he did once characterize a product he considered useless to be as "practical as a crocheted pisspot."

His indulgences were modest. The first years of their dating were the last years of Prohibition, which ended in 1933, and he and Ethel occasionally frequented a blind pig, an illegal establishment selling alcohol. They would drink and stay out late at wedding dances. A decade later, with his date of induction into military service imminent, he took up smoking a pipe, thinking that his would give him something to do with his free time in the service. He was deferred several times, given his age and vital occupation at Western Union, but he continued to smoke his pipe for twenty years until one day he up and quit.

"ET-tella," Welcome to Rosalia's

Ethel gained access into Joe's family as easily as he had into hers. However vast the cultural differences were between the Linsdeaus and the Amatos, Ethel entered Rosalia's home with an open heart and mind. With no impeding prejudices, my mother understood that the core aspirations and basic needs of Rosalia's family were essentially the same as her own. Yet, she understood that this family lacked a father—and learned the painful details of the failed second marriage. Their five-year engagement testified equally to Joe's unalterable pledge to support his mother until his sisters were raised and to Ethel's fidelity to Joe. So trust bridged time, making their words honorable and their lives morally dignified.

In fact, Ethel, whom Rosalia always called "ET-tella," liked each other immediately: They were both peppery, and were astute about people in general and the wishes and motives of Rosalia's adolescent daughters in particular. Ethel helped Rosalia in raising and marrying off Joe's sisters, which required observing the oldest Sicilian courtship laws regulating a daughter's honor while shepherding them in successful American ways of "getting a man." Aside from listening to Rosalia pour out rivers of feeling and passion, which no doubt embarrassed Joe, Ethel's duty as a second mother was to chaperone Joe's sisters at dances during a period when more and more young men of the working class had fifty-dollar used Model Ts for their steeds and ungallant interests far from a young woman's honor.

Ethel practiced the womanly art of sympathy well. She best showed her love for the family when she named me Joseph Anthony, making this first (and only) grandson the namesake of both Rosalia's son and her first and truly loved husband. Ethel and Rosalia learned to tease and coax each other about life's primary matters. Ethel laughed when Rosalia's malapropisms identified "a two bit whore" as a "two by four," and with Yogi Berra wisdom declared, "Every day has a dog!" On festive occasions, Ethel enjoyed the bawdy jocularity of a Sicilian song, "La Luna Mezz'o Mare" about a young girl who implores her mother to marry her off. Her mother lists what kinds of endowments a bride might expect from a sailor, a butcher—or a gardener, "Who will have a cucumber in his hand." In concert with the sisters, Ethel even succeeded on a few Easters, when I was young, in convincing Rosalia to put aside her customary black and wear a bright flowered dress; then they pinned a corsage on it and told her how good she looked. After World War II, my parents took Rosalia with us on our Sunday outings into the countryside around Detroit to see the fruit trees at harvest time. In all her married years, Ethel never shirked her Sunday obligation to visit Rosalia, even if Joe happened to be working. Mom also joined fully into family celebra-

Ethel and Rosalia, May 1936

tions of weddings, baptisms, and funerals, which were still held at home.

Ethel had no trouble in grasping the primacy of food in Joe's home. Before anyone in the family was accustomed to dining out at anything other than a hamburger joint or a bar that served fish and chips on Friday night, we ate five-course meals at Rosalia's. Starting with a lettuce and tomato salad, we advanced to chicken noodle soup, then to spaghetti, meat balls, and anise-spiced Italian sausage, then to chicken or my favorite, breaded veal with potatoes and vegetables. We finished up with dessert, *i dolci*, which was often an array of Italian cookies, *spumone* ice cream, and once in a while, the Sicilian specialty of almond- and cream-filled *cannoli*. Finally, there were offers of another bottle of beer, a glass of homemade red wine—a zinfandel (made with four boxes of red grapes, one of white), or a shot of inexpensive whiskey, while out came a bowl of fruit, with grapes and possibly pomegranates. At Christmas the nut tray brimmed over with walnuts, chestnuts, Brazil nuts, and hazelnuts, which one of my uncles—I have forgotten who—could crack by pressing two together in his hand.

Christmas was the longest and most social of all holidays. It wove the family tight with visits, meals, and gifts. Lasting from Christmas Eve to Epiphany, it was the season of obligatory visiting, especially in the 1940s and into the early 1950s before the family began to disperse across the east side. A strict order ruled the family proper. We had to visit all the families of my mother and father's brothers and sisters, and they had to visit us. We could walk across the street to visit Rosalia's brother John and his wife, Margaret (the sister of Rosalia's beloved Antonino), and then go two blocks over to visit Rosalia's sister Paulina, her husband, Joe DeCarlo, and their son Joe Jr. in the flat above them. These visits, which honored families and their homes, involved a lot of preparation—dressing in good and new clothes; the exchange of three-to-five-dollar gifts (especially for the children); plentiful meals, drinks, sweets, and chocolates, by which one's hospitality was measured. My father's youngest sister, Pauline, and her husband, Benny, usually won out, with wonderful selections of Italian cookies and obligatory half-size and full *cannoli*. As standard fare, men were offered beer and shots, while women were given a mixed drink, usually a highball: a shot, big or small, of cheap whiskey, local Vernor's

The older generation from the Hillger neighborhood in front of the church at my parents' wedding, 1937: Rosalia's brother John and his wife, Margaret; Rosalia; Rosalia's sister Pauline and her husband, Joe DeCarlo

Ginger Ale, with or without ice. After preliminary holiday greetings, ritual-
ized praise of the Christmas tree as "full," the history of the tree's purchase and
its price, the saga of bringing it home, tales of the insubordinate tree stand
that refused to hold the tree straight, and mention of other Christmas decorations and new furniture, the visit formally began when the men adjourned
to the kitchen to play cards and women initiated their long and more intimate gossip about pregnancies, marriages, deaths, absent children, family
members, neighbors, and acquaintances. After two or three hours of cards,
usually poker for small stakes, the game was suspended around ten o'clock
for a snack of sandwiches and dessert (Ethel loved to make pineapple upside-
down cake). Then, after the table was cleared, the women were invited to
play poker in the simple form of show down, which was five cards up, with
high and low cards winning side pots. This would go until midnight or so. I
would always fall asleep to wisecracking, large "ahs" and "oohs" accompanying wins and losses, and the most comforting hushing sound of my youth,
rising and falling familiar voices, the very tide of human community.

The Old East Side

In joining Joe's family, Ethel was joining a generation of urban villagers. At its
heart for Joe and Rosalia was first the house on Beniteau Street, which the 1930
census listed as being worth nine thousand dollars. In the early 1930s, Joe purchased the duplex on Hillger, just a few blocks away, and the family moved to
the downstairs apartment; the rent from the upstairs apartment helped make
house payments. In a neighborhood of mixed ethnicities, with residents'
birthplaces identified in the 1930 census in Italy, Germany, Canada, the East
Coast, the South, the Midwest, and predominantly Michigan, relatives and
Sicilian friends lived across the street and were scattered on nearby streets.

   As intently as any of my nineteenth-century rural families, Joe and Rosalia focused on getting money for food and homeownership. They bought
food in bulk, raised small gardens, canned food in large jars and tins, and
kept caged rabbits and chickens in the basement, along with a barrel or two
of homemade wine and root beer. They and their relatives hunted empty

lots for dandelions, burdock (*carduna*), and other greens, fished in the nearby Detroit River, and walked the tracks to gather or even steal coal. They took in boarders, bought and rented half of their duplexes; Rosalia worked as a wet nurse, a factory hand, and a school janitor. Life was, as it had been for their ancestors, first and foremost an economic enterprise.

The old east side formed a relatively new industrial landscape, which in the 1920s and 1930s still offered the semblance of a rural community with horses kept in garages, pigeon coops (a clear identifier of Belgian residents) at the back of the lot, and essential for most home-owning ethnics, a garden. Like nearby concentrations of Germans, Belgians, and Poles, the Sicilians and Italians had their own village on this landscape. They had their own churches, social halls, hardware stores, grocery stores, doctors, dentists, funeral directors, violin instructors, real estate salesmen, and even an Italian newspaper or two. Also, along with abortionists and fortunetellers clandestinely tucked in here and there, in continual circulation were street vendors of greens and household goods, knife grinders, rag pickers, and icemen, whose dripping carts spelled summer relief for children begging a chip of ice.

Our Italian neighborhood, near the center of the east side in the Kercheval and St. Jean area, was bounded by Gratiot and Jefferson, two of Detroit's great spoke avenues that formed a great pie-shaped piece radiating from the center of Detroit to the city and county limits at Eight Mile Road. On the downtown end of Gratiot Avenue, Joe and Ethel attended weddings at Roma Hall and shopped at Eastern Market. In the opposite direction, near the original city airport, they visited relatives and attended funerals in a neighborhood known to its residents, and the city Italians as *Caca di lupo*, the boondocks where "the wolf shits." (The people, places, and things of the area bore the corresponding adjective, *cacadilupesi.*)

Jefferson Avenue, which followed the Detroit River east from downtown, formed the southern spoke of Detroit's transit system. In contrast to Gratiot Avenue, which centered the old German neighborhood and ran roughly north of the Italians and south of the Poles, Jefferson Avenue opened the door to a dynamic industrial Detroit. Along Jefferson, going from Grandma's toward downtown, one passed the Chrysler factory at Conner Street and came to the U.S. Rubber Company plant and the Detroit Stove Company at East Grand Boulevard, which opened to the Belle Isle Bridge. Along the way, you passed the pride of Detroit: the stone-gated Detroit Waterworks Park, which once delivered water taken from the Detroit River in greater quantities than in any other industrial city in the nation. The park, which featured ball fields and picnic areas, made Detroit, a city of manufacture and immigrants, a national model of cleanliness and shade. This was no small matter of both civic and class pride at a time when immigrants, especially Italians, were stereotyped as dark, criminal, and huddling masses.

The Detroit River, which had attracted French explorers and settlers in the 1600s, joined the Great Lakes and the North Atlantic to Chicago and the American hinterland and pushed even the most closed minds of urban villagers to imagine distant worlds, as big and mighty rivers do. On the east end of the Detroit River stood Gross Pointe Farms, where the mansions of the nation's industrial elite, including the stone-walled estate of Henry Ford, were on full and ostentatious display. Adding to the romance of the river and adjoining Lake St. Clair, rumrunners and whiskey smugglers chased from prohibition-free Canada to Detroit in their high-powered watercraft. In the winter they drove their booze-filled cars and trucks across the ice. Also, beginning with Gar Wood's powerboats in the teens, and lasting for the next three decades, hydroplanes—the world's fastest boats—raced the river to win the prestigious Detroit Gold Cup. The deep roar of their airplane motors resonated throughout the east side during racing days. For more serene and sentimental summer amusement, excursion boats offered moonlight cruises and dance music, as they headed south down the river for the island amusement parks of Bob-lo and Put-in-Bay.

But our greatest nearby escape, just down Jefferson Avenue, was the city's large and singularly wonderful Belle Isle, a thousand-acre island park, roughly two by three miles in size. Originally known as "le aux Cochons (Hog Island), Belle Isle was—and still largely is—a mixture of woods and open grassland, ponds, and beaches. Landscaped in the 1880s by Frederick Law Olmstead, known as the designer of New York City's Central Park, Belle Isle

My parents at Belle Isle, around 1935

had a half-mile long beach facing the city skyline, a yacht club for the wealthy, a boat club for those who aspired to be wealthy, a canoe livery for adventure-some youth, as well as a riding stable, a small municipal golf course, and a tiny zoo. Inviting our kind and the city at large to participate in the middle-class pleasures and refinements of urban life, the island also boasted the large and ornate Scott Fountain, a luxurious casino, a fine botanical garden, and America's oldest public aquarium, inspired by the Naples aquarium. Our family frequently took visitors to Belle Isle to show them just how great Detroit was—and how well they had done by coming to it. With pride my parents also pointed to the constant parade of passing giant freighters, proving that Detroit was a vital connection to the Great Lakes, the Saint Lawrence, and the world at large.

On Belle Isle the young ethnics of the east side celebrated and projected new images of themselves. They went to the island to hold family picnics and reunions, to kiss at night by Scott Fountain or have their wedding photographs taken there, and to walk their children through the zoo and the island's amaz-ing aquarium. All eyes and ears turned to see and hear the nearby chiming Nancy Brown Bell Tower, which stood on the edge of a main canal, only a few hundred yards from the Conservatory. Amorous young Detroiters took some of their first solo car rides to the island to "watch the submarine races," to use a phrase that passed from generation to generation. In the summer, the masses piled into canoes, some with the intention of capsizing in their mind before departing, while in the winter, the bold, like my Uncle Bill and me, skated on the island's extensive canal system. On the island, my father—not much of an athlete—tried his hand for a season or two at tennis, and my mother, as she repeated many times, once ran hurdles in an all-city grade school track meet. Belle Isle furnished our family album with several photographs. In one, my parents pose affectionately at the base of a large tree. But romantic sensibility did not hold forever. Another family photograph from the island shows how people found lighter things in heavier matters: several generations of Amatos (perhaps taking their cue from a well-known Coney Island photo) lie on their stomachs on a beach in their bathing suits, making a comparative display of their ample behinds. Whose exactly was biggest was always worth a laugh.

Life on the east side convinced Joe and Ethel that they had a front row seat to history in the making, and they and their generation cheered the city, despite the Great Depression, as if they were members of its chamber of commerce. The foundries and presses of the auto industry that made the world go round glowed and reverberated throughout their neighborhood.[10] The completion of both the Ambassador Bridge in 1929 and the tunnel to Windsor, Canada, in 1930, added to Detroit's status as an international port.[11] In the same period, the new Detroit Zoo became one of the first in the nation to exhibit its animals without bars. In 1929 booming Detroit ranked third in the nation in building and construction, behind only New York and Chicago.

As the Depression slowed the city's growth, my father and his generation continued to cheer for Detroit in the most constricted but symbolically concentrated terrain of the sports fields. In 1935 Detroit fans experienced ecstasy. In that single remarkable year, the Detroit Tigers claimed their first World Series Championship in baseball, the Lions won the National Football League championship, and the Red Wings concluded the 1935–36 season by winning the Stanley Cup. In 1935, black heavyweight boxing champ Joe Louis—Alabama-born, Detroit-bred, and unmatched in popularity—had a stunning year. Fighting thirteen times, the "Brown Bomber" most notably knocked out former world heavyweight champion Primo Carnera in six rounds and former heavyweight champion Max Baer for the first time in the German's career. In a 1938 rematch, Louis avenged his 1936 defeat at the hands of Germany's world heavyweight hero, Max Schmeling, by knocking him out in the first round. Detroiters celebrated Louis's victory as a triumph over Nazi superiority, anticipating what the city would gloriously do as freedom's "Arsenal of Democracy" in the coming war.

The Most Compelling Art of All

However, my young parents were intent on the more serious competition, that of family economics. They met in 1932, when they were both twenty. As the oldest children in working-class families, each had already been out working full time on the family's behalf for almost four years. Ethel, who had quit school after tenth grade, worked at a variety of jobs, including the one at Sobin's Five and Ten Cent Store. Good with her hands and fast with her lips, she liked to interact with people and always, bubbling over with energy, had a project underway.

If Ethel were a good and energetic worker, Joe belonged to that breed born to work. He got his first lessons in diplomacy selling fruit off his step-father's horse and cart to factory workers, learning how to convince workers not to return hard fruit, but to take it home and allow it to ripen. He worked through his school years at the Italian store in Eastern Market, graduated early from Southeastern High School, and went to work for Western Union.

The young Ethel and Joe understood the first challenge of all mill-town and city workers: finding steady work that paid a decent and dependable wage. They embraced unionism, which grew dramatically in Detroit in the 1930s. Ethel, who had gone on more than one walk-out strike and had theo-logically instructed a boss or two where they might deliver themselves for long-term keeping, observed picket lines her whole life. Joe was a union man almost from the day he entered the labor force until the day he died sixty years later. Acknowledging his membership in the working class and his alle-giance to the Democratic Party, especially to Franklin Delano Roosevelt and Harry S. Truman, Joe endorsed unionism as a collective way to improve con-ditions and create a fairer and better nation.[12] He faithfully attended union meetings, mastered bylaws and rules of order, held union offices, bargained contracts, represented grievances, went on two or three short-lived strikes, and ran the union's credit union. In the post–World War II period he trav-eled to national union conventions, making Mom jealous when he went to Boston in 1948, and taking Mom, recently widowed Aunt Milly, and me to Miami in 1951. His union was not aggressive, but he welcomed the affiliation of his AFL Chapter of Western Union with the CIO. On a principal battlefield between management and labor, Joe welcomed the phenomenal growth of unions, whose membership went from one in eight workers in 1930 to more than one in four in 1940.[13] He cheered the outcome of the successful Flint Sit-Down Strike against General Motors in 1936 and a run of union victories in Detroit on the streets and at the bargaining tables in 1937. He also recognized labor's indebtedness to FDR's National Labor Relations Act (the Wagner Act) of 1935. No one in the family disputed Joe on the matter of unionism and the Democratic Party. When once I thoughtlessly confessed, sometime in the 1980s, to having voted for my first and only Republican, my father instantly and aggressively labeled me "Judas!"

But the war followed close on the Depression, and the military heroism of his younger brothers-in-laws' generation quickly eclipsed the labor heroism of my father's. Indeed, family historians must critically examine how long are the shadows cast by "the greatest generation." Going on strike or fighting the Communists in his union did not make my father a warrior. Certainly, his courage did not match the heroic deeds of his brothers-in-law, navy corpsman Uncle Bill, who survived the sinking of his ship in the Mediterranean, and infantryman Jimmy Messina, who once causally mentioned to me that he had killed "ten or so Germans" on his way up the Italian Peninsula and later on the way from Normandy to Paris.

The whole family took up the mantle of the war. Grandpa and Grandma Linsdeau flew a service star banner in their front window for son Bill. Brother-in-law Benny used his tool and die expertise to make military parts, while cousin Rose Notaro actually gave the family its own "Rosie the Riveter." The whole family worked long hours, rationed goods (which we also hoarded and exchanged in small quantities), grew victory gardens, turned in coat hangers for scrap iron, and took in boarders because of a housing shortage. Working two and three shifts for extended periods, Detroiters, amid thuds of mighty presses and the flashing blue of arc-welding torches, filled the city's supply yards and fields with the tanks, jeeps, trucks, planes, and ducks (amphibious landing craft) that secured victory in Europe and the Far East. After fashioning our own celebration for Victory over Japan, which boisterously amounted to a handful of us going about the neighborhood and randomly tipping over garbage cans in a few alleys, as if it were Halloween, I went to downtown Detroit with my father to join the city's celebration. In a Mardi Gras atmosphere, which killed two and wounded some fifty others, masses of people were spontaneously mingling, embracing, hugging, and kissing. Young men sat on the tops of disabled streetcars, which stood like

little islands in the surging human tides that filled Woodward Avenue and poured onto adjacent streets and avenues. It was a parade without an end, not even an idea, only the indisputable certitude of victory, the emotional relief of having at last won, the chance again to be something else. Such incomprehensible jubilation—and never did we so decidedly belong to Detroit and Detroit so decidedly belong to America as then, the year we—as family, city, and nation, hand in hand—defeated the Axis powers. In the fall of '45 our beloved Detroit Tigers again beat the Chicago Cubs in the World Series.

A New Home Front on Evanston Street

In some way, the war was only a diversion on my parent's mission to secure a home, which was the great prize for a life well spent. The stage for this intense and unrelenting competition was the Great Depression and undefined but certain past poverty. They came of age during its first three years, when national unemployment soared by 25 percent and production, consumption, and wages sank proportionately.[14] In 1931, the year of the international banking crisis and the year the Federal Reserve determined to maintain the value of the dollar, Detroit entered the doldrums. A million auto workers were laid off, with production down four million units, or 80 percent. The city defaulted on a $400 million debt and began to pay city workers with its own scrip, which stores accepted as currency.[15] The unemployed sold apples, soup lines swelled, thrift gardens sprouted up around the city, and a U.S. census considered Detroit, with 223,500 unemployed, the hardest hit of the country's nineteen largest cities.[16] The scoreboard registered scarcity and downward mobility for many.

Yet, for Detroiters like Joe and those who kept their jobs, the sky had not fallen. In fact, at work Joe had advanced from his starting position to mail clerk. Although I don't have old pay stubs, checkbooks, and other financial records, which would have proven so important to a full economic history of the family, general indexes of wages in the telephone and telegraph

In front of the Amatos' duplex on Hillger Street during World War II. By rows, from top: Phil Trupiano; Ethel, Benny Rizutto, and his wife Pauline; Jimmy Messina (in cap), his wife Josephine, Rosalia, and Millie; myself and my cousin Angel.

industry suggest that his wages sank by less than 10 percent between 1930 and 1934, from $1,410 a year to $1,338. Between 1934 and 1939, while food and other prices stayed the same or fell, telephone and telegraph workers' wages had increased to an average of $1,600 a year. This put Joe's wages, nationally, half again higher than the average worker's annual wage. Indeed, an income of $30 a week bought a fair amount of goods when a loaf of bread cost only five or six cents and one paid $5 for a suit or pair of shoes. Dad's income in the 1930s accounts for how he successfully purchased the Hillger duplex in which Rosalia and his sisters lived.[17]

Nevertheless, for my father to abandon the small second-floor flat he and Mom rented just south of Jefferson Avenue and to buy his bride the new house she was pushing for, my father really had to sharpen his pencil. The real and relative deprivation of his youth still remained fully alive for him and his generation, in what historian David Levine calls "the immediacy of the past-in-the-present."[18] He could trust, as much as one can in such fickle matters, that he would keep his job at Western Union and that wages would incrementally improve relative to the cost of living. He was, after all, simply joining the national trend; the 1930 census saw the majority of the U.S. population living in homes of their own. Furthermore, all his sisters were married, or soon would be. All would be out of the Hillger home except Milly, who stayed on with Grandmother Rosalia. At the same time, with Ethel having suffered a serious miscarriage that precluded the possibility of her having another child, Joe could safely deduce that he would have only a small family of his own to support. However, other factors dictated against taking on another mortgage. First, the least controllable factor: Ethel's determination to have a better brick home in one of the newer developments on the far east side, some three or more miles from the old neighborhood. At the same time, Joe, a Sicilian traditionalist, refused to allow Ethel to work outside the home. His desire to have a well-kept home, his advancing white-collar worker's desire to imitate the wealthier classes, the shortage of decent jobs for Ethel—whatever the exact combination of these factors might have been, they formed a whole on which he wouldn't budge. Like so many men of that era, he never anticipated how much energy, leisure, and individual character he was sequestering in our comparatively small and relatively isolated home.

Sometime early in 1941, before the declaration of world war, Ethel and Joe reached an agreement: she would have a new home and be a stay-at-home homemaker and mother. Taking on a 25-year mortgage for $5,000 at 3 percent interest, they bought a small, two-story, Tudor-style brick house on the far east side on Evanston Street, in the McNichols (Six Mile) and Harper Avenue area. Owning a home whose value put them at the time in the top 25 percent of city homeowners, Ethel and Joe began life in a subdivision built in the 1920s, whose streets bore such pretentious names as Buckingham, Nottingham, and Berkshire. But the neighborhood held a mix of Yankee, Canadian, German, Irish, Hungarian, Polish, and Slavic families, whose bread earners worked in factories, sold insurance, owned small stores, served as city police, or were retired. With two or three bedrooms, unfinished basements, and finished or unfinished attics, most of the homes had single-car garages. They were situated on gravel-covered alleys along which hollyhocks grew and down which an occasional ragman came, perched on his cart and bellowing on a small silver horn to announce his coming. Out front, a milkman on a horse-drawn truck passed, as did chanting fruit sellers, with voices so similar to those still heard in the markets of Palermo and on the streets of Cerda and Montemaggiore Belsito. They called us from our homes to see their "Green beans, sweet potatoes, and strawberries." Occasional vendors, peddlers, and knife sharpeners came to our door, but we did the majority of our shopping a block away on Harper Avenue, which had a couple of grocery stores, a hardware store, and various other shops—including one that, to my youthful puzzlement, sold horse meat for a while during the war. Also nearby, and readily reached on foot, were dentists, doctors, movie theaters, my grade school and a Lutheran grade school, numerous churches, and our own Catholic St. Matthews.

Beyond greetings and occasional conversations carried on outdoors with rakes in hand, adults in our neighborhood carried on their own private lives, while children percolated throughout, playing on the streets, in the alleys, vacant fields, and lots on which new homes were being built. What transpired behind the walls of neighbors' houses remained largely a matter of

guess and gossip, but more than one on our block of twelve homes was lubri-
cated and sequestered by alcoholism. By almost any measure, family privacy
and individuality superseded community, even though during the war we
shared infrequent air raid drills, occasional social visits, and some of the men
like my father found a way to rake leaves while listening to a Detroit Tigers
baseball game, blaring from a well-positioned radio.

Ethel and Joe began a cautious, but constant, embrace of consumerism,
which, with its origins in the nineteenth century and despite the Depression,
had inched its way forward in the 1930s. Brand names of foods and cleaning
products punctuated the conversations of those who knew the muck of farm
and the grime of the factory. Radios, furniture, and cars transformed everyday life into distinct pleasures to be sought out and experienced rather than
a succession of inescapable pains to be endured. Entertainment and recreation became the assumed and deserved reward for the working classes, as,
dressed in style, they stepped out to dances, bars, and weddings, or ventured
from the city for weekends in a cabin or small vacations in northern Michigan. Joe sported a nice suit for high school graduation and proved himself to
be a snappy dresser from then on, even wearing two-tone shoes, an impressive overcoat, and a broad and soft fedora from the days he courted Ethel. For
the next three decades Mom, who was a handsome woman, wore fashionable though moderately priced clothes, higher or lower heels, and a smaller
or bigger hat, as the year's trends dictated.

Their ascent to the world of abundance arose out of their economic planning. But it also had its course in the revival of national industrial commercial society and the reemergence of the automobile industry, foretold in 1937
when national car registrations returned to 90 percent of what they had been
in 1929. During the war, the city's workforce increase by two hundred thousand and its income tripled. By 1950, the auto industry was in overdrive and
the Depression was visible only in the pessimists' rearview mirrors. Detroit
was the richest city in the nation, with its 489,300 families enjoying a median
income of $4,090.[19]

As prices increased, so did Joe's wages. He was promoted from clerk to
manager of the messengers, to head of collections, and to branch office super-

visor. (Telegraphers and telegraph workers reported average wages increasing from $2,250 in 1945 to almost $3,000 in 1950.[20]) Progress meant increased consumerism, which could be inventoried by a string of electric appliances, power tools, a new sewing machine, and for me a succession of new Western Union bicycles, which my father bought at a discount. Changes in our unfinished basement after the war showed the progress: a new gas furnace displaced our sooty coal furnace and bin. My father built himself a workroom in one corner of the virtually empty furnace room, while a pool table and ping-pong table occupied the non-partitioned remainder of the basement. The mechanical wringer washing machine, scrub board, and clothesline were the last to be updated, to an electric washer and dryer.

Appreciative of what hard times and work meant, my father embraced the new material order. At every turn he had learned to accept and impose order on the world emerging around him. He mastered its schedules, made inventories, kept accounts, even ordered his gestures: he argued that you should wear your watch on your left wrist if you were right-handed, in order to protect the watch. He kept his closet in perfect order and always flattened and organized the money in his wallet by denominations, face-side up and forward. He never did yard or housework without putting on work clothes, and he always had the right brushes and brooms for cleaning the screens and sweeping the floor, the proper sponge and chamois for cleaning glass, and so on. Everything he painted got a second coat. His work spaces and tool bench showed the same order as his files and bedroom drawers.

A quick and keen counter, my father kept numeric tabs on the world. He filled in scorecards at ball games, was designated scorekeeper of all card games, and noted all personal documents with careful and neatly written annotations and dates. To my amazement, he kept his mechanical pencils in lead and functioning. My father economically accumulated, used, and kept things, with a skill his son never mastered, or had even the least inclination to learn. More romantic and obsessed, I sought a state of mind and being, rather than a way of doing and performing. I couldn't equate my need with work or my leisure simply with time to be spent away from work. After running an errand, paying bills, and doing exterior household chores, my father was

My father in his easy chair

content to sit down and read the paper, do the daily crossword puzzle, which he usually finished, and listen to a ball game, and then fall asleep in his easy chair before going to bed, as ritual required, at 10:00 PM. His weekend routine was much the same, except he added visits to relatives, more shopping, and Sunday morning Mass.

My father never went out with friends. He wouldn't try his hand at golf, although he did try a little backyard bocce ball when I brought home a set of wooden balls. He did nothing as a lark; there was no spur of the moment for him. He belonged to no clubs, did no politics, and sat on no church or civic boards. At one period in the middle 1950s, my mother incongruously outfitted him with a homemade plaid shirt and a string tie and set him on

The square dancing couple

the square dance trail, which for a few seasons led from public gym to public gym, an exhausting two and three nights a week.

Shy, reserved, my father never agonized or philosophized about life. He did good work, married, and in the process became a Detroiter and an American who knew how to handle life, money, and his family affairs.

Driven to a New Place

The car was the prow of my parents' consumerism. After all, the car was the invention that invented Detroit—what would we have been without it? We looked at the world through its windshield. Putting your hands on a car, even an old jalopy, indicated that you were on the go, and when you had enough money to purchase a new car, it meant you had really gotten somewhere. It truly reordered our senses of place, speed, and self.

Cars wrote the biographies of my parents and their generations. During or just before World War II, Grandpa Linsdau got his hands on a wonderful, used, forest green '37 Chevy convertible, with a fashionable rumble seat. It was so flashy a stranger once offered to buy it when Grandpa stopped at a red light. Aunt Mabel, who too had a new home on the east side, thanks to her husband Jimmy's small but prospering refrigeration repair shop, drove a new '47 Chrysler coop with "fluid drive." Uncle Bill, who had just purchased his first home with a popular FHA government loan earmarked for veterans, had a used '47 Studebaker with overdrive. The cars my father bought marked off stages of his life. Giving up his old Model T in about 1938, he bought a used Model A to bring me home from the hospital. Shortly after buying the Evanston Street house, he bought a slightly used, four-door, white 1941 Plymouth, whose value was enhanced because in 1942 Detroit automobile production was fully converted to military production. My father paid around five hundred dollars and threw in his Model A as part of the deal. Of course, except for Sunday trips to the grandparents and short vacations, the Plymouth took back seat to the more economical city bus, which stopped just a block from our house and allowed my father to read the daily newspaper, which he folded neatly into squares for confined bus reading. (Mom learned to drive after the war, but she could never back the car out of the garage, down the driveway, along the side of the house, and past the great maple tree.) Dad next bought a succession of economical new Chevys—a 1947, a 1951, and the 1953, on which I learned to drive and whose gearbox I wrecked.

Acquiring a car afforded modern men as important a ritual as buying a team of horses in earlier times. The process always started with extensive but imprecise shopping, took more concrete form with general bargaining, advanced to fine haggling, and was summarized by self-congratulations. My father conducted the process over weeks and even months, ending it only when he was satisfied he had squeezed everything he could from the salesman, who usually capitulated by throwing in free undercoating, floor mats,

My parents with me and our new 1941 Plymouth

and stories of losing money on the deal. My father had to satisfy my mother on the matter of color, which usually meant green, giving her another way to tell the world she was Irish. The final ceremony required showing off the newly purchased car to the relatives. It began with a walk around the car, then proceeded to a sit behind the wheel and the opening of the hood to inspect the motor and of the trunk to gape at its spaciousness. It ended with a test spin around the block, which invariably proved that the new car was as good as it looked.

Cars took us on our first long vacations "up north," as Michiganders say, or yet all the way down to Florida, where Michiganders in large numbers were learning to vacation and, like Aunt May, to winter. Uncles returned home from family vacations to brag about total miles they had driven, the most miles traveled in a single day, and miles achieved per gallon. The automobile found its more plebian but important use in the 1940s and 1950s by keeping the family in contact. The car assembled the family for birthdays, weddings, hospitals visits, and picnics. Extending our normal weekend or even evening trips by ten miles in all directions, it tied the near east side to the far east side and its suburbs, while making Sunday and holiday visits to grandparents Rosalia, Frances, and Bill more obligatory than going to church.

The car facilitated relatives' moves to the suburbs. They had been migrating eastward almost since their arrival in Detroit. On one count they followed the rich industrialists who, before World War I, fled the dust, din, and tumult of downtown, which was largely of their own making.[21] But my relatives moved to the far east side in the 1950s and 1960s for two reasons. Their improved wages allowed them to buy better homes, on the one hand. But there was also a push factor: the astronomically growing black population, which having suffered deep unemployment during the Depression was identified with increased crime, social disorder, and depreciating property values, began renting and buying homes on the near east side. The whites, especially the younger generation, were unfortunately in flight, simultaneously to improve and to save themselves.

But my parents' move from Evanston Street to the near suburb of East Detroit (recently renamed Eastpointe to disassociate itself with troubled

Detroit) was necessitated by something different. In 1954 their home was condemned for the construction of Interstate 94, part of the 42,500-mile Eisenhower Interstate Highway and Defense System. This single act took the boyhood home I knew and sliced my childhood world in two.

For our Evanston Street home the city made a payment of approximately $16,500, which tripled the price my parents had paid fifteen years before and slightly more than doubled the unadjusted rate of $7,500 for a median home in Michigan.[22] Its replacement, a two-bedroom ranch home with an attached single-car garage (and no alley) in East Detroit, cost $19,500.[23] Only six blocks from the city limits, it meant a longer bus ride, with a transfer, for my father. The Lincoln Avenue house had an ample yard with trees, a small living room and kitchen, and no dining room, although it had a three-season porch and a large unfinished basement. The new neighbors, which included alcoholics, old bachelors, juvenile delinquents, a Pole who had been in a German POW camp, and a new convert to Buddhism, led Ethel to call her new neighborhood "Lincoln Place," after the popular, scandalous, and decadent new television show, *Peyton Place*.

Besides getting to know several immediate neighbors, gregarious Ethel ventured out into the surrounding blocks to meet people. She organized a group of young neighborhood girls around seven or eight years old into what she dubbed her junior nurses. At nearby St. Veronica's, she and Joe joined in card games, rummage sales, and dances, turning a few retired Italian and mixed-ethnic couples into close friends; my father, changing his habit, sat on the church board. At the same time, they learned to shuttle their way among various stores, which sat a mile or two away in all directions. Their new home in East Detroit spelled the dawn of economic security and enhanced material goods for my parents, but that did nothing to quell Ethel's mood swings, which became increasingly severe. More and more alone, she was forced to try to talk and think her way into the community she didn't have. She abandoned what little canning she had done. She set her sewing aside. With still plentiful energy, she had less and less to do other than shop, put a shine on her household possessions, and carry on ever-longer conversations on the telephone.

Her isolation deepened in the middle 1950s, as branches of the extended family simultaneously grew further apart, and it intensified in 1956, when I left for the university. The problems of the grandparents escalated as they entered fully into the pains, maladies, and ordeals of old age. The families of brothers and sisters increasingly withdrew into their own lives. Nieces and nephews did not go on to college, but rather married and took up their isolated places as small families. In the world of new goods, suburban homes, and annual trips to Florida or Las Vegas, there were divorces, interfamilial fights, mental disorders, and serious illnesses. Family visits diminished, and when they did occur they were shorter and there was less card playing. They frequently provoked one of Ethel's talking jags. In truth, the order that she and Joe had built sequestered and caged my mom. Her undiagnosed mania and depression oscillated back and forth with greater depth and frequency. It was as if the unused energy of a lifetime surged back and forth within her. She was one generation too early and one class too poor to have the world as her worthy opponent. Yet, to the end of her life she supported the notion that a woman's place was in the home.

By the middle of the 1950s Ethel and Joe had culminated what could be called a long family journey. It began fifty years before when Antonino and Rosalia left the mountains of western Sicily, or two hundred years before when the Acadian Boodrys were uprooted from the swamps of Nova Scotia. Now by language, consumption, experience, and identity, Ethel and Joe had become true Detroiters, car owners, suburbanites, and real Americans. Their journey, following the main arc of modernity, had traversed an immense distance between pain and comfort, scarcity and abundance, collectivity and individuality, and necessity and choice. Joe was tired and content with what they had accomplished, while restless Ethel, true daughter of Frances, did not find a terrain adequate to her spirit and energies. After my father's death, when she was living in Minnesota, her illness was diagnosed and treated, and she found some measure of peace. Outliving my father by thirteen and half years, Ethel lived until she was ninety. She never lost her keen mind and able tongue, but without a victorious narrative to relate, Ethel, a common soul, battled the world daily with the word and wit she could muster. She never lost sight of the fact that her son would write of her and the family.

Home, Always But One Identity Away

I found no new home in East Detroit and made no sure step from youth to maturity. I was sixteen when we moved, the first "only child" in all the known generations of my ancestors, and I had no idea who I was, what I could, would, or should make of myself. The cement canyon of the I-94 expressway cut across my heart just as the cruel doubts of adolescent self-consciousness shredded what I had inherited. Detached from my childhood home, I did not know where, when, or how I would ever be at home again.

The Evanston Street house had formed the first skin of my senses. It was the hub of my first experiences. In it I came to know my mother and father; I had a bedroom of my own; and I learned the meanings of kitchen, living room, basement, and attic. From it I ventured into the world, I went out on the grass, down the sidewalk to make friends, or along the crushed limestone alley, where rats ran and hollyhocks grew, to climb a tree, to wade in a spring-filled pond, to go to the store to buy a loaf of bread, or to take a shortcut to school. But now Evanston was gone, and my compass for being at home in the world was set awhirl.

The dismantlers of my home picked it clean of bricks, detached it from the basement, and left the skeleton of an empty wood frame. They set great beams under it, jacked it up, and slowly towed it away, as if a solemn cortege, to a waiting foundation about a mile away. I never wanted to visit the reborn house, even though it stood only a few doors down from my Uncle Bill's small FHA home on Wayburn Avenue. I was detached, displaced like the Joads, the Okie family of John Steinbeck's *Grapes of Wrath*, which I read that very year. My sympathies joined all who suffered the ravaging armies of progress.

They cut down the giant maple tree at the end of the drive, the tree into which I had once futilely pounded nails, seeking to tap its spring sap. The neighbors' houses, the backyards, the fences and alleys, the fields and stores out back—all that was mine they excavated with a twenty-foot-deep trench,

without beginning or end, on whose flat bottom six concrete lanes of traffic still speed and stream, day and night. For this kind of common modern
loss, be it the slums of London for the Metro or the arid hills of Los Ange-
les and the farmland of Minnesota for freeways—there is no corresponding
common rite. Only a single pedestrian bridge stands where I once lived and
from which I can peer down to the bottom of the great gulf of no more. The
loss of the Evanston home anticipated my approaching darker visions of the
emptying conformities of business and the pending obliterations of nuclear
bombs.

By the time we moved to East Detroit, I had become captive of the automobile that built the throughway, created the suburbs, and took away my
home. It drove me to and from friends' houses. It chauffeured me to my
old high school, Denby, which I continued to attend even though we had
moved outside its boundaries. And I went by car to the Country Club of
Detroit, in Grosse Pointe, where I caddied and ran the driving range, and
to the municipal courses where I played and captained a champion high
school golf team.

I decided that I wanted to go to college inexplicably, out of the blue. I
was sixteen and just starting my junior year. While driving alone to buy milk
in the fall of 1954, I got the idea that I might go to college, and by the time I
started back home, I had decided that, yes, I would. Whatever its source, the
effect of conversion could not be doubted. The Cs, Ds, and even an F or two I
had earned as a freshman and sophomore turned into As and Bs, and I started
to dress and act like a future college kid. The turnaround won me a generous
four-year Chick Evans Caddy Scholarship, which offered room and tuition at
the University of Michigan.

When I left for the university in the fall of 1956, I didn't own a car. Like so
many others, however, I carried with me a variety of sentiments and sensibilities that would spawn a generation of "beats" and "existentialists." I was not
at home in East Detroit and I would not be at home in Ann Arbor. For four
years, on foot, and living in the Evans scholarship house at the University of
Michigan, with two, three, and four sharing a room, I, who had been raised

A full follow-through by the high-school senior in the backyard of the Lincoln house

My high school graduation photo, 1956

in a bedroom of my own, tried to puzzle out a career, a future, and a home of my own. I went to the university without a close friend or an articulate and confident defining tradition. My roommates, mostly engineering and business majors who strove for an immediate place in fraternity society and an ultimate place in the world of money, provided no companionship. In fact, they became the antithesis of what I thought the good life should be.

As no one in my family's past had ever been, I was detached from necessity, drinking at the well of judgment, choice, and self-definition. My father's model, acceptance of fate, did not help me with self-invention. I burdened my nervous, energetic, depressed mind, as if I were Frances or Ethel. Books were my addiction. I subverted every conversation with my interest in ultimate questions.

To get up in the morning was to resume my previous day's self-interrogation: Who was I, what I was doing, and what did it meant anyhow? My mother's declaration that I would lose my faith by going to the university soon turned into an accurate prophecy. Her fear that I would become different from the family, and her well-rehearsed accusations that I would never find a job, get married, and have children, furthered my sense of alienation. Reversing the assumptions of scarcity that shaped my family's past, I judged contemporary America to be vulgar and materialistic. I could make nothing out of my Italian or ethnic background to define world or self. With questions of all sorts roiling about in my head, for a short period, I anointed myself a rational philosopher and promptly gave proof to Alexis De Tocqueville's idea that "Nothing is more unproductive to the mind than an abstract idea."[24]

Fortunately, three things spared me this void and returned me home to myself. I reconverted to my Catholicism, not just as a faith but also as an intellectual well. It connected me in eternal time to my parents and grandparents. Rome gave me Europe and the world as a surrogate for the United States I had lost; Catholic doctrine furnished me in time a universality—the Middle Ages, and a whole western tradition of Jew, Greek, and Roman—for the place I no longer held in contemporary society.

Second, my marriage to my beloved wife, Catherine Bavolack, which took place in 1966, when I was in graduate school at the University of Rochester, saved me more than anything from my indwelling. It reconnected me to flesh, love, and family. With my anxious, idea-laden head reattached to my body, I was restored to my senses. I bought a set of used clubs and returned to the links. I took my skates out of the closet and again flew around the ice. Over time, with a good wife and four children, I found a fleshy niche in this world of matter and things. Though of Eastern (Byzantine) Rite, Cathy was also Catholic, and religion, as it did for Jacob Linsdau and Mary Jane O'Brien, formed an all-important bridge across ethnic differences. Her grandparents, members of a non–nationalized people from the Carpatho-Rusin Mountains, were most striking of all from McAdoo, Pennsylvania, a town bordering Kelayres, the tiny coal village to which Antonino and Rosalia first immigrated. Cathy and I were doing what villagers have been doing since time immemorial: We were marrying a cousin.

Third, for us to have and know our place in the world, I needed only to fashion our marriage and religion into a tradition. As a highly mixed matter of discovery and purpose, in which words and concepts evolve only slowly, I first crafted parents, grandparents, and my own family into new ethnics, the ranks of the Catholic working classes, and a type of personal, historical, and ethical unit. Over time, and satisfying my exaggerated tendency as a philosopher and historian to order the world, I located our family roots among the European peasantry and the rural poor of the American countryside. There I knitted together lives and fates of my family. Finally, detaching my quest for tradition from a distinct people, a fixed class, or a place on land or in village, I transformed family into this ongoing story of settlement and migration, a two-hundred-fifty-year history of the American poor and their search for home.

Proving how porous American society is to mass, popular, and ethnic cultures, as well as to high traditional culture, I became a college teacher and a professional historian. I was the first in the family to have had the leisure, training, compulsion, and, I believe, actual need to utilize the past to establish a meaning in the present. Memoirs, genealogy, and family history are recent and novel undertakings for the poor. Up to the last hundred years, the act of writing family history to define one's inheritance belonged to the upper classes and those who presumed a superior lineage. Individualizing and personalizing memory has been until recently a modern and exclusive sentiment.

But individuals can now do for themselves what historians in the last two or three centuries have done for public causes, institutions, nations, and ideologies: give themselves a history.[25] Individuals need no longer be subservient to the narrow elite that would deny the majority particular histories of their own and restrict history to those with "significance"—power, money, and influence. Indeed, if God and his son have deemed the individual worthy of covenant and salvation, does not each person merit a history? And, in turn, should not a pluralistic democracy welcome individual and family histories, in all their variety?

Writing family history acknowledges, commemorates, and teaches. Paying a debt and doing a duty, it assembles and distributes a singular inheritance. Even though it may record only ordinary journeys, mundane work, common ordeals, and all-important everyday sacrifices, family history honors the dead and forms a crucial inheritance for the living. In our own small way, family historians recognize the humble living truth in the words the great Shakespeare had written on his tombstone: "I have affirmed the distinction of my mother's name and restored my father's honor; I have laid claim to my lost inheritance; I have created that inheritance."[26]

The Reason For,
and The Matter Of, Family History

I begin this conclusion with a three-part confession. First, I plead guilty to having ended this work in a state of ecstasy and exhaustion. I have taken too much of my family into myself and, at least for the time being, depleted my empathy and imagination in recomposing their lives. I have grown weary over anguishing, especially in the case of my parents and grandparents, whether I have divulged too much and yet said too little about their lives. As much as the dead deserve to be remembered, they also merit the cool shade of selective forgetting, rather than the continually glaring light of revelation. There comes a time when to heal I must heed Christ's advice: even historians must let the dead bury the dead. If we are to meet again, let it be in raiment free of leaden memory and the embroidered mazes of an intricate past.

Second, I must confess that I have also used the doors of my family's past to enter the dwellings of others. Their lives have indulged me in my pursuit of history and humanity itself. Their migrations forged a path tracing my own route to the present and modernity. They gave me a narrative and a philosophy of home.

Third, as much as I have tried to make *Jacob's Well* a truthful family history, I also admit that it is in some ways an invented story. No family history can be reduced to simply pursuing last names, bloodlines, or most recently, DNA identification; no family, in turn, can be fixed over time in immutable beliefs, ways, and practices. Any family history that spans multiple generations can only be considered as a complex, constantly mutating, and ongoing historical creation.

In creating *Jacob's Well*, I have drawn on the trinity of family history: gene-alogy; history, especially local and micro-regional history; and storytelling. Genealogy, which at times seemed a fumbling, clumsy, and expensive craft aimed at casting scanty stick-and-rope bridges across time, proved absolutely indispensable. The turn of the microfilm reader, the click of a computer, and the aid of all those amateur and professional genealogists identified a majority of my family's members. Local history, also commonly ignored and even disdained by some professional historians, introduced me to the land they walked—the landscape and environment they inhabited, their neigh-bors, institutions, churches, economies, and social circumstances. Stories, the most precious cargo a family carries, were my guiding threads though the labyrinth of time. They individualize and universalize the family past to which I belonged.

In so far as *Jacob's Well* is the measure, family history is created against the background of obscure origins, in the face of missing evidence, with reference to unfathomable stories and persisting ambiguities. While my family history acknowledges a whole past, it was constructed out of a pau-city of information. My questions about roles and changing family rela-tions exceeded my evidence. Genealogy and local history, the best tools I had, proved insufficient. The speculation that rushed in to fill the void did not produce a spine for a narrative or the substance for anything rep-resenting certain explanations. Hypotheses and conjectures never com-pensate for missing facts; generalizations, though they can be subtle and insightful, can stifle a living past in conjecture and rumination.

In a family's past we chew on a cud of memory never to be entirely digested. Borders and boundaries forever need deciphering. The dead, who can be entirely forgotten, often survive only as ghosts of myth and unverified stories. And even the best-known and most documented dead are refracted in the mirror of present views, interests, passions, and sen-sibilities. The ultimate consolatory appeal of Judaism, Christianity, and Islam forever lies in the belief that the one and great God jealously, lov-ingly, and unfalteringly listens to human hearts and all the stories of Jacob's rich progeny.

Why?

Family history teaches what abstractions cannot. It offers wisdom about life that springs like a cat from a pointed story or cunning proverb. Irish poet Michael Coady, in his memoir *All Souls*, wrote that genealogy "should not be the neat assembly of pedigree culminating smugly in self, but its exact opposite: the extension of the personal beyond the self to encounter the intimate unknown of others in our blood." And yet, it does more. Producing the fruit of all true historical study, it expands us, far beyond blood and name, to acknowledge and imagine, to imagine and acknowledge, how vast the variety of other places and peoples.

These possibilities attracted me as I grew older and the immediacy of the present loosened its grip on me. Public life increasingly invited me to a party I do not enjoy. Approaching seventy, I have wrapped myself tighter in the details of the past. I egotistically yearn for the community in which I was truly an *Amato*, a beloved child! I would be without gratitude if I did not cast, with my whole heart, a long, deep, and grateful glance back toward those who made my childhood so rich in personalities and senses.

On this count, *Jacob's Well* is an act of piety. I intend my work to be as the tightest grained and the most lasting stone I could hew out of words. I join the family dead in the fight against oblivion, which the course of time and the earth's turn counsel. From history's crossroads, I brought into me multitudes of the family. I assembled therein a tribe of Jacob—and I found assurance in Walt Whitman's justifying words, "Do I contradict myself? Very well then I contradict myself, I am large, I contain multitudes." The dead are wild within me. I have puzzled them, sought their identities, queried their stories, and heard their advice: Take care lest you drown in the past that you have allowed to well up within you. The dead can shout down the living.

Finally, one command deserves attention: Do not convert your familiarity with the dead into a belief about the great reach of your spirit. The dead exist beyond the sum of thought, and no matter the multitude of them you take in, you will remain one and here of this earth and this time. However, if you think deep on the dead, you do, as if participating in a sacrament, commingle yourself with them. They lead you to strange and out-of-the-way places, which they make familiar. They become the saints of your daily liturgical calendar, providing models of such ordinary virtues as hard work, tenacity, loyalty, and self-sacrifice.

But more than an attraction for the dead turned me to the writing of *Jacob's Well*. I am a voracious historian. Although I am a trained and writing European intellectual and cultural historian, I have spent more than two decades creating local and regional history, which, as I spelled out in *Rethinking Home*, shares long and open borders with genealogy and family history. Having learned to give life to the dead of other tribes, it followed that I should seek to animate my own—to go a step further and make them the measure of nations and empires.

Family history enriched and consoled me. It filled my soul with other souls, and there can be no better sustenance. It offered examples of cleverness, wit, kindness, and charity—each, in a distinct way, so necessary to keeping everyday household life afloat. Wives and husbands, starting with my parents and going back across the generations, repeatedly displayed that unexplained willingness to sacrifice for mate and child. Whether they did so because they did not know how to do otherwise, or for their own self-interest, or for love, the family of Jacob defined a common and unheralded loyalty and tenacity to family, this institution older than state and church.

Writing family history also chastened me. It reminded me that we are of flesh, born of our biological inheritance and made of material conditions, local circumstances, and historical change. Things outside and beyond influence us. A season's rainfall, the opening of new lands, the work of a horse, a shift in trade, a spike in credit rates, a new road, or yet the spread of an idea, all played their part in the twists and turns of a family's fate.

But family history can also augment our wisdom. Knowing the detail of one's own family spares its historian from being taken in by groundless collective histories of others. It rescues one from the claims of official political history and imperializing ideologies. Abstractions cannot withstand the prick of experience, the piercing power of an anecdote. The history of a family constitutes a reply to generational solipsism: We are decidedly not alone. Contradicting contemporary society's specious claims to mastery over nature and its pervasive belief that choice exists in all things, family history points to limits, compromises, forgiveness, and judgments, a more complex, frail, and elemental environment in which we live cheek to jowl, wit to wit, day by day. Generations, in truth, do not live independently of the past that begat them or separately from the gradual incursion of future that displaces them. In writing family history, we enroll ourselves in our own kind, and thus embrace our own limits.

And What Will Come of It

I ask, as writers of their own family histories inevitably do, what will come of this family history—and the very memory of the family I have inherited, invented, and re-animated. Reflecting a common prejudice of the old, I struggle with the idea that future generations will not take the dead to heart, as my generation did. Modern times have driven Rosalia's *miseria* into the shadows and put Heaven and Hell themselves in retreat. Styles and fashions fill the present with itself; the working middle class accepts the economic rewards of bigger homes, more goods, and greater leisure at the cost of the subordination of household to work, on almost all counts. The young suffer the old less—and the old, multiplying in age and numbers, take themselves to be young. With fewer fears of and hopes for the afterlife, younger generations, I conjecture, do not look to familial reunification in the thereafter.

I do not ask aloud who among my four children will read *Jacob's Well*—or even keep its long-researched and supporting documents. As confident as I am that all of my children will show some interest in the past, I also know that this story will undergo the present's triage. Obviously, it is idle—even emotionally ensnaring—to pursue this line of thought. We corrupt ourselves by asking about the inner hearts of others and the future minds of the young. We do best, as in fact we finally must, to make the past a free gift to the present. But for the tenacious authenticity of our memories and the earnest art of our histories, tomorrow produces illusions, the future is a thief against which the past has no security, and nothing is spared the flood,

So in the end, I find consolation in being a historian. The present, I concede, is beyond my command, and the future is not for me to guess. Time, thank goodness, will reveal what I cannot imagine. But I know, and this truly does console, that the past is an inexhaustible storehouse that belongs to me; that rich memories and stories thread past and present together; and that those of us who follow Ariadne's thread through the past escape today's narrow reasoning and parsimonious diversity. In this age of cruel and demented abstractions, family history offers endless testimonials to ineffable individuals and families. And on this basis, it only seems seemed fitting and just that I, as the keeper of the graves, should tell of our family's search for home and Jacob's well, at which my mother drank.

APPENDIX

Select Genealogy of Amato, Linsdeau, Notaro, Sayers, O'Brien, and Broody (Boudrot) families

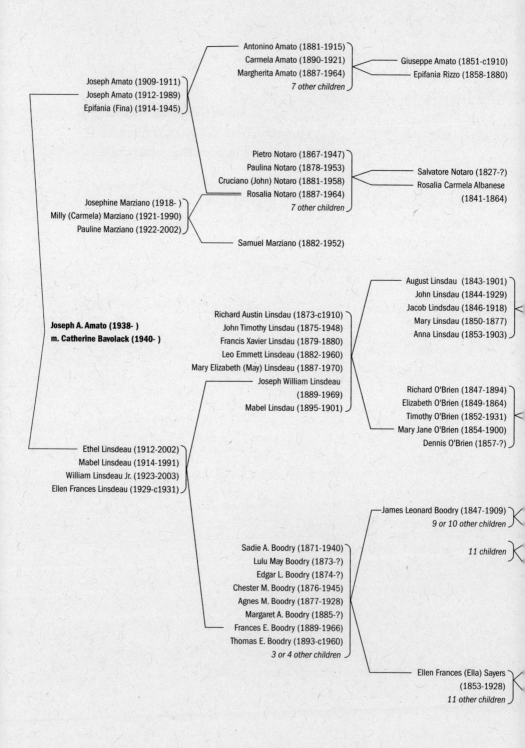

Antonino Amato (1881-1915)
Carmela Amato (1890-1921)
Margherita Amato (1887-1964)
7 other children

Giuseppe Amato (1851-c1910)
Epifania Rizzo (1858-1880)

Joseph Amato (1909-1911)
Joseph Amato (1912-1989)
Epifania (Fina) (1914-1945)

Pietro Notaro (1867-1947)
Paulina Notaro (1878-1953)
Cruciano (John) Notaro (1881-1958)
Rosalia Notaro (1887-1964)
7 other children

Salvatore Notaro (1827-?)
Rosalia Carmela Albanese
(1841-1864)

Josephine Marziano (1918-)
Milly (Carmela) Marziano (1921-1990)
Pauline Marziano (1922-2002)

Samuel Marziano (1882-1952)

August Linsdau (1843-1901)
John Linsdau (1844-1929)
Jacob Lindsdau (1846-1918)
Mary Linsdau (1850-1877)
Anna Linsdau (1853-1903)

Richard Austin Linsdau (1873-c1910)
John Timothy Linsdau (1875-1948)
Francis Xavier Linsdau (1879-1880)
Leo Emmett Linsdeau (1882-1960)
Mary Elizabeth (May) Linsdeau (1887-1970)
Joseph William Linsdeau
(1889-1969)
Mabel Linsdau (1895-1901)

Joseph A. Amato (1938-)
m. Catherine Bavolack (1940-)

Richard O'Brien (1847-1894)
Elizabeth O'Brien (1849-1864)
Timothy O'Brien (1852-1931)
Mary Jane O'Brien (1854-1900)
Dennis O'Brien (1857-?)

Ethel Linsdeau (1912-2002)
Mabel Linsdeau (1914-1991)
William Linsdeau Jr. (1923-2003)
Ellen Frances Linsdeau (1929-c1931)

James Leonard Boodry (1847-1909)
9 or 10 other children

11 children

Sadie A. Boodry (1871-1940)
Lulu May Boodry (1873-?)
Edgar L. Boodry (1874-?)
Chester M. Boodry (1876-1945)
Agnes M. Boodry (1877-1928)
Margaret A. Boodry (1885-?)
Frances E. Boodry (1889-1966)
Thomas E. Boodry (1893-c1960)
3 or 4 other children

Ellen Frances (Ella) Sayers
(1853-1928)
11 other children

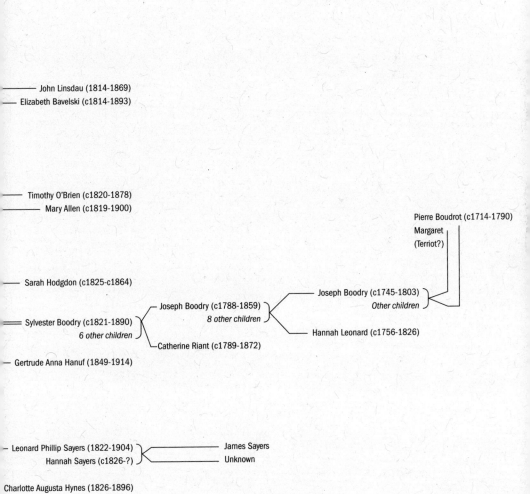

John Linsdau (1814-1869)

Elizabeth Bavelski (c1814-1893)

Timothy O'Brien (c1820-1878)

Mary Allen (c1819-1900)

Pierre Boudrot (c1714-1790)

Margaret

(Terriot?)

Sarah Hodgdon (c1825-c1864)

Joseph Boodry (c1745-1803)

Other children

Joseph Boodry (c1788-1859)

8 other children

Sylvester Boodry (c1821-1890)

6 other children

Hannah Leonard (c1756-1826)

Catherine Riant (c1789-1872)

Gertrude Anna Hanuf (1849-1914)

Leonard Phillip Sayers (1822-1904)

James Sayers

Hannah Sayers (c1826-?)

Unknown

Charlotte Augusta Hynes (1826-1896)

Source Notes

Preface: Family History

1. For the quotation and the development of these ideas, see John R. Gillis, *A World of their Own Making* (New York: Basic Books, 1996), 14, and xv-xvi.

2. Historian David Levine conceives the family not as a distinct result of the "'Christian marriage ideology', a 'homeostatic demographic system', or a 'feudal mode of production', but an interconnection of these elements within a quite distinctive ecological environment." Levine, *At the Dawn of Modernity: Biology, Culture, and Material Life in Europe after the Year 1000* (Berkeley: University of California, 2000), esp. 268–69.

Introduction: Putting on the Coat of the Past

1. For a historiographical introduction to the sundry dimensions of family history, see Lawrence Stone, "Family History in the 1980s," *Journal of Interdisciplinary History*, 12 (1981): 51–87; Tama Hareven, "The History of the Family and the Complexity of Social Change," *American Historical Review* 96 (1991): 95–124; Katherine Lynch, "The Family and the History of Public Life," *Journal of Interdisciplinary History* 24 (1994): 665–84; Louise Tilly, "Women's History and Family History: A Fruitful Collaboration or a Missed Connection?," *Journal of Family History* 12 (1987): 303–15. Representative books include Peter Laslett's classic, *The World We Have Lost*, 2d ed. (London: Methuen, 1971); Jean-Louis Flandrin, *Families in Former Times: Kinship, Household and Sexuality* (Cambridge: Cambridge University Press, 1979); Jack Goody, *The European Family: An Historico-Anthropolgical Essay* (Oxford: Basil Blackwell Publishers, 2000); Martine Segalen, *Historical Anthropology of the Family* (Cambridge: Cambridge University Press, 1986); Michael Mitterauer and Reinhard Sieder, *The European Family: Patriarchy to Partnership from the Middle Ages to the Present* (Chicago: University of Chicago Press, 1997); and David Levine, *At the Dawn of Humanity: Biology, Culture, and Material Life* (Berkeley: University of California Press, 2001).

2. Joseph Amato, *Rethinking Home: A Case for Writing Local History* (Berkeley: University of California Press, 2002), Valery quotation cited p. 3.

3. Cited in Greg Dening, *The Death of William Gooch: A History's Anthropology* (Honolulu: University of Hawai'i Press, 1995), 13.

4. Cited in David Levine and Zubedeh Vahed, "Ginzburg's Menoccio: Refutations and Conjectures," *Histoire Sociale/Social History*, 34 (2001): 437.

Chapter 1: Rosalia, a Misery as Ancient as Sicily

1. The name Amato is common in parts of Sicily and southern Italy, and thanks to emigration it can be found throughout Europe, Latin America, the United States, and elsewhere. It is also a name used by Spanish or Mediterranean Jews.

2. Walter Nugent, *Crossings: The Great Transatlantic Migrations, 1870–1914* (Bloomington, Ind.: Indiana University Press, 1992), xii-xiii, 11–14. For Italian emigration, see also Gianfusto Rosoli, ed., *Un Secolo di Emigrazione Italiana, 1876-1976* (Rome: Centro Studi Emigrazione, 1978).

3. Central for the formation of the European peasant is Levine, *At the Dawn of Modernity*, 43–44, 192–95, 208–9. A few works of interest on the peasantry are Emmanuel Le Roy Ladurie, *Montaillou: The Promised Land of Error* (New York: Random House, 1979); Piero Camporesi, *Il pane selvaggio* (Bologna: Mulino, 1983); Carlo Ginzburg, *The Cheese and the Worms* (Baltimore: John Hopkins University Press, 1980); and Arthur Imhof, *Lost Worlds: How Our European Ancestors Coped with Everyday Life and Why Life Is So Hard Today* (Charlottesville: University of Virginia Press, 1996).

4. Jules Michelet, "The Bondage of the Peasant," *The People* (Urbana, Illinois: University of Illinois Press, 1973), 30–31.

5. Jane Schneider and Peter Schneider, *Culture and Political Economy in Western Sicily* (New York: Academic Press, 1976), ix-x.

6. For this quotation and two books on the transformation of the countryside and its people in late nineteenth-century western Sicily, see Donna Rae Gabaccia, *Militants and Migrants: Rural Sicilians Become American Workers* (New Brunswick: Rutgers University Press, 1988), 1–36 (quotation p. 7), and *From Sicily to Elizabeth Street: Housing and Social Change among Italian Immigrants, 1880–1930* (Albany: State University of New York Press, 1984). For a worthy examination of economic conditions in western Sicily precipitating migration to the United States, see Virginia Yans-McLaughlin, *Family and Community: Italian Immigrants in Buffalo, 1880–1930* (Ithaca: Cornell University Press, 1977).

7. Cousin John Notaro believes that our Amato family, whose origin is the southern Sicilian coast town of Licata, did not arrive in Cerda until the middle of the nineteenth century. Of course, the number of generations a family spends in a particular town can be an indicator of its well-being, as migration, which accelerated throughout rural Europe, Italy, and Sicily in the nineteenth century, indicated need and dissatisfaction—and now frustrates genealogists and family historians who seek singular origins in Europe.

8. Every August, the *villici* appeared before the local *gabellotti* (land agents) to seek a contract for the next growing season. Because the contract called for delivery of a specified amount of grain, the desperate *villici* constantly had to increase the promised yields in order to assure the rental of their land. This harsh arrangement forced the impoverished sharecroppers to exhaust the land they tilled and would eventually abandon. John W. Briggs, *An Italian Passage: Immigrants to Three American Cities, 1890–1930* (New Haven: Yale University Press, 1978), 19–20.

9. For a classic portrait of the nineteenth-century Sicilian peasant, see Giuseppe Pitré's mon-

umental *Biblioteca delle tradizioni popolari siciliane*, 25 vols., published between 1871 and 1913, which was complied contemporaneously with the lives of young Antonino and Rosalia. Also, see Salvatore Salomone-Marino, *Customs and Habits of Sicilian Peasants* (London: Associated University Presses, 1981); Charlotte Gower Chapman, *Milocca: A Sicilian Village* (Cambridge, Mass.: Schenkman, 1971); and Cristoforo Grisanti, *Folklore di Isnello* (Palermo: Sellerio, 1981).

10. Yans-McLaughlin, *Family and Community*, 25–34.

11. Over the course of three centuries, commercial agriculture dismantled traditional Sicilian landholding institutions. Distant European markets came to dictate regional changes. Baronial hamlets became embryonic towns, and towns, especially those along the coasts, grew larger. Coincidentally, absentee landlordism spread and estates fell under the management of hated middlemen, *gabellotti*. As cash increasingly determined transactions in the countryside, traditional contractual relationships, which once provided a measure of security, vanished. Landlords invited in laborers from Greece and Albania, which may account for the origins of Rosalia's mother's maiden name, Albanese. During these centuries, and with accelerated intensity in the nineteenth century, Rosalia and Antonino's ancestors were metamorphosed into economic beings, and a new money class composed of bankers, tax collectors, and landlords took hold of the island. No longer concentrated in the upland grain lands, which travelers today see as vast and empty expanses, the rural population steadily relocated to larger towns and along the coasts. The development of Sicily required reforesting mountains, launching irrigation projects, building villages, hamlets, and roads, and planting diversified labor-intensive crops. Instead, government removed protective trade barriers and re-imposed a grist tax, which worked against the locally based economies of Sicilian peasants and craftsmen. See Francesco Renda, *L'emigrazione siciliana* (Palermo: "Sicilia al Lavoro," La Cartografica, 1963), 24–25; Schneider and Schneider, *Culture and Political Economy in Western Sicily*, 7, 118–20.

12. Schneider and Schneider, *Culture and Political Economy in Western Sicily*, x, 9, 114–15. Also useful for the Sicilian Mafia is Anton Blok, *The Mafia of a Sicilian, 1860–1960* (New York: Harper and Row, 1974).

13. *Inchiesta Jacini Atti della Giunta per Inchiesta agraria e sulle condizioni della classes agricole* (Rome, 1886), 8:667.

14. Emilio Sereni, *History of the Italian Agricultural Landscape* (Princeton: Princeton University Press, 1997), 281–82, and Salvatore Francesco Romano, *Storia della Sicilia Post-Unificazione, Parte Seconda* (Palermo: Società siciliana di Storia Patria, 1958), 140–65.

15. Briggs, *An Italian Passage*, 7.

16. The *Marco Minghetti*, which would have taken weeks to clear the Mediterranean and cross the Atlantic, carried 960 passengers (24 first class, 936 third class) and would have cost Antonio between $15 and $25, with no food provided en route. This, I calculate, could have amounted to a half-year's salary, or more.

17. Largely ignored by historians, the Kelayres Massacre arose out of intensifying local political struggle over patronage between the controlling Republican family, headed by Joseph Bruno, and the aspiring Democrats. Seven members of the Bruno family were convicted

of firing on the parading protesters on the eve of the election, killing six and wounding twelve. Tony told a story of an Italian immigrant in Kelayres who was annoyed with the Irish immigrant baseball players who chased pop flies into his garden. He retrieved from his dresser a pistol he had brought with him from the old country, returned to his garden patch, and shot both the catcher and the pitcher in the leg. "No authorities came and arrested the Italian, and the Irish thereafter quit chasing pop-ups in his zucchini," Tony concluded. A useful study of contemporary Sicilian immigration to and settlement in Buffalo, New York is Yans-McLaughlin, *Family and Community*. Also useful for early Sicilian settlements and Italian communities are Jerre Mangione's memoir of Sicilian settlement in Rochester, New York, *Mount Allegro* (New York: Columbia University Press, 1981); Gabaccia, *From Sicily to Elizabeth Street;* Marie Hall Ets, *Rosa, The Life of an Italian Immigrant* (Minneapolis, University of Minnesota, 1970); and Rudolph Vecoli's seminal critique of Oscar Handlin's failure to recognize continuities and communities among immigrants, "Contadini in Chicago: A Critique of *The Uprooted,*" in *Journal of American History* 51 (1964–65): 404–17.

18. "Mother Give Me a Hundred Lire," folk song transcribed by Carla Bianco in Roseto, Pennsylvania, *The Two Rosetos* (Bloomington: University of Indiana Press, 1974), 37.

19. An urban family lived on $10 a week, with a five-room downstairs flat renting for only $14 a month and a man's overcoat costing $10; William Adams Simonds, *Henry Ford: His Life, His Work, His Genius* (New York: Bobbs-Merrill, 1943), 137.

20. On occupations, see Victor Re, *The History of the First Presbyterian Church of Detroit* (n.p., n.d.), 1. Not surprisingly, the host community didn't distinguish among the new immigrants, which it classified as "obscure working folks," in the words of local historian Louis Rankin; "Detroit Nationality Groups," *Michigan History Magazine* 23 (Spring 1939): 163. The Sicilians came to Detroit first as fruit vendors. Under the leadership of Genoese John Schiappacasse, they turned their gardening skills to economic advantage at Eastern Market and pioneered the import, the ripening, and the sale of tropical fruits, especially bananas, throughout southern Michigan and nearby Ontario. See Joseph John Giglio, "An Historical Survey of Italian Immigration to Detroit," published typescript in Burton Historical Collection, Detroit Public Library, esp. 14.

21. My cousin John Notaro and I have not yet identified the family and friendships from Sicily and Pennsylvania that undoubtedly supported Rosalia and Antonino, but we have found clues. Antonino's sister Carmela was married to Giacomo Bomegna, who came on the ship with Antonino to America; his final destination was not Pennsylvania, but Detroit. Giacomo came from the Sicilian seacoast town of Carini, where the Amatos of Cerda might find their origin.

22. Report from Men's Probation Department, Recorder's Court, Oct. 14, 1929, in Recorder's Court of the City of Detroit *vs.* Samuel Marziano, Case No. 91342, Aug. 1929.

Chapter 2: "Forty Acres, and All Mine"

1. Madison Peters, ed., *The Great Hereafter, or Glimpses of the Coming World* (New York: J. A. Wilmore & Company, 1897).

2. Richard Bushman, "Family Security in the Transition from Farm to City, 1750–1850," *Journal*

of Family History 6 (Fall 1981): 248–49. For additional comments on the importance of home ownership for the American working class, see Harvey Green, *The Uncertainty of Everyday Life, 1915–1945* (Fayetteville: University of Arkansas Press, 2000), 91–118.

3.   For a provocative treatment of the transformation and the dissolution of German identity in the context of Philadelphia, see Russell A. Kazal, *Becoming Old Stock: The Paradox of German-American Identity* (Princeton: Princeton University Press, 2004).

4.   In *Measuring America: How an Untamed Wilderness Shaped the United States and Fulfilled the Promise of Democracy* (New York: Walker Publishing Company, 2002), Andro Linklater points that government lands were first sold in 1796 in a minimum of a half a section (320 acres) at $2 per acre. In 1804 they were sold in a quarter section (160 acres), and then half a quarter section (80 acres), with a price reduced to $1.25 an acre. In 1832, the government universalized landholding by permitting bids on a quarter of a quarter, 40 acres. Railroads, granted vast acreages, frequently sold their lands in forty-acre units. Adopting General Sherman's characterization, liberated slaves in 1865 were reckoned to be "self-sufficient with forty acres and a mule" (p. 166). Testifying to the small units in which American farming was parceled out: in 1880, no Midwestern states had farms averaging more than 160 acres. For land and its divisions, also see the summary of Paul Gates, *The History of Public Land Development* (Washington, D.C.: Zenger Publishing, 1968), 765–72.

Chapter 3: Banished from Acadia

1.   Almost a hundred years before the Acadian expulsion, the policy of expelling and selling Indians into slavery, even those who surrendered their weapons and pledged loyalty to the king, had become common. See Nathaniel Philbrick, *Mayflower* (New York: Viking, 2006), 252–53, 345.

2.   *"Arcadie,"* or *"Arcadia,"* evoked the idealized garden of antiquity. Taking their cue from explorer Verrazzano, early day mapmakers used the name Arcadia to designate the land corresponding to present-day Maine and the Canadian Maritimes. The name *"Acadie"* appears to have dropped its "r" as a consequence of increased interaction with the native Mi'kmaq Indians. The territory increasingly became known as *la Cadie,* resembling native names like Shubenacadie, Tracadie, and Passamaquoddy, and then became *l'Acadie,* according to Sally Ross and Alphonse Deveau, *The Acadians of Nova Scotia: Past and Present* (Halifax: Nimbus, 1992), 8.

3.   One English count at the time of the deportation numbered the Acadians having as many as 120,000 head of cattle. See Pierre Belliveau, *French Neutrals in Massachusetts: Story of the Acadians Rounded up by Soldiers from Massachusetts and their Captivity in the Bay Province, 1755–1766* (Boston: Kirk S. Giffen, 1972), 46.

4.   Ross and Deveau, *Acadians of Nova Scotia,* 15.

5.   Knowledge of diking, it is conjectured, came with the early setters from France, who had seen the reclamation of the marshes of Poitou, initiated by Henri IV as early as 1599 and carried out by Dutch engineers. The key device in controlling the waters was the *aboiteaux,* a primitive wood valve inserted at the center of a dyke complex that opened to drain excess inland waters and closed shut against rising tidal bay and river waters. Diking began as

early as 1650 in the Bay of Fundy (known as the *Baye Francaise*) and the adjoining Minas Bay (*Bassin des Mines*), whose principal settlement was Grand Pré. By 1710 the Acadians turned the marshlands in and around the Bay of Fundy into rich farmland. By the end of the seventeenth century, Acadians had already begun to develop the marshes of the Minas Basin and the immense zone of Beaubassin, located around present-day Amherst, New Brunswick. From 1700 to 1750, Port Royal, the mother colony, grew from 446 to 1,750 inhabitants; Grand Pré grew from 487 to 5,000 inhabitants; and Beaubassin grew from 188 to 2,800. See Ross and Deveau, *Acadians of Nova Scotia*, 32–33, 47; Pierre Belliveau, *French Neutrals*, 47.

6. For reasons of orthography, I refer to the Acadian Boodrys as the Boudrot, in accord with standard work of Acadian genealogist Bona Arsenault, *Histoire et Généalogie des Acadiens*, vols. 1–3 (Annapolis Royal, Nouvelle-Ecosse: Leméac, 1978). However, among the many spelling variations of the name (including the most common, Boudreau and Boudreaux), genealogist Frederick Boyle identified my first Acadian ancestor in Massachusetts as Peter Boudriott, perhaps accounting for source of the spelling Boodry. However, we also encounter in the same period such varying orthography as Boodery, Boodrey, Boudrott, Boudroitt, Boudreau, Budro, Beaudroe, Boudrix, and Powdry.

7. The birthplace of Michel Boudrot in France is highly contested and conjectural, as explored at http://perso.orange.fr/froux/boudrot/boudrot.htm.

8. Stephen A. White, *English Supplement to the Dictionnaire Généalogique des familles acadiennes*, première partie 1636 à 1714 (Moncton: Centre d' études acadiennes, 2000), 38.

9. Http://membres.lycos.fr/ancetre/boudrot.htm.

10. Bona Arsenault, *Histoire et Généalogie des Acadiens*, 441.

11. Http://www.membres.lycos.fr/ancêtre/boudrot.htm. For the content of the king's order, see White, *English Supplement*, 38.

12. The 1752 Inspection Voyage of Sieur de la Roque tallied animals—oxen, cows, pigs and sheep, hens, and geese—and watercraft such as canoes, rowboats, and skiffs (*esquif*). Several Boodrys are identified in a partial translation offered by Steven DeRoche at http://www.geocities.com/Heartland/Valley/2229/laroque.html.

13. White and Arsenault agree on his having eleven children.

14. Http://www.acadian-cajun.com/boudreau.htm.

15. Http://membres.lycos.fr.ancetre/boudrot.htm.

16. Arsenault, *Histoire et Généalogie des Acadiens*, 442, 1108.

17. Stephen A. White, *Dictionnaire Généalogique des Familles Acadiennes*, vol. 1 (Moncton, N.B.: Centres d'Etudes Acadiennes, Université de Moncton, 1999), 211, 212.

18. British Lt. Col. John Winslow's classic list of expelled Acadians from Grand Pré, which forms a census of Grand Pré residents, has been published in a bilingual edition as *Lt. Col. John Winslow's List of the Acadians in the Grand-Pré Area in 1755* (Grand Pré: Société Promotion Grand-Pré, 2002).

19. In a lengthy interview at the University of Moncton, June 8, 2004, and a subsequent telephone conversation in Aug. 2004, Stephen White argued that documents showed that Mar-

guerite Terriot married Pierre Boisenneau, not Pierre Boodry. This claim, he remarked, was substantiated by the testimony of Marguerite's son, who contends that she was not deported to Massachusetts but was sent to Virginia and then England. He has drawn the conclusion that Pierre was a grandson of Charles, who settled at Pisiquid. He identifies, without precision, either Denis or Pierre of Pisiquid as the probable sons of Charles. Genealogist Frederick Boyle, C.G., who did extensive and revelatory work for me on the Boodry family, argues that Arsenault "is more reliable," than White, since, first, the former "connects Pierre with Marguerite, which coincides with Massachusetts records," while White never establishes a marriage. Arsenault also connects Pierre with the resettlement of Neutrals, and he connects Marguerite (b. 1716) to the Terriot. His date for the marriage of Pierre and Marguerite, 1736, also coincide with the birth of son Pierre Jr., and son Joseph would coherently carry the name of his grandfather, Joseph Boudrot of Grand Pré. Finally, the Pierre identified in Pisiquid does not correspond to any Pierre found in Massachusetts records. Letter from Frederick Boyle, Aug. 21, 2004.

20. Andrew Hill Clark, *Acadia: The Geography of Early Nova Scotia to 1760* (Madison: University of Wisconsin Press, 1968), 218.

21. Some of them emigrated to back country, seeking refuge in the more remote inland regions of the Chignecto Isthmus, which defined the Chipoudie, Peticoudiac, and Memramkouke rivers in southeastern New Brunswick. With the English authorities near at hand in Halifax, Pisiquid's inhabitants were conscripted to work on the east-west road that ran from Halifax to Minas Basin, and, more ominously, they were increasingly blamed for the grave wrong of supporting Indian and French attacks on English settlements. Clark, *Acadia*, 218.

22. Belliveau, *French Neutrals*, 46.

23. For the connection between the mentality of the Acadian and sixteenth-century French cultures, see Antonine Maillet, *Rabelais et les traditions populaires en Acadie* (Quebec: Les Presses de l'université Laval, 1980), esp. 5.

24. Ross and Deveau, *The Acadians*, 38–39, 42. For charges surrounding Abraham Boudrot as a spy for the French, see Margaret Melanson, *The Melanson Story* (Toronto: Self-published, 2003), 67–68, 71–74, 77–79.

25. Cited in Bernard DeVoto, *Course of Empire* (Boston: Houghton Mifflin, 1952), 227.

26. For a useful introductory survey of Acadian history, its prosperity, and the deportation, see N. E. S. Griffiths, "The Acadians," *Dictionary of Canadian Biography* (Toronto: University of Toronto Press, 1979), 4:xvii–xxxi.

27. Geoffrey Plank, *An Unsettled Conquest* (Philadelphia: University of Pennsylvania Press, 2001), 137–38.

28. The governor of Nova Scotia acted with the agreement of his newly appointed head of court, with the cooperation of English Royal Navy and government, and in unity with the governor of Massachusetts, who raised an army of 2,000 soldiers and assembled a fleet of ships—including those of Boston merchant John Hancock. In effect, a handful of men in England, Nova Scotia, and Massachusetts had determined that the hour had come to implement Halifax's order, which is described in telling detail in John Mack Faragher, *A*

Great and Noble Scheme: The Tragic Story of the Expulsion of the French Acadians from Their Ameri-can Homeland (New York: Norton, 2005), especially for Grand Pré, 340–46, and for Pisiquid, 361–62.

29. Cited in Chief Justice Cushing Chapter of the Daughters of the Revolution, *Old Scituate* (1921; repr. ed., Scituate, Mass.: The Chapter and the Scituate Historical Society, 2000), 81.

30. Belliveau, *French Neutrals*, 4, 32–33. In southern New Brunswick, in the general region of Moncton, Acadian rebels gave rise to a prolonged and heroic guerilla war that lasted until the fall of Louisbourg in 1758 and of Québec, the great French North American bastion, in 1759; Paul Sourette, *Memramkouke, Petcoudiac et la Reconstruction de l'Acadie*, vol. 1 of *Histoire des Trois-Rivières* (N.C.: La Société historique de la Vallée de Memramcook, 1981), 10.

31. Parkman, whose adult life was almost exclusively devoted to writing about the epochal English and French struggle for North America, judged the Acadians to have been too closely associated with the "troublesome" Indians and too much under the influence of both the meddlesome Catholic church and France, which played the Acadians as pawns in their diplomatic machinations. Additionally, Parkman believed that the Acadians matched their ingratitude for what the English had offered with an obtuseness about what England threatened. For Parkman's original judgment, which was amended after the completion of his major work, see *Montcalm and Wolfe*, part 7 of *France and England in North America* (in vol. 1–3, Frontenac ed.; Boston: Little, Brown, & Co., 1902), 1:243–95; for his concessions about Acadian suffering, see p. 268.

32. Clark, *Acadia*, 346.

33. For a succinct account of the numbers and places involved in *le Grand Dérangement*, see Carl A. Brasseaux, *Scattered to the Winds: Dispersal and Wanderings of the Acadians, 1755–1809* (Lafayette: Center for Louisiana Studies, University of Southwestern Louisiana, 1991), esp. 1–8. Also, see Clark, *Acadia*, 344–51, and "Acadie, Odyssey of a People" (1989, rev. 1993), a poster published by Parks Canada.

34. With the fall of the principal French maritime fort at Louisburg in 1755, the deportation was extended to the entirety of Acadia, including Québec's eastern Gaspée Peninsula and the Isle St. Jean (Prince Edward Island) from which 3,500 Acadians were deported mainly to France. Seven hundred were set to sea in rotten ships and drowned, and only a few of those who safely reached France found a home there. At the end of the war they were returned to the Maritimes and Louisiana. Small numbers of Acadians in other places continued to be rounded up and held in fortresses, while yet others were deported to France and even the fever-ridden West Indies. Many Acadians who had fled into the woods were burned and starved out or were greeted in distant Quebec "with hostility and hardship." It is esti-mated that "a third of the existing eighteen thousand Acadians, some six thousand people in all, perished because of the *Grand Dérangement*"; Belliveau, *French Neutrals*, 33; Griffiths, "The Acadians," xxviii.

35. See *Lt. Col. John Winslow's List*. Aside from twenty-six Boudrots, three of whom were named Pierre Boudrot and one Joseph Boudrot, the list included such associated family names as Terriot, Como (Comeau), Tibodo (Thidodeaux), Trahan, and Aucoin, the maiden name of patriarch Michel Boudrot's wife, Michelle. Acadian historian and genealogist Paul Surette

furnished me with the count of approximately sixty-three individuals named "Pierre Boodry" in pre-deportation Acadia; he says that twelve to fifteen of them were deported. Interview, June 9, 2004.

36. Parkman, *Montcalm and Wolfe*, 1:289.

37. Starting on the week of November 12, English ships jammed the Boston port with two thousand Acadians; Brasseaux, *Scattered to the Winds*, 25.

38. Ross and Deveau, *The Acadians*, 64.

39. For decades Massachusetts disputed Maine's borders with France. "In 1754, the Great and General Court committed Massachusetts to take part in the full possession of Acadie and the seizures of Louisburg and Québec.... Massachusetts sent two thousand men, at England's expense, to carry out the great deportation. At the same time the colony's merchants and ship owners scented profitable opportunities in the venture of removing the competitive Acadians and annexing land to Massachusetts' northern frontier." Belliveau, *French Neutrals*, 3, 7, 9–14.

40. In Boston an entire day was dedicated to a parade that blasphemed the Pope (Belliveau, *French Neutrals*, 42), but the province's concern for the condition of the ships and the health of the Acadian arrivals in port can be found in the *Journals of the House of Representatives of Massachusetts, 1755* (Boston: Massachusetts Historical Society, 1957), 180, 218, 220, 226. On provisions, see Belliveau, *French Neutrals*, 29–40, 124, 248.

41. Belliveau, *French Neutrals*, 1, 119, 131, passim; Richard Lowe, "Massachusetts and the Acadians," *William and Mary Quarterly* 25 (Apr. 1968): 212.

42. Lowe, "Massachusetts and the Acadians," 215. For an introduction to the matter of colonial government and debt, see Parkman, *Montcalm and Wolfe*, 2:290–92, and Robert Zemsky, *Merchants, Farmers and River Gods* (Boston: Gambit, 1971), esp. 129–56.

43. See "Order Restraining the French Neutrals from Traveling About," in Province Laws, 1756–57, Vol. 5, Chapter 68, *Acts and Resolves of the Province of the Massachusetts Bay* (Boston: State Printers, 1908), 556–57. See also Belliveau, *French Neutrals*, 93, 107, 109–10, 113, 133, and 214. At one point, the Massachusetts Court ruled that Neutrals not "be absent from town for more than six days at a time and were forbidden from Sunday travel under threat of being put in jail with sparse rations and yet charged for their keep and board"; cited in Lowe, "Massachusetts and the Acadians," 219, 221.

44. "Warning out of town" was used widely in New England to pressure or to coerce "outsiders" to settle elsewhere, according to Josiah Henry Benton, *Warning Out in New England, 1656–1817* (Boston: W. B. Clarke, 1911), 106–13, 115, 117.

45. Massachusetts itself teetered on bankruptcy after the Neutrals arrived. "Leaving out the Puritan immigration of 1630–40, not less than half, and perhaps considerably more, of all the white immigrants to the colonies were indentured servants, redemptioners, or convicts." Richard Hofstadter, *America at 1750: A Social Portrait* (New York: Random House, 1973), 34.

46. Lowe, "Massachusetts and the Acadians," 224.

47. The names of Peter Boodry's children are inconclusive, according to Frederick Boyle's

complete genealogy for Pierre Boudrot/Boodry of Raynham, Mass., Sept. 30, 2003, which is my possession and ownership. In one petition, signed Mar. 21, 1757, he claimed that he was "formerly an inhabitant of Nova Scotia with wife and family being seven in number" (Mass. State Archives, 23:373–75). According to Boyle, four of his and Marguerite's children were:

    i (probably) JOHN, no further record after 1760. A John Boodery, French Neutral, was also at Scituate June 3, 1760 (Mass. State Archives, 24:323). He may have been an older son of Pierre and Marguerite or perhaps a brother to Pierre Sr. However, Bona Arsenault shows no brother of Pierre Boudrot named "Jean" or "John."

    ii Joseph, b. ca. 1745, m. Hannah Leonard in Taunton in 1773, d. in Raynham in 1803. He is the father of Joseph, who settled in Maine.

    iii FRANCIS, no further record after 1760.

    iv PETER JR.; m. "of Raynham" (int.) Raynham Sept. 21, 1779 (1:248) [int. Freetown, Mass. July 15, 1779] *Vital Records of the Town of Freeport, Mass.* LOVINA/VENIA ANDREWS/ANDROSE. He apparently was the "Peter Boodrey" who served as a private in Capt. Samuel Warner's Co., Col. Abiel Mitchells's Regt., from Aug. 8 to Oct. 31, 1780 (2 months, 26 days) in a company raised to reinforce the Continental Army. Secretary of the Commonwealth, *Massachusetts Soldiers and Sailors of the Revolutionary War* (Boston: 1896), 2:270.

    v FRANCIS, no further record after 1760.

48. Cushing Chapter of the DAR, *Old Scituate*, 81–82. According to city minutes, Scituate's Acadians came from Grand Pré, which, if taken to be a true and complete statement, supports Arsenault's contention that Pierre and Marguerite came from Grand Pré, not Pisiquid.

49. At the time of incorporation in the seventeenth century, Scituate was seventy square miles. However, as a consequence of eighteenth-century population growth along the northeast seacoast, Scituate was forced to surrender approximately thirty square miles to surrounding communities for their expansion and incorporation.

50. Today Jacob's Pond is under the control of the Norwell Conservation Commission, and the commission's literature describing the pond makes no mention former Acadian residences. A description and a nineteenth-century photograph of Cricket Hole is found in Cushing Chapter of the DAR, *Old Scituate*, 81–83, 217.

51. In 1760, the town selectmen requested that the colony pay 9 pounds and 16 shillings for providing for "the French people from Nova Scotia," on the basis that the province, implying Nova Scotia, not the town, should pay for them. The request was declined. "Selectmen Notes, Scituate," Mar. 10, 1760.

52. *Journals of the House*, 235.

53. *History of the Town of Hingham*, vol. 1, part 1 (Hingham, 1893), 256–57, passim.

54. Cited in Cushing Chapter of the DAR, *Old Scituate*, 81; also, for their and other Acadians' complaints in the period of 1756 to 1757, see Belliveau, *French Neutrals in Quebec*, 162–63; Lowe, "Massachusetts and the Acadians," 221–22.

55. Pierre's petition is found in Mass. Archives, 23:373–75. The fact that Pierre signs with an "X" does not necessarily testify to his illiteracy. As Kenneth Lockridge pointed out, the practice of signing with an "X" had become a widespread convention used by literate and illiterate

alike at this time; cited with a discussion of matter of colonial illiteracy in John Demos, *A Little Commonwealth* (Oxford: Oxford University Press, 1970), 22n2. That Pierre was French and didn't author the document might not have been additional reasons for marking X. On the other hand, literacy among Acadians declined throughout the first half of the eighteenth century as they came under British control and they had fewer priests and schools to educate their youth.

56. John Boodery, French Neutral, was at Scituate in June 1760, Mass. State Archives, 24:323. Probably an older son of Pierre and Marguerite, he was deemed to be bedridden for four years and in care of Barnstable County, *Acts and Resolves*, 1760–61, Chaps. 389–91, 736. A full construction of Pierre's family in Massachusetts would require a gigantic genealogical project of identifying twenty different "Boudreau" (Budroe, Budro, Boodery, Boudot, Boudrix, Boudrot, Beaudroe, and Boudrix) found in the Massachusetts State Archives.

57. *Acts and Resolves*, 1756–57, Chapter 56, 754.

58. Belliveau, *The French Neutrals*, 132–33.

59. Document dated May 24, 1760, in Mass. State Archives, 24:355.

60. Belliveau, *French Neutrals*, 160–61.

61. For the care of the two French neutrals in his charge, Colonel Leonard's bill itemized such charges as 14 shillings for two flannel waistcoats; 1 pound, 17 shillings for four flannel shirts ready made; 17 shillings, 8 pence, for four pair yarn stocking home made; 12 shillings for two pair of shoes; 12 shillings for two hats; Raynham, Selectman Records, Jan. 22, 1759, Mass. State Archives.

62. Rev. Fobes expended only 52 of those pounds, saving 18 pounds for lending, as derived from Rev. Fobes's Bill, Oct. 13, 1766, in Old Colony Historical Society, Taunton, Mass. Also at the society, see his will, in file F681P. For a short introduction to Fobes and Raynham's Congregational Church, see Rev. James Tilbe, *If These Stones Could Speak* (Raynham: First Congregational Church, 1994) and the *Taunton Daily Gazette*, Apr. 16, 1925.

63. Belliveau, *French Neutrals*, 113.

64. Mass. State Archives, 24:488. Also, see Belliveau, *French Neutrals*, 227.

65. Mass. State Archives, 24:526. Also, see Belliveau, *French Neutrals*, 228.

66. Under the name of "Pete Powdry," Pierre joined the Jan. 1, 1765, petition of the four hundred Acadians asking the Governor for transportation to San Domingo (Mass. State Archives, 24:515; also see Belliveau, *French Neutrals*, 146, 228). Many Acadians fled to San Dominque, part of the Spanish-controlled island of Hispaniola (today the independent nation of Haiti).

67. Belliveau, *French Neutrals*, 230–32.

68. Belliveau, *French Neutrals*, 236.

69. Belliveau, *French Neutrals*, 146, 245.

70. Belliveau, *French Neutrals*, 236–37.

71. Belliveau, *French Neutrals*, 238.

72. Bristol Co. deed 51:263, Bristol County Court House, Taunton, Mass. The acreage calculation is based on the amount sold off and identifying last name of purchaser to be "Gushee,"

whose property is located on Titicut Pond, which is on the west end of town on the edge of Titicut Swamp.

73. The Old Colony Historical Society has in its archives several letters from prominent individuals and the selectmen voicing the struggle over the new meeting house's proposed site and the history of the church.

74. G. Marston Leonard, "James Leonard of Taunton, Massachusetts, Ironmaster," 1960, Old Colonial Historical Society.

75. Recorded in Vital Records, Raynham, Sept. 21, 1779 (1:248), and Vital Records of nearby East Freetown, Mass., July 15, 1779.

76. Secretary of the Commonwealth, *Massachusetts Soldiers and Sailors of the Revolutionary War* (Boston: The Commonwealth, 1896) 2:270. An unidentified "Lewis Boudre" also served in the American Revolution from Massachusetts.

77. For a short treatment of Shay's rebellion, see James A. Henretta, David Brody, and Lynn Dumenil, *America: A Concise History* (Boston: Bedford/St.Martin's, 2002), 198–200.

Chapter 4: Up and Down the Hills of Maine

1. An account of a typical New England family is found in James Henretta, "Families and Farms: *Mentalité* in Pre-industrial America," *William and Mary Quarterly* 35 (Jan. 1978): 3–32. On the dominance of the family in social life, see Darrett Rutman, "Assessing the Little Communities of Early America," *William and Mary Quarterly* 43 (Apr. 1986): 163–78.

2. Rutman, "Assessing the Little Communities of Early America," 173 (relying in part on anthropologist Marvin Harris); Henretta, "Families and Farms," 5–7; David Danbom, *Born in the Country: A History of Rural America* (Baltimore: John Hopkins University Press, 1995), 35.

3. For history and description of the mismatch, see Danbom, *Born in the Country*, 34, 35, 55, 56–57. Lockridge's work is in "The Evolution of New England Society, 1630–1790," *Past and Present* 39 (Dec. 1968): 63–67, 70, 77–79, 80. For a searching discussion of Massachusetts agricultural communities neither composed of self-sufficient farms nor sustained by markets but "integrated, economically as well as socially and culturally," see Bettye Hobbs Pruitt, "Self Sufficiency and the Agricultural Economy of Eighteenth-Century Massachusetts," *William and Mary Quarterly* 41 (July 1984): 333–64.

4. Bristol Co. Deed 51:264.

5. Bristol Co. Probate 51:563.

6. Bristol Co. Probate 51:563.

7. Bristol Co. Probate 56:60.

8. The *Gran Rétour* of 1776 was an expedition of eight hundred Acadians who set out from Boston in 1776 to return on foot to their former home in Nova Scotia. Their march led across the New Hampshire and Maine wilderness. Though ill clad and ill equipped, they subsisted on the way by hunting and fishing. Their epic journey lasted four months, during which time children were born and many deaths occurred. Cushing Chapter of the DAR, *Old Scituate*, 83.

9. Joseph's birth and tie to Pierre are confirmed by two important death records for Nathan and Hannah Boodry, children of Joseph and Hannah (Leonard) Boodry, which both give "British Dominion, Canadian French" as the birthplace of their father.

10. At the time Hannah (d. Taunton Sept. 19, 1826, aged 70), one of eight daughters, received her inheritance, it could have purchased several small farms or one large one in Ohio, Illinois, or Michigan, where one of Joseph Boodry's children immigrated. Leonard, "James Leonard of Taunton."

11. Children of Joseph and Hannah (Leonard) Boodry, b. Taunton and Raynham:

    i   JOHN, b. say 1775

    ii   (probably) TRIFENA, b. 1765–1784 (census), a resident of Livermore, Oxford Co., Me., 1810, living alone, aged 26–45. No other records for her have been found. However, Joseph Boodry Jr. named a daughter "Tryphena," presumably after her aunt Trifena.

    iii (possibly) LUCINDA, b. c. 1782 (1880 census) lived in Oakham, Worcester Co., Mass., 1880 with John and Prudence Dean, aged 46/43.

    iv   NATHAN, b. Jan. 10, 1785 (DVR)

    v   SYLVESTER, b. say 1787

    vi   JOSEPH [Jr.], b. c. 1788 (GS)

    vii BENJAMIN LEONARD, b. c. 1794 (IGI), lived in Fairhaven, 1840, with a wife the same age; m. Raynham Mar. 1815 LYDIA RICHMOND, b. Raynham c. 1796 (DVR), daughter of Seth and Hannah (Paddleford) Richmond, d. Rochester Sept. 9, 1849, aged 53 (VR, p. 352).

    viii HANNAH, b. c. 1795 (DVR), d. Mattapoisett Jan. 9, 1871, aged 76 (Me. VR 239:246).

12. The warning out of Joseph and his family is found in the Raynham City Records, Jan. 12, 1790.

13. See Henry, *Warning Out.*

14. A copy of the Bellfery Subscription, Jan. 1991, Raynham Church, is found in the Old Colony History Society.

15. *A Sermon; the substance of which was delivered to Taunton, November 11, 1784, upon the Day of the Execution of John Dixson, for Burglary, with an Appendix on the Nature and Enormity of Burglary and a Sketch of his Life* (Providence: Bennet Wheeler, n.d.,), located in the Old Colonial Historical Society.

16. In January 1787 Daniel Shay, a destitute farmer who served as a captain in the Revolutionary War, led an army of 1,200 men, which was defeated after a month of serious fighting in Springfield. Defeat, in this case, had its spoils. There was pardon for all who joined the rebellion. The legislature decided not to impose a direct tax in 1787, as well as lowering court fees and exempting clothing, household goods, and tools of one's trade from the debt process. Richard B. Morris, ed., *Encyclopedia of American History* 6th ed. (New York: Harper and Row, 1982), 137–38.

17. Frank Walcott Hutt, *A History of Bristol Massachusetts* (New York: Lewis Historical Publishing Company, 1924), 1:n.p.

18. In *The Peopling of British North America* (New York: Random House, 1986),10, American historian Bernard Bailyn offers reasons for us to consider the American migration in measure as

a set of migrations at work in the British countryside which peopled North America itself. He writes that the peopling of British North America must be understood as an expansion of domestic mobility patterns—of such a scale, however, as to alter European population and its patterns.

19. The battle between large land proprietors, speculators, settlers, and squatters in the last decades of the eighteenth century and the first of the nineteenth is a subject of Maine historian Alan Taylor in "'A Kind of Warr': The Contest for Land on the Northeastern Frontier, 1750–1820," *William and Mary Quarterly* 46 (Jan. 1989): 3–26, and his *Liberty, Men, and Great Proprietor: The Revolutionary Settlement of the Maine Frontier* (Chapel Hill: University of North Carolina Press, 1990), which contains Dwight quotation, p. 155. For background on the selling and dividing of Maine, see Paul Gates, *History of Public Land Law Development* (Washington, D.C.: Zenger, 1968), 45.

20. Sylvester acquired property in Taunton in the 1820s and sold it in the early 1830s, then in 1834 made two separate purchases, totaling 240 acres, west of Adrian, in Rollin Township, Lenawee County, in southern Michigan. As was common, the families of cousin Sylvester, his father-in-law John Haskins, and his brothers-in-law Luther and William Haskins—twenty-three people in all—arrived together and settled on adjacent farms, making a micro-community of neighbors and family. Richard Bunner, ed., *Memoir of Lenawee County* (Madison, Wisconsin: Western Historical Association, 1909), 1:324, 325. The Boodry family, however, never succeed in its transplant from New England to Michigan. Before and after father Sylvester and mother Lydia died, all the brothers and sisters died by disease and accident, until only Nathan, the fourth child of thirteen, survived. Bachelor and family caretaker, Nathan stayed on the homestead until he died of cancer in 1896. See biographical files in Lenawee County Historical Society and W. A. Whitney and R. I. Bonner, eds., *History and Biographical Record of Lenawee County, Michigan* (Adrian, Mich.: Williard Stearns, 1880), 2:336–37.

21. The marriage was recorded in Avon Vital Records in 1811. While Catherine's birth date is given as 1789 in a death record from Rangeley, Francis Gould Butler offers the birth date of 1791 and lists her brothers and sisters in *A History of Farmington, Maine* (Farmington: Press of Knowlton, McLeary, 1885), 562. Joseph Riant's pension application for service in the Revolutionary War indicates that he served in a Massachusetts unit, even though he was born in Connecticut.

22. For a painfully detailed accounting of his poverty, see his petition in 1818 to the state of Massachusetts and a subsequent petition in 1829 to the newly formed state of Maine, in the file of Joseph Riant of Farmington, Me.; the original documents, though generated in Massachusetts up to 1820 and in Maine thereafter, are found in the War of 1812 Pension Application Files, National Archives, Washington, D.C.

23. Although there is no record of Joseph Boodry serving in the War of 1812, his widow unsuccessfully filed a claim for a military pension for his service in it. She claimed that her husband had served in Capt. Ladd's Co. of the Maine Militia; W.O. 3845, War of 1812 Pension Application Files, National Archives.

24. The work of Frederick Boyle, with partial support of Shirley Adams, self-appointed town

genealogist of Rangeley, Me., determined the children of Joseph and Catherine (Riant) Boodry to be the following (the first six born in Phillips, Me. [VR, p. 57]):

i   JOSEPH, b. Dec. 7, 1812.

ii   SARAH, b. Dec. 26, 1814; m. c. 1833 CALVIN KINNEY.

iii   TRYPHENA, b. Feb. 28, 1816, d. Weyauwega, Wisc. Dec. 13, 1888; m. Rangely, Me. June 1, 1833 DANIEL HOAR, b. Jan. 26, 1811, son of Luther and Eunice (Lakeman) Hoar, d. Weyauwega Jan. 16, 1884.

iv   SYLVESTER, b. Mar. 4, 1819; m. May 26, 1842 SARAHH HODGDON; m. (2) ANNA, b. Prussia c. 1849 (1880 census).

v   THOMAS, b. June 8, 1821, d. Weyauwega, Wisc.; m. EUNICE ABBOTT, b. c. 1822, d. Rangely, Me. c. 1859. [1850 census shows him married to NANCY, b. c. 1824 (1850 census) in Rangely.]

vi   LEONARD, b. May 10, 1822, d. "on board the Antarctic bound for Liverpool" Jan. 1855 (obit.).

vii   LUCINDA/LUCY P., b. Avon, Me. June 9, 1830 (From age at death), d. Rangely May 21, 1904, aged 73–11–12 (Me. VR); m. "of Benton" at Clinton, Me. Nov. 16, 1852 ANDREW J. THOMPSON of Clinton, d. before 1880.

viii   ELEANOR THERESA, b. Rangely, Me. c. Aug 1839 (DVR), d. Rangely Oct. 20, 1905, aged 66–2 (Me. VR); m. JAMES H. COLLINS, b. Me. 1837 (GS), son of Barnabas A. and Nabby ( ) Collins, d. 1914 (GS).

25.   Deeds and Mortgages, 45:146, Franklin County Court House, Farmington, Me.

26.   Carole Shammas, *Pre-industrial Consumer in England and America* (Oxford: Clarendon Press, 1990), 299.

27.   For everyday life in rural Maine in the late eighteenth and early nineteenth century from the perspective of a midwife, see Laurel Thatcher Ulrich, *A Midwife's Tale: The Life of Martha Ballard, Based on Her Diary* (New York: Random House, 1990).

28.   For a discussion of how an expanding market can chase the poor toward temporary self-sufficiency, see Winifred Barr Rothenberg, *From Market-Places to a Market Economy, 1750–1850* (Chicago: University of Chicago Press, 1992), 46–48.

29.   "Southeast of Rangeley in the town of Phillips, was the birthplace of fly-fishing legend Cornelia T. ('Fly Rod') Crosby (1854–1946), recipient of the first Registered Maine fishing license issued by the state." Kathleen Brandes, *Maine Handbook* (Chico, Calif.: Moon Publications, 1998), 573. Sometime in the 1950s, as if the natural potency and fertility of Joseph and Catherine's sexuality had to be studied and joined to spiritual liberation, the controversial Austrian-born psychoanalyst William Reich moved to Rangeley and established a research center devoted to studying sexual energy and discovering the liberating power of the orgasm.

30.   Henry D. Kingsbury and Simeon L. Deyo, "Town of Clinton," *Illustrated History of Kennebec County, Maine* (New York: H.W. Blake, 1892), 1243–56.

31.   For a start on the complex issue of soldiers' pay, see E. B. Quiner, *A Military History of Wisconsin* (Chicago: Clarke, 1866), 73, 74, and Charles E. Estabrook, ed., *Records and Sketches of Military Organizations* (Madison: State of Wisconsin, 1914), 197.

32.   For outlines of the campaign of Wisconsin's 32nd Infantry, see Estabrook, ed., *Records and Sketches*, 154, and William Deloss Love, *Wisconsin in the War of Rebellion: A History of All Regiments and Batteries* (Chicago, 1866), 737, 961–64, 1002–6.

33. Sylvester's service record is in Wisconsin Adjutant General's Office, Regimental Rolls, 1861–68, Wisconsin State Archives, Series 1142.

34. Kingsbury and Deyo, "Town of Clinton," 1246. For understanding how the "Towne of Main [*sic*]" as a colony of Clinton Mainites fits a larger New England pattern, see Lois Kimball Mathews, *The Expansion of New England: The Spread of New England Settlement and Institutions to the Mississippi River, 1620–1865* (Boston: Houghton Mifflin, 1909), 221–49; Stewart Holbrook, *The Yankee Exodus: An Account of Migration from New England* (New York: Macmillan, 1950), 108–30; David Curtis Dearborn, "Ancestors on the Move: Migrations Out of New England," *New England Ancestors* 3 (Spring 2002): 12–16; and Wisconsin Cartographers Guild, *Wisconsin's Past and Present: A Historical Atlas* (Madison: University of Wisconsin Press, 1998), 16–17.

35. The deed to Sylvester's property, which can be located on the 1881 Plat of Main, in Outagamie County, was only filed in 1879. He sold a half-acre of his property for $5 in 1871, and his widow sold the remainder, over 39 acres, for $400 in 1894.

36. For a significant consideration of the interplay between narrative, explanation, and historiography, when considering the formation, development, and transformation of families across large units of time and space, see Levine, *At the Dawn of Modernity*, esp. 1–16, 411–28.

37. Emmanuel Le Roy Ladurie, *The French Peasantry, 1450–1660* (Berkeley: University of California, Press, 1987), and *Histoire du Languedoc* (Paris: Presses universitaires de France, 1962).

38. For a recent exploration of the evolution of the household, see Carole Shammas, *A History of Household Government in America* (Charlottesville: University of Virginia Press, 2002).

Chapter 5: Migrants West

1. Kathleen Neil Conzen, "A Saga of Families," in *The Oxford History of the American West* (New York: Oxford University Press, 1994), 341.

2. This portrait of Charlotte is based on her eulogy, delivered by Rev. J. Hamline Smith, Oct. 16, 1896, Milan Cemetery, Milan, Kans.

3. This information is found in Bernard Bailyn's magisterial treatment of immigration from the British Isles on the eve of the American Revolution, *The Peopling of British North America: An Introduction* (New York: Knopf, 1986), 9. Also worthy of consideration are his *Voyagers to the West: A Passage in the Peopling of America on the Eve of the Revolution* (New York: Vintage, 1988), and Conzen, "A Saga of Families," 328–29.

4. Henry Adams, *The History of the United States of America During the Administration of Thomas Jefferson* (New York: Literary Classics of the United States, 1986), 5–6, 8, 19.

5. The Sayers name itself is common in England, Scotland, Ireland, New Zealand, Canada, and the United States. The origin of the name is ambiguous, stemming from one of several different occupations, including a sawer of wood, a sayer (pronouncer), a silk salesman, and someone who tries things (from French "essayer") such as a metal tester, food taster, and so on. It has many variants of spelling, including Sayers, Sayre, Saer, Seyers, Sear(e)(s), Seear and Seers. Subsequent New York and Wisconsin censuses identify Leonard as born in 1822 in St. Lawrence County, New York, the son of James Sayers of England, born c. 1780. St. Lawrence County, where Leonard was married, has a Norfolk Township, the suspected source of James and Leonard Sayer's ancestors and well-documented descendants of

Thomas Sayers of Carbrooke, Norfolk, England, and his identified brothers and children; "Descendants of John Sayer," a hundred-page document, was furnished to me by Earl Sayer Cory on Jan. 2, 2005. William and Elizabeth had four daughters, Mary, Elizabeth, Martha, and Rebecca, to match their four English-born sons Fortunatus (1807–1889), James (1809 [or 1801]-1868), William Jr. (1812–1865), and Thomas (1814–1885). Two helpful sets of documents on William's family and the township's cemetery record list are housed in the archive at the Macomb Township Building. One set, complied by India Burton, Macomb Town Historian, includes "Sayer" genealogy, penciled L[atter] D[ay] S[aints], July 1981, 1; "Sayer" genealogy, one page; and "Sayer," Pioneers of Macomb, St. Lawrence Co., New York. A relatively thorough set of records, making use of censuses, the Oldsville Cemetery Book, Town of Macomb, and Civil War records, is titled "Family Group Record on Sayers," by Ann M. Patch of Cicero, New York, Apr. 7, 1993. There are inconsistencies on the birth date of William's son James, which is one of the Norfolk Sayers's most popular first names. One genealogy and cemetery record places James's birth in 1801, whereas on his tombstone and other genealogies it is 1809. The latter date more accurately corresponds with James and eliminates him as the father of Leonard.

6. Leonard's mother may have been named Hannah, providing Leonard's younger sister with her name and a name used by the following generation in the family.

7. Information supplied by genealogist Don Burke, spring 2000.

8. Macomb township records, 1847. In the 1850 census her age is given as 24.

9. One Rosegrant family lived next to Leonard and Charlotte Sayers, in Oswegatchie Township. The whole family included Elizabeth (Rosegrant) Tallman, with a husband and a number of children; Nicholas, with a wife and ten children; and Franklin Rosegrant, with a wife and five children.

10. Brother-in-law Franklin Rosegrant was born in 1816 in Little Falls, Herkimer Co., N.Y., according to Carla Hoffman's twelve-page genealogy, which furnishes information of his will and other matters. In 1838, in partnership with a second party, he bought 18 acres for $300 in Heuvelton. The following year Franklin married Frances Hynes, Charlotte's older sister, in Ogdensburg, where the 1840 census identifies them as living. In 1854 Franklin bought 71 acres for the significant sum of $1,375. He held that land until 1863, when he sold it for $3,675, an amount equal to eight years of income for the average county worker or farmer. In 1865, he, Frances, and eleven children emigrated to Russia Township, Lorain County, Ohio, three miles west of Oberlin, where they prospered. He left a hundred acres of land to his wife and family and was eulogized in 1882 by his minister not as a farmer, but as a successful businessman. Up to the hour of his death, the eulogist exuded, "Franklin carried out practically his favorite motto, 'Owe no man anything!'"

11. Aaron M. Sakolski, *The Great American Land Bubble: The Amazing Story of Land-grabbing, Speculations, and Booms from Colonial Days to the Present* (New York: Harper & Brothers, 1932), esp. 65–68.

12. Paul Gates, *History of Public Land Law Development* (Washington, D.C.: Zenger, 1968), 43.

13. In the Town of Macomb, along Fish Creek, William and his last son Thomas bought property on May 10, 1851, for $294. In the same year, William's son James purchased another piece

of property there for $250. In 1852 Thomas paid Samuel Sayers, son of Fortunatus, $400 for a lot along the Oswegatchie River in Town of Dekalb. William Jr. bought a piece in Macomb in 1854 for $262.99. James bought a 1.25-acre lot in 1857 in Macomb for $50. Then, suggesting how much the Sayers worked in concert and resembled a colony, Fortunatus purchased from his father William and son Thomas a 58.5 acre piece of property on Fish Creek for the large sum of $1,200.

14. Edgar Blankman, *Geography of St. Lawrence County* (Canton, New York: Plaindealer Presses, 1898), 39.

15. According to an 1845 county census, Macomb produced 15 acres of turnips, 389 acres of wheat, and nearly identical acres of corn and oats. Small amounts of land were dedicated to potatoes, beans, buckwheat, and flax. Evincing the land's appropriateness for grazing, the agricultural census inventoried 1,266 sheep, 724 hogs, and 448 milk cows, which produced 80,000 pounds of butter and 50,000 pound of cheese; India Murton, Macomb Town Historian, "Macomb History of Census, 1845," 1957.

16. For Pope's Mill, see Willis Kittle, Macomb Town Historian, "A Short History of the Town of Macomb," 1964. The 1845 census recorded a human population of 1,113 people, 206 farms, a tavern, a retail store, a grocery store, an uncounted number of churches, and, notably, nine public schools, which testified both to the dispersal of the population and to a determination to educate its children. Murton, "Macomb History of Census, 1845."

17. Notes on Civil War Pension Records, in Patch, "Family Group Record," Macomb Township Building.

18. Information on the number of children is from family pedigree chart in Patch, "Family Group Record," Macomb Township Building. Benjamin was born shortly after the family's arrival in Heuvelton.

19. Without calculating debt on land, in 1860 Thomas had only $600 in real estate; William Jr., $1,000; Fortunatus, $1,600. Indeed, by virtue of having $1,800 in real estate and $650 in personal property, it appeared that James and Jane were the best off. The 1870 census, taken two years after James' death, recorded that their land had appreciated to $2,850 and personal property to $1,200. By the end of the 1880s, Jane's claim to survivor dependent benefits rested on her puny assets and her indigence, as seen in 1880 census.

20. Data taken from Murton, "Macomb History of Census, 1845."

21. Elliot West, "American Frontier," in *Oxford History of the American West*, 144–45.

22. For a general accounting of New Englanders moving as communities to and settling the West, see Andrew R. L. Cayton and Peter S. Onuf, *The Midwest and the Nation* (Bloomington: Indiana University, 1990), 25–42; Holbrook, *The Yankee Exodus*, chap. 4 note 33; and Kimball Mathews, *The Expansion of New England: The Spread of New England Settlement and Institutions to the Mississippi River, 1620–1865* (Boston: Houghton Mifflin Company, 1909), esp. 221–49.

23. Additional facts confirmed that Hannah Pope, Eliphalet's second wife, was Leonard's sister. Leonard and Charlotte's third daughter's was named Hannah. The 1840 census notes that Hannah and Leonard previously lived in Morristown, Lawrence County, next to Eliphalet, his first wife, and their five children.

24. Reuben manifested the kind of mobility we identify with Leonard Sayers. Immigrating to Wisconsin as part of a large family from Nova Scotia in 1842, this family first settled in Milwaukee, then moved to Manitowoc County and Sheboygan. Reuben volunteered to fight in the Civil War. In his last of three terms of enlistment, Reuben participated in General Sherman's Georgia campaign. After marrying a Boodry woman, his second marriage in 1870 was to Charlotte Sayers, with whom he had nine children. They moved to Fond du Lac, Wisc.; Waterloo, Iowa; Neenah; back to Town of Maine, where he stayed until 1890; then to Clinton, Me., and a farm near Bear Creek. Like Leonard and Sylvester Boodry, Reuben was a carpenter.

25. Family member Laurie Evans remembers reading Charlotte's stories of pioneer days in an unidentified local newspaper.

26. The *Kansas Chief* printed Lucy Larcon's "Call to Kansas," 1876, cited in Allan Bogue, "Agricultural Empire," *Oxford History of the American West*, 287.

27. Telephone interview, Lura "Irene" Kolman, Nov. 22, 2004.

28. Less than half of the county's 376,000 acres were in agricultural production, and of that total, farmers dedicated 82,000 acres to the settler's preferred crop, corn, in contrast to putting only 8,000 acres in what would become the preferred crop, winter wheat. Seven thousand horses, 7,000 milk cows, 35 hogs, and 17,000 cattle further defined the emerging landscape. *An Illustrated Atlas* (Philadelphia: Edwards Brothers, 1878), 3–30.

29. Of the twenty-one households in the 1870 census, which formed the neighborhood into which the Sayers moved in 1877, all had lived in at least one other place. Sixteen of the families were split evenly between having lived in two or three places. Only three households noted in the 1870 census can be identified in the 1880 census. By 1880, 17 of 20 households had members born in two or three places other than Kansas. One family had lived in four locations. The 100 people total in the 20 households were born in 16 different states, with Kansas supplying 29 (mainly children). For an overall consideration of westward migration based on birthplace and "latitudinal zonation," see John Hudson, "North American Origins of Middlewestern Frontier Population," *Annals of the Association of American Geographers* 78 (1998): 395. See also A. Gordon Darrock, "Migrants in the Nineteenth Century: Fugitives or Families in Motion?" *Journal of Family History* 6 (Fall 1981): 257.

30. Danbom, *Born in the Country*, 133.

31. Danbom, *Born in the Country*, 147; also see James Malin, *History and Ecology: Studies of the Grassland* (Lincoln: University of Nebraska, 1984), 244.

32. Of them, 200,000 were born in Illinois; 136,000 were born in Missouri; 100,000 were born in each Iowa and Indiana; 75,000 were born in Ohio; and significant numbers with origins in Kentucky, New York, and Nebraska. About 100,000 were foreign born—Germany, England and Wales, British-American, Scandinavia, and Irish—of whom less than 50 percent came directly to Kansas, and in a ten-year period approximately 60 percent of the farmer-newcomers disappeared. Malin, *History and Ecology*, 245, 248.

33. Craig Miner, *Kansas: The History of the Sunflower State* (Kansas: University of Kansas Press, 2002), 22.

34. Fred Shannon, *Farmer's Last Frontier* (Armonk, N.Y.: Sharpe, 1973), 306.

35. Walter Nugent, *Into the West: The Story of Its People* (New York: Alfred A. Knopf, 1999), 67.

36. *Argonia Clipper*, Mar. 15, 1884 and 1884, *passim*.

37. Julie Roy Jeffrey, *Frontier Women: The Trans-Mississippi West, 1840–1880* (New York: Hill and Wang, 1979), 27. For a breakdown of the numbers, see John Unruh, *The Plains Across: The Overland Emigrants and Trans-Mississippi West, 1840–60* (Urbana: University of Illinois Press, 1979), 119–20.

38. John Hudson, *Across This Land: A Regional Geography of the United States and Canada* (Baltimore: John Hopkins University Press, 2002), 258.

39. Born in New York a generation after Leonard in 1836, Charles Ingalls moved his family from New York to Wisconsin, to Missouri, to Kansas, back to Wisconsin, then to Walnut Grove on the banks of Plum Creek, forty miles from where my wife and I have lived for the last forty years. He then went to Iowa, only to return to Walnut Grove, to finally set out for DeSmet, S.D., where he died in 1902, two years before Leonard. The books formed the basis for the popular television series, "Little House on the Prairie."

40. Interview with Irene Kolman on tour of region and Sayers farm site, June 24, 2003.

41. Genealogical materials on Leonard and Charlotte's daughters and son were furnished to me by Irene Kolman, June 24, 2003, and also a telephone interview, Feb. 2005.

Chapter 6: A Memorable Death, a Common Lot

1. Referring to Joshua, verse 14:5, in which the people of Israel allotted the land, as the Lord commanded Moses, Henry Gariepy points out the connection between a lot of land and a man's fate. *Treasures from the Psalms* (Grand Rapids, Mich.: Erdmans, 2002), 21.

2. A rough formula might be: we bring the sum of our cultural, intellectual, and religious resources to give meaning to death, and death, in all forms experienced and imagined, tests the meaning of what we think of this world and the next. I suggest this in *Death Book: Terrors, Consolations, Contradictions, and Paradoxes* (Peoria, Ill.: Ellis Press, 1985).

3. This poem was first published in Amato, *Death Book*, 98–100.

4. For the settlement of Town of Maine, see Thomas H. Ryan, *History of Outagamie County* (N.p.: Goodspeed Historical Associations, 1911), 1339–41. Also for surrounding area see Gordon Bubolz, ed., *Land of the Fox: Saga of Outagamie County* (Appleton: n. p., 1949). For the historical context of its settlement, see two works from the multivolume *The History of Wisconsin*: Richard Current, *The Civil War Era, 1848–1873*, vol. 2 (Madison: State Historical Society of Wisconsin, 1976), 89; and Robert C. Nesbitt, *Urbanization and Industrialization*, vol. 3 (Madison: State Historical Society of Wisconsin, 1985), 3.

5. This idea was borrowed from Levine, *At the Dawn of Modernity*, 286.

6. Teamsters, the largest group of workers in the lumber industry, earned only $2 more a month than the sawyers, approximately $10 less than the cooks, and half of the foreman's $50 a month, according to Nesbitt, *Urbanization and Industrialization*, 72–73.

7. I was unable to determine why James and Ella left their land. For a description of Appleton, see Nesbitt, *Urbanization and Industrialization*, 187.

8. For origins and development of the Appleton system and street scenes, see http://www.triviaasylum.com/parks/hydro/hydro.htm; for origin and historical notes, see http://www33.brinkster.com/iiiii/inventions/trolley.asp.

9. Bubolz, ed., *The Land of the Fox*, 156, 157.

10. For Shiocton, see *Outagamie County History* and John Lammers, Richard Leitch, et al., *Shadows on the Wolf* (Shiocton: Shiocton History Project Committee, 1987).

11. This judgment of inequality and calculations of wealth are found in Harold U. Faulkner, *Politics, Reform and Expansion, 1890 to 1900* (New York: Harper and Row, 1959), 72, 74.

12. For a portrait of contemporary Appleton, see the Wisconsin *Blue Book, 1911* (Madison: State of Wisconsin, 1911), 19–27, passim. This is a biannual publication of Wisconsin's Legislative Reference Bureau.

13. Born Erik Weisz in Budapest, Hungary, on Mar. 24, 1874, Houdini came as four- or five-year old boy to Appleton, where his father Mayer Weiss served, until his death in 1892, as rabbi of the German-speaking Zion Reform Jewish Congregation.

14. Edna Ferber, "A Peculiar Treasure," reprinted in Richard O. Davies, Joseph A. Amato, and David Pichaske, eds., *A Place Called Home: Writings on the Midwestern Small Town* (St. Paul: Minnesota Historical Society Press, 2003), 196.

15. I had numerous telephone conversations and exchanged letters and information with amateur Boodry genealogist Delores Johnson, granddaughter of Chet, of Crandon, Wisc., in 2002 and 2003.

Chapter 7: Jacob, the Rise and Fall of a Plebian Patriarch

1. The death certificate of Jacob's sister Mary states that she was born in the village of Neudorf. With nine Neudorfs in West Prussia, I locate their village, for a series of circumstantial reasons, in the upland region around Gdansk. Of course, this only assures us that they lived there at the time of her birth, approximately 1850.

2. Prussia was two-thirds rural, one-third urban, in 1867. By 1910 this ratio was exactly reversed, according to Klaus J. Bade, *Migration in European History* (Oxford: Blackwells, 2003), 43. For the effect of industrialization on Germany, see p. 34–35.

3. The Gambsky (aka Gambaski, Gambske, and Gamski) also arrived in Menasha from Paterson, N.J., in 1866 and intermarried with the Linsdaus. They are most likely the family that welcomed the Linsdaus to Menasha. Possibly the Linsdau family's migration intersected with that of Mary's husband, Jacob Gambsky, and his family, who came from what is today Lezno, Poland, south of Poznan or possibly Lesna, a mountain village, farther to the south. They arrived in New Jersey in 1852, and then went to Menasha in 1866.

4. The 1850s witnessed the birth of the first white child, the installation of a post office, the beginning of the dredging of the upper Fox River, the arrival of the first steamboat, and the building of a warehouse; Richard Harney, *History of Winnebago County Wisconsin* (Oshkosh: Allen & Hicks, 1880), 215–18.

5. One of the two routes to Lake Michigan ran east along Plank Road to Kaukauna, where a steamboat could be taken to Green Bay; the other route started with a steamboat to Fond

du Lac, then proceeded forty miles along a toll plank road to Sheboygan, located on Lake
Michigan. Only in 1874, after constant rivalry with adjacent Neenah over the use of the Fox
River, did Menasha incorporate as a town.

6. While Menasha continued to open both parochial and public schools to keep pace with its
    growing population, it did not offer high school classes until required to do so by state law
    in 1875; Harney, *History of Winnebago County*, 153.

7. Making business its business, as did the paper of every growing town in the Midwest, the
    Island Times bugled the town's immediate advantages and long-term prospects. It also sup-
    ported the building of a new public school and welcomed new stores and industries, like
    the newly constructed woolen mill, to the town's commercial community. For paean, see
    Feb. 6, 1866.

8. The *Island Times* demonstrated the underlying class, ethnic, and associated religious divi-
    sions separating more Catholic Menasha from more Protestant, English, and Scandina-
    vian Neenah by recording all church services in the two towns, except those of Catholic
    masses.

9. In a single issue, the *Island Times* reported a $1,600 robbery of the Express Office, tallied
    the costs to the public of the local poor house, and noted the discrepancy in Civil War
    bounties between those who enlisted early and those who joined near the war's end. Base-
    ball games between intense rivals Menasha and Neenah provided common fare for the
    paper's readers, as did a naming of recent installation of Masonic officers. Issue after issue
    voiced dangers from the excesses of drink and pointed out "the perils of accouchement,"
    the creeping presence of "houses of ill-fare," the assembling of mobs, cases of hydrophobia
    and robbery, rapes and attempted rapes, and a local delivery man who insisted on a kiss
    from a lady for having delivered a letter from her distant husband.

10. For a short introduction to Irish and Germans immigration, see Stephen Flanders, *Atlas of
    American Migration* (New York: Facts on File, 1998), 93–95.

11. The Linsdau siblings illustrate this. Older sisters Mary and Anna married promising young
    Polish men, or Germans with Polish names, in the family home church of St. Mary's. Anna
    espoused Michael Poplinski in 1874 and lived with her mother on his farm. Mary married
    successful Jacob Gambsky in 1871.

12. As late as 1901 St. Patrick's Irish church only had 300 members in contrast to German St.
    Mary's with 1,500, and Polish St. John's with 800; Charles Glaab and Lawrence Larsen, *Facto-
    ries in the Valley* (Madison: State Historical Society of Wisconsin, 1969), 213.

13. In 1894 Richard, judged insane, was committed to the county asylum. His widow's struggle
    for military benefits, reminiscent of the struggle of that of Benjamin Sayers's mother, pro-
    voked years of redundant inquiries, which surely cost more than the total pension ever
    allotted, revealing how bureaucracies purloin issues for their own profit.

14. For an overview of German immigration and ethnicity in Wisconsin, see Wisconsin Car-
    tographers' Guild, *Wisconsin's Past and Present*, 18–19.

15. The Allens first appeared in the records of Rochester, Monroe County, in 1837. The O'Briens

were of unidentified Irish origin. The migration of Timothy and Mary (Allen) O'Brien can be traced by their children's birthplaces: they were probably married in Rochester, c. 1845, where their oldest son Richard was born in 1847. In 1849, daughter Elizabeth was born in Indiana, where they were probably working a segment of the state's long Wabash and Erie Canal. Children Timothy Jr., Mary Jane, and Dennis were born in Menasha in 1851, 1854, and 1857, suggesting that the family arrived with development of the Fox River transportation system. See correspondence with professional genealogist Kris Beisser Matthies, Jan. 7, 2005, on the Allens and Apr. 23, 2003, on the O'Brien children; for the story of the canals and their building, see *A Tale of Twin Cities, or the Development of the Fox River Waterway* (Neenah: Neenah Historical Society, 1993), esp. 163–69.

16. The Foxes, who were in Upper Ontario as early as 1825, may have immigrated to the New World with the assistance of the British government. Irish immigration to Canada was both an answer to overcrowding in Ireland and a means to colonize its contested southern border against the United States in the wake of the War of 1812. The crown sponsored two Irish settlements, one of which probably brought Fox ancestors, known as *Sheneck* (the Gaelic word for "fox") from County Cork to the vicinity of present-day Peterborough, Ontario, a difficult three-day trip inland from Lake Ontario. For a useful genealogical guide, see Carol Bennett, *Peter Robinson's Settlers, 1823–1825* (Renfrew, Ontario: Juniper Books, 1987). Remote, rocky, and subject to long, cold winters, the land placed prospective colonists on a continuing migration for better land elsewhere. Some sought refuge in lakeside towns such as Port Hope, where Richard Allen's wife, Elizabeth (Fox) Allen—daughter of English-born Cornelius Fox and his unnamed Irish wife—was born on Sept. 16, 1825.

17. Doty Island, between Menasha and Neenah, was the site of a major Ho-Chunk (Winnebago) village, visited by Jean Nicolet as an agent of Samuel de Champlain in the seventeenth century. With the Indians removed and sequestered on reservations by a succession of treaties from the 1820s through the 1840s, Wisconsin statehood established in 1848, the political and economic forces of Milwaukee and southern Wisconsin began their relentless advance northward; http://www.mpm.edu/wirp/ICW-150.html and *Wisconsin's Past and Present,* 2–15.

18. August's wife Catherine Hughes Linsdau inherited half of her parent's three acres along Plank Road in 1879 and bought the other half from her sister for $100 the following year. With only two daughters, one who remained in Menasha and bore an illegitimate child, the family was chained to mill wages until the second half of the twentieth century, when August's grandson Bernard started a small greenhouse that grew a full-time business under the supervision of his three daughters. Because of military service, debt, or work, Jacob's brother John arrived in Wisconsin in 1872, six years after the rest of the family and at the onset of a national depression, and he promptly married Mary Tumet in St. Mary's Church. He found work in Milwaukee as a streetcar conductor. In 1879, he and his wife went north to the woods of Langlade County, Wisc., where they were early settlers near the northern Wolf River, on the edge of the Menominee Indian reservation. A man of many talents who spoke five languages and completed eight years of schooling in Germany, he survived by skidding logs and building homes and the very school his eight children attended. They lived partially off the land, especially its readily available deer meat. Surviving until he was

in his eighties, he died in 1929, outliving his wife by twenty-five years. In way of an obituary, local newspaper editor generously wrote, "He was not a prominent man, but one that gave his strength and support to his community to help make it what it is. His kindheartedness led him to help neighbors in many ways." Perry Gillett, *Antigo Daily Journal*, Dec. 30, 1929.

19.   Arthur F. Burns, *The Business Cycle in a Changing World* (New York: Columbia University Press, 1969), 42–43.

20.   Alice E. Smith, *Millstone and Saw: The Origins of Neenah–Menasha* (Menasha: State Historical Society of Wisconsin, 1966), 138–39. The paper industry in Menasha was led by the Gilbert Paper Company, which produced 30 million pounds each year, with a value of $800,000. The paper plant workforce of 110 workers, including Linsdau family members, had a payroll of $52,000, for a roughly calculated annual worker salary of $500 dollars a year, or about $1.50 a day; Glaab and Larsen, *Factories in the Valley*, 285.

21.   Menasha Wooden Ware manufactured barrels, tubs, kegs, pails, and other wooden containers. As lathe foreman, Jacob earned an extra fifty cents a day over the average base salary of $1.00 or $1.25 a day. The *Semi-Centennial Edition of the Menasha Press: Historical, Biographical, and Descriptive* (June 1898), 166, touted the Menasha Wooden Ware Company as the largest woodenware plant in the world. During its first years, the company took advantage of excess seasonal agricultural and timber workers to pay only minimal wages. One man recalled working as a child for the company's predecessor before the Civil War for two cents an hour, paid out in credits for use at the company store. Labor's rising expectations and growing need for cash, and the company's use of lay-offs, brought unionism to Menasha in 1896, when workers joined the Amalgamated Woodworkers Union. Begrudgingly given raises, joined to demands for higher daily production, produced an ongoing friction and strikes in Menasha, whose labor protests bore no semblance to the violent disturbances that overtook nearby Oshkosh; Glaab and Larsen, *Factories in the Valley*, 240–41.

22.   The Menasha Wooden Ware Company employed as many as 300 workers in its peak periods and 176 men and 50 children in its normal times; Glaab and Larsen, *Factories in the Valley*, 224.

23.   Glaab and Larsen, *Factories in the Valley*, 222–24; also see Smith, *Millstone and Saw*, 87. Also, see Menasha Register "Mill Towns," *The Emerging Cities: Menasha/Neenah: Stories of the Nineteenth Century* (Menasha: Neenah Citizen Sesquicentennial Edition, 1998), 40. In 1890, with workers working approximately sixty hours a week, the national income for industrial laborers was $486. Ten years later, with wages increased to only $490, typical expenditures for a factory worker's annual budget would be $205 for food, $108 rent, $26 gas and coal, $24 clothing, $8 baby clothing, $45 furniture, $8 books and paper, $3 charity, $7 recreation, $6 gifts, $27 loan, $8 kitchen needs, $14 miscellaneous needs (stamps, paper, thread, pins, etc.); Harold U. Faulkner, *Politics, Reform, and Expansion, 1890–1900* (New York: Harper & Row, 1959), 80, 92–93.

24.   Glaab and Larsen, *Factories in the Valley*, 229–31.

25.   Glaab and Larsen, *Factories in the Valley*, 37.

26.   "The Fine Print of Smith's Park," *Emerging Cities*, 69.

27.   A reading of the town notes for the eight years Jacob was in office suggests that he could be

accused of self-interested behavior for having once voted in favor of paying his son John $12 for working for the city and compensating his brother-in-law Michael Poplinski $240 for sewer work. In his last term in office, he supported his brother-in-law's request for a liquor license and later led a successful motion that Poplinski receive a rebate for the first-year cost of the license fee, since Poplinski did not set up his establishment until the second year of the license. He also authorized payment of $1.50 to his brother-in-law, the grocer J. J. Gambski, for filling a welfare order.

28. Glaab and Larsen, *Factories in the Valley*, 40.

29. In one instance, he urged the immediate payment of a gas bill for the city lights, and in another, he pushed the city to settle a $40,000 debt on bonds owed to the Central Railroad Company.

30. In the spring of 1885 Jacob joined Irish aldermen Fitzgibbon, McFadden, and Walch, along with Mangold, in defeating Strange and Jennings's amendment to raise liquor fees. On a subsequent referendum on the same issue in September of that year, Jacob's ward resoundingly joined him in saying no to raising the annual fee of a liquor license. His ward registered 517 votes to leave the fee of $200 unchanged, against 15 to raise it to $350, and 173 to $500—the annual wage of an average worker.

31. In 1893 Jacob's brother-in-law Michael Poplinski, running as an Independent candidate, failed in his bid to be a Menasha alderman.

32. Here and below, see the *Menasha Evening Breeze*, Jan. 14, 1897.

33. Peter J. Adams, "The New of 1897: Saloon Keepers under Fire for Serving Minor," *Menasha Register*, Dec. 16, 1998.

34. The foreign born in Menasha were composed of 1,071 Germans, 667 Poles, and 117 Irish. Neenah, which also had a nearly identical ratio of two foreign-born residents to one native American, seemed less "foreign" and more American to nativists, when it is noted that the foreign born included no Poles, only 60 Irish and 710 Germans, and northern European peoples, including 510 Scandinavians and 175 English and Canadian; *Emerging Cities*, 22, 69.

35. *Semi-Centennial Edition of the Menasha Press: Historical, Biographical, and Descriptive* (June, 1898).

36. The sharpest strike among the women mill workers occurred at the nearby Neenah Boot and Shoe Factory, where management tried to reduce wages in 1896 with a reduction of the daily rate from the low rate of a dollar to ninety cents a day.

37. "Mill Towns," *Emerging Cities*, 40.

38. "Mill Towns," *Emerging Cities*, 56–60.

39. In the 1920 directory, with Jacob's family gone, the Linsdaus remaining in Menasha were Dorothy Linsdau, daughter of his missing son Austin and his wife Theda, who worked as a telephone operator, while Bernard Linsdau and his daughter Helen were employed by paper companies.

40. The indenture document of 1889 was provided by Kris Beisser Matthies in correspondence, Apr. 23, 2003.

41. Ethel Amato, my mother, provided the fullest variant of this story on July 1, 1991.

42. Theda Linsdau's obituary in the *Menasha Register* (Dec. 6, 1908), described her as "this well-known Menasha lady," who was born in Denmark, Sept. 6, 1874, and lived at 538 Board Street with Jacob Linsdau. The obituary listed her three children Dorothea, Donald, and Robert, her five sisters and two brothers, but did not mention her vanished husband, Austin. Her funeral was to be held in St. Mary's, not in St. Patrick's, where up to then Jacob and Mary Jane's children had been baptized.

43. For some hundred of Emmett's photographs, see Menasha Advancement Association, *Illustrated Menasha, 1913* (Sheboygan, Wisc.: National Publicity Association, 1913).

44. The conflicted choice between the freedom and opportunity of the new land versus the inheritances and traditions of the old constitutes a principal and well-articulated theme of Jon Gjerde's *The Minds of the West: Ethnocultural Evolution in the Rural Middle West, 1830–1917* (Chapel Hill: University of North Carolina Press, 1997), esp. 129–31. A history of the complex formation of German identity is the central theme of Russell A. Kazal's insightful study of Philadelphia's German communities, *Becoming Old Stock* (Princeton: Princeton University Press, 2004).

45. The Sedition Map, now offered for sale at Wisconsin State Historical Society and elsewhere, was first published in the *New York Sun*, Mar. 21, 1918.

46. Barbara Linsdau, letter to husband John Linsdau, Feb. 14, 1919.

47. Jacob and Mary Jane are not found in the 1907 church census of St. Patrick's.

48. Patricia Walker, William brother's granddaughter, Jan. 21, 1999, related to me what her Aunt Toots (Barbara Marie), her grandfather's youngest daughter, reported.

Chapter 8: Cousins of the Tongue

1. Following the general European plane of prejudice of Poles to define themselves as Germans and Germans as French, rather than in the probably more accurate and opposite historical direction, one relative transformed Jacob Linsdau's wife, Elizabeth Bavelsky, into Louisa Bevaire. With this mistaken assumption, I followed the origins of the family to Strasburg, mentioned in a newspaper obituary, in the west, rather the Strasburg in West Prussia, now located in Polish territory and known as Brodnica.

2. I doubt Ethel ever knew that Bernard was the illegitimate son of her great-uncle August's daughter Nellie, or kept track of his three articulate and generous daughters, Helen Wiatrowski, and unmarried Gertrude (recently deceased), and Corrine, whom thanks to genealogy I had the great pleasure of re-discovering more than fifty years later. The family florist shop only recently closed, had its origins in 1932, when their father Bernard, working only three days a week, "had time on his hands and three daughters and wife to support"; Arlen Boardman, "Family Florists: Two Sisters Are Flower Children from the '30's," *Appleton-Neenah-Menasha Crescent* (Feb. 13, 1990), C 1.

3. Property records indicate that Mary Jane, its owner, borrowed $550 against her property in 1890 and $900 again in 1895.

4. Mary Jane Linsdau's will, dated Sept. 29, 1919, is found in the Lake Winnebago County Court

House in Oshkosh. Before mortgages and expenses were deducted, she had $2,000 in real estate property and $950 in personal property.

5. Vernon Linsdeau, printed-produced loose-leaf journals, held by his wife in St. Clair Shores, Mich., entry for Aug. 27, 1998.

6. Linsdeau journals, May 7, 1997.

7. Linsdeau journals, Aug. 25, 1996.

8. Linsdeau journals, Feb. 22, 1995.

9. Linsdeau journals, Feb. 22, 1995.

10. Linsdeau journals, Feb. 22, 1995.

11. Linsdeau journals, Aug. 27. 1994.

12. Linsdeau journals, Nov. 16, 1994.

13. Linsdeau journals, Aug. 22, 1995.

14. Linsdeau journals, Aug. 22, 1995.

15. Linsdeau journals, Apr. 22, 1995.

16. Linsdeau journals, Aug. 27, 1994.

17. Linsdeau journals, Feb. 9, 1997.

18. Linsdeau journals, Aug. 2, 1995.

19. I fashioned this view of the transformation of American society and its pressure on family in part from Samuel Hays, *The Response to Industrialism, 1885–1914*, 2d ed. (Chicago: University of Chicago Press, 1995), 7–46, and Irving Howe, *World of Our Fathers* (New York: Harcourt Brace Jovanovich, 1976), esp. 73–74, 77, 117.

Chapter 9: Workers to the Bone, East Siders to the End

1. For this characterization of the modern family I drew on the work Steven Mintz and Susan Kellogg, *Domestic Revolutions: A Social History of American Family Life* (New York: Free Press, 1988), xv.

2. Cited in Joseph Amato, "Review of Russell A. Kazal, *Becoming Old Stock*," in *Journal of Social History* 40 (Winter 2006): 528.

3. Hays, *Response to Industrialism*, 61–63.

4. English and European historian David Levine used this phrase to describe a collection of biographies of British workers from 1870 to the end of the 1940's found in Jonathan Rose's *The Intellectual Life of the British Working Classes* (New Haven: Yale University Press, 2001), in "Review Essay: Re-membering the Past," *Journal of Social History* 40 (Fall 2006): 209.

5. For a useful social study of dance halls in ethnic Chicago in the 1920s and 1930s, see Randy D. McBee, *Dance Hall Days: Intimacy and Leisure among Working-Class Immigrants in the United States* (New York: New York University Press, 2000).

6. Plummeting auto sales, which were Detroit's bread and butter, reduced the wages of city's privileged auto workers from $1,600 to $1,000 in the early 1930s.

7. In 1930, Italians made about 4 percent of the city's multi-ethnic total population of 1,700,000 inhabitants. Having expanded from 2 percent in 1910, Italians still lagged far behind Poles who constituted 13 percent; Canadians, 11 percent; Germans, 8 percent; Blacks, who suffered the Depression worst of all, 7 percent (and up from 1 percent in 1910). In fact, the numbers of Italians were equivalent to people of English background and were ahead of numerous other groups including Russians, Scotts, Irish, and others who were 2 percent or less, according to Steven Babson, *Working Detroit: The Making of a Union Town* (Detroit: Wayne State University Press, 1986), 27.

8. The tax filing would come later; in the 1930s, only the elite, estimated to be less than ten percent of Americans, had sufficient income to file and pay income tax.

9. Presbyterian missionaries, charged with such unbounded hope that they would try to convert even Sicilians to their faith, thought that these new immigrants were not saying *caca di lupo* but were saying "car loops," referring to the fact that the streetcar looped on its return to downtown Detroit at this point along Gratiot.

10. By the 1890s, Detroit was already a national leader in carriage making, with 125 carriage companies was spurred to manufacture iron machines, stoves, and gasoline engines for ships. This alone sharply differentiated Detroit from worlds of stone and wood my relatives had inhabited since time immemorial.

11. Simultaneous with the beginning of the Depression, Detroit continued its conquest of the river and surrounding lake system. Its location on the water defined the city since French explorer Cadillac's discovery of Detroit in 1701 and the 1818 arrival of the first steamboat, *The Walk in the Water,* which reduced travel time from Buffalo to Detroit from ten days to forty-two hours. Providing fishing, yachting, powerboat racing, and access to recreation on twenty islands in Ontario and New York, Detroit stood as a central port along the Great Lakes waterways, on which the Boodrys, Sayers, O'Briens and Linsdaus all traveled west.

12. For a nice photographic depiction of workers, unions, and strikes, see Debra E. Bernhardt and Rachel Berstein, *Ordinary People, Extraordinary Lives: A Pictorial History of the Working People in New York City* (New York City: New York University Press, 2000).

13. Robert VanGiezzen and Albert E. Schwenk, "Compensation from before World War I through the Great Depression," U.S. Department of Labor, http://www.bls.gov/opub/cwc/archive/fall2001ᵃrt3.pdf, 8.

14. In an article on the Depression, Peter Temin wrote, "Industrial production fell by 37 percent, prices by 33 percent, and real GNP by 30 percent." Stanley Engerman and Robert Gallman, eds., *The Cambridge Economic History of the United States,* vol. 3: *The Twentieth Century* (Cambridge: Cambridge University Press, 2000), 301.

15. Scott Derks, ed., *The Value of a Dollar* (Lakeville, Conn.: Grey House Publishing, 1999), 311–12.

16. "How the Great Depression Changed Detroit," *Detroit News Rearview Mirror,* http://info.detnews.com/history/story/index.cfm?id=49&category=life; *Time Magazine,* Mar. 30, 1931.

17. *Monthly Labor Review* (Jan. 1939):2, 186, 208–22; in 1938 wages were 50 cents an hour nationally, over 60 cents in California and Massachusetts, and below 30 cents in seven southern states (118–92). For long term trends, see *Monthly Labor Review* (Jan. 1945), 142–238.

18. David Levine, e-mail note to author, Feb. 5, 2007.

19. James Haswell, "U.S. Rates Detroit Most Prosperous Big City," *Detroit Reporter*, Sept. 14, 1951, p. 7. For Detroit and the nation's improved condition during and as a consequence of the Second World War, see Harvey Green, *Uncertainty of Everyday Life* (Fayetteville: University of Arkansas Press, 2000), 70.

20. Derks, *The Value of a Dollar*, 254.

21. The rich left East Grand Boulevard and residential homes along Jefferson for Grosse Pointe and Grosse Pointe Farm and its estates, where they established their impressive lakefront mansions, and riding, golf, and yacht clubs.

22. See U.S. Census Bureau, Census of Housing, Historical Census of Tables–Home Values found on http://www.census.gov/hhes/www/housing/census/historic/values.html.

23. To suggest the story of accumulating wealth, a principal theme of this work, beyond its present narrative, my parents sold their Lincoln home in 1983, for $40,000. They had modestly doubled their money in twenty-eight years.

24. Alexis de Tocqueville, *Democracy in America*, vol. 2 (New York: Vintage Books, 1957), 243.

25. These consideration about family as a creation of the historian rather than a reality of the past were in part taken from John R. Gillis, *A World of Their Own Making: Myth, Ritual, and the Quest for Family Values* (New York: Basic Books, 1996), esp. 3–19.

26. Shakespeare's tombstone is cited in Stephen Greenblatt, *Will in the World* (New York: Norton, 2004), 86.